SAMURAI
and NINJA

Acknowledgments

I would like to thank the following people for them continuing support. Firstly, to Yoshie Minami and Mieko Koizumi for their constant help and translation, without them the world of the samurai and shinobi would still be dark. Next is Daniel Tennent, I would like to thank him for his ever encouraging words and his insight into warfare. Also, to Paul Martin, who has a great understanding of the Japanese sword, a researcher, who has dedicated his life to samurai history. Appreciation must go to Richard Gillies who has helped fund the acquisition of rare books and scrolls and also to Rob Simmons, Kevin Aspinall and Robert Lee, who have created the wonderful images found within these pages. To Gian Piero Costabile for his image of the Fukushima-Ryu boat and to Rien de Rooij who generously supplied me with the Fukushima-Ryu documents from his own collection. Ben Morgan for his continued and very 'English' style of support. Lastly to Jacob Sipes, for editing early drafts.

SAMURAI
and NINJA

The Real Story Behind the Japanese Warrior
Myth that Shatters the Bushido Mystique

by
ANTONY CUMMINS

TUTTLE Publishing

Tokyo | Rutland, Vermont | Singapore

Published by Tuttle Publishing, an imprint of Periplus Editions (HK) Ltd.

www.tuttlepublishing.com

LCCN 2014042316

ISBN: 978-4-8053-1334-3

Distributed by

North America, Latin America & Europe
Tuttle Publishing
364 Innovation Drive
North Clarendon, VT 05759-9436 U.S.A.
Tel: (802) 773-8930; Fax: (802) 773-6993
info@tuttlepublishing.com
www.tuttlepublishing.com

Japan
Tuttle Publishing
Yaekari Building, 3rd Floor
5-4-12 Osaki, Shinagawa-ku, Tokyo 141 0032
Tel: (81) 3 5437-0171; Fax: (81) 3 5437-0755
sales@tuttle.co.jp
www.tuttle.co.jp

Asia Pacific
Berkeley Books Pte. Ltd.
3 Kallang Sector #04-01, Singapore 349278
Tel: (65) 6741-2178; Fax: (65) 6741-2179
inquiries@periplus.com.sg
www.tuttlepublishing.com

First edition
27 26 25 24 23   10 9 8 7 6 5 4 3   2311VP
Printed in Malaysia

Contents

Question: There are some clans which adore those people who know much about archery, horse riding, swordsmanship, spearsmanship, etc., and who encourage their men to practice and practice; on the other hand there are those clans who do not. What can be said about this?

Answer: While practicing with sword and spear is not so useful, it can be an appropriate pastime for samurai, and therefore it is called Heiho— "the Way of the Soldier." Contests with bamboo swords can be of some use—however, you should not think that you can escape death by practicing such things. That being said, with those skills, you may be seen as blessed and formidable when fighting the enemy. Also, even if things result in you being killed, you will not have died in vain if you injure the enemy, be it even a small amount. This is the real goal to be achieved at the cost of your life. As you are from a samurai clan, it is important to know the ways of archery, horse riding, the sword and spear, etc.

Generally in Budo, you should hope to be regarded as honorable after your death through the preparations you have made while living. Know that even if you are killed during a spectacular combat but [died] due to ill fate, if you were deeply determined and were fully prepared for everything at all times, and if you have realized that lady luck has left you but you still fight a spectacular fight—your death will be mourned.

The Gunpo Jiyoshu Military War Manual, *Volume I, c. 1612–19*

The Search for the Samurai and the Shinobi

As the twentieth century came to a close, something quite special happened. The study of Western knights and medieval combat shifted. Movies began to change, imagery began to adapt, and ingrained ideas began to fall away. The medieval knights of Europe were transformed from a clunking shiny Victorian hero figure into a dynamic, powerful and robust specialist practiced in war craft. He no longer swung a heavy sword with bent back, nor was he lifted onto a horse with a mechanical pulley system. Now the knight flashed with deadly skill as the intricate art of Western swordsmanship was rediscovered. In addition, we discovered that the knight was a very complex character. They were war masters, trained from youth to serve a lord, be experienced in the arts of the siege and defense, and master the various machines of his time; all with an aim bent on killing the enemy. The knight was no longer a two dimensional figure who sang beneath ladies' bedrooms in the evening and fought the unholy dragon in the red light of dawn. His identity changed to the noble killer with a chivalric code that was an *ideal* and not a *reality*; a trained warrior wrapped in the fervent dedication of Christianity. This was all polished with education in various forms, the strings of ritual and an appreciation for beauty, all of which brought about a much more complex figure than previously believed.

In full contrast to this, the samurai and the shinobi of Japan remain in the looming shadow of modern fantasy and romance. The samurai is now widely believed to be a knight who charges headlong into death for the love of a lord. They also have a mysterious and magical blade, which can cut through any material. In the day he meditates on loyalty and is gifted with blessed enlightenment, but in the night, he fearfully protects against his famously dreaded enemy—the ninja. This outline is as redundant as the knight fighting a dragon next to a maiden locked in a tower, and it belongs in one place; story books. Of all the associations that exist for the samurai, one of them has fallen from grace, which by rights should not have. The samurai were classically termed as the "knights of the East," the Japanese equivalent to the European warrior class. This connection has fallen by the wayside in recent years, yet it is one founded in reality. The samurai share so many common traits with the European knight that the differences are found in the details, not in the principles. Therefore a revolution of the samurai should be moving in tandem with the revolution of the knight.

The increasing interest in the European knight has not been replicated for the samurai or the shinobi. In fact, quite the reverse has taken place. With the craze of Mixed Martial Arts (MMA) taking the world by storm, things Japanese have been pushed back into the realm of cliché and comedy. The samurai are fast becoming a vague, diluted shadow of a reality that once existed. They were real warriors, but with little or no respect in a modern fighter's world. It is now time for the *revolution of the samurai*, and like his Western counterpart, he too will undergo a change of image. Here you will see the samurai change from the obedient, enlightened, Victorian-style super warrior to the very real, very deadly, medieval Japanese knight. These warriors were trained in military arts, siege warfare, and castle defense. They were trained as mounted riders who tore through enemy territory in scouting war bands. The Samurai were educated scholar-warriors who attempted to understand the mysteries of the world through a deep and religious philosophy. Contrarily, there were also those whom threw philosophy away for personal advance, treachery, wealth, and above all, bloodlust. Observe the military headhunter, the head-taker who, like the tribes of old, took the heads of their enemies as gruesome trophies to be displayed as a measure of his prowess. You will also find the tactician, a mastermind of war alongside the *chi* masters; those select few who scan the enemy for omens of doom in the *chi* riding above them in the sky. There will even be fire-masters, the owners of flame and explosives. Therein will be standard-bearers giving forth their war cries to a backdrop of flame and smoke. Yet above all of these, we will investigate one special samurai military entity—the infamous ninja.

The ninja were a specialist branch of samurai warfare and were an integral part of the Japanese war machine. They were not outside of the samurai system and nor was their task the duty of lower people, under the iron fist of samurai rule. The ninja were a selection of specially trained people—often from specialist families— who concentrated on systems of espionage and infiltration. They maintained spy networks across the different principalities of Japan and gathered information from the highways of the world. Meeting in secret and in dark corners of enemy territory they plotted against each other and against enemy lords. They built complex pictures of a clan's resources, the feel of the people, the standards and banners used by its officers. The ninja also drew detailed plans of enemy castles, towns, highways and byways. They could be hidden in the ranks of an army, waiting for secret orders to be given for them to move on a mission of stealth, or alternatively, they could be hired to defend a lord and his castle. However, what is fixed in our minds is what ninja are famous for above all things: stealth. They skulk in the black of night, climbing a castle wall in windy rains, or creep through bamboo groves hiding from the moon, moving in the silhouette of a target's house, to murder everyone in their beds. All of these things are part of the samurai way of life. Now is the time for these truths to catch up with the rest of history. That is to say, restore the samurai to his rightful place as one of the most professional and deadly warriors of all time.

The history of the samurai and the ninja has previously followed two paths; the *academic* and the *fantastical*. Both have been rolled together to form a complex mess of half-truths. An extreme and impressive level of historical detail has been studied, yet forged with hearsay and romanticism. Therefore, this book has two simple aims: make that which is complex easy, and in doing so, eradicate that which is false. This means that this volume will purposely avoid an overuse of Japanese, it will not ask you to remember lists of names and dates. It will not bog you down in technical trivia. This book will destroy the half-history and deliver a solid, yet simplified, realistic foundation. From this you can return to other more complex books on medieval Japan and appreciate them with a new depth of understanding. Overall it will be a series of steps that act as a map, allowing you to journey through samurai life without the confusion of having to understand the intricacies of Japanese history.

It is my ardent wish that you now wipe your mind clean of all the movies, the comics and the stories you have read. Right now, imagine your mind as a blank sheet of paper. In beautiful, dark calligraphy the word "samurai" appears at the top of this parchment. Then as you move forward, chapter by chapter, allow a new historical image of the Japanese knight to draw itself on the page. In the end you will be left with a clearer understanding of this warrior class. From this fresh image, a new respect will grow for these historical warriors and, ultimately, a thirst for more historically accurate knowledge on the long-dead knights of the East.

Antony Cummins
Shiki, Japan
2013

Part I

TEARING THE WORLD OF THE SAMURAI AND NINJA APART

Introductory Observations

The following elements are considered true in the world of the samurai, yet are actually not wholly accurate. I have raised these questions at the start, in order to examine where the image of the samurai has come from. More specifically, I would like to explore how a truer picture can be created.

The Honorable Duel

The image of the samurai meeting his nemesis in a fair fight to the death is a hang over from the romance of American western films. Also it stems from samurai cinema in the twentieth century. Gang fights and riots were perfectly acceptable behavior for duelling samurai. A group of friends could attack and kill their enemy, who may be walking alone; they would not feel it shameful. Samurai duelling can be identified in three basic formats:*

1. *Kenka*—When angers have arisen and tempers have flared, this is spur of the moment combat through insults given, drunkenness or through simple bloodlust.
2. *Uchihatashi*—When there is a deep hatred between people, a family feud, or a situation has made two samurai become enemies, or that they have a simple dislike of each other. Pledges are made in writing or spoken to kill the opposition. War between families, groups or individuals is initiated.
3. *Adauchi*—Revenge killings. If a member of a samurai's family has been slain or a friend has been killed, a samurai must venture on a mission of *adauchi*—"a journey of revenge"—even if it means his own death. Lafcardio Hearn in his early writings on Japan states that a person on a mission of wrath may walk fifty miles in a day, carry nothing but a small package, kill ten men in under a minute, and then turn the sword upon himself to die. Acts of vengeance are truly in the blood of the samurai.

---

* Remember, terminology can change depending on both chronology and time; the terms here are taken from Natori-Ryu.

In samurai society it was perfectly acceptable to come across a duel in a field or forest, and then lend aid to the man attempting revenge. The level of help given can differ. It can be simply a distraction in the background, such as shouting and giving false commands while the revenge-seeker kills their enemy; or it could be a group of friends making their way out together to take down a formidable foe.

The Sword is the Soul of a Samurai

Without doubt one of the greatest symbols of the samurai is the katana—the mythical sword of the Japanese. It has taken on such proportions that it is compared to Excalibur and other magical swords. However, the katana rarely featured as a principle weapon in the Sengoku, or Warring States period (1467–1573). That specialty goes to the bow, the spear, and other pole-arms. For a samurai who was alive in the period of the country at war, the main weapon would be a spear, or another form of pole-arm. Alongside his horse, his servants and squires would carry his spear, bow, and helmet. The sword *was* important and was a key feature of the samurai class—to accidently brush or knock a samurai's sword was a serious *faux pas*. However, it was not essential to the identity of the samurai, like we have been led to believe. In fact, when charging into battle, the first samurai to clash with the enemy is called *ichibanyari* ("the first spear"), while the second samurai is called *nibanyari* ("the second spear"). The sword became a symbol of the samurai at a later date.

The Katana is the Greatest Sword on the Planet

The katana has led the image of the sword in modern times and it is said that it can outperform any sword in the world. It is believed to be the sharpest and most perfect blade, beyond the affordability of most people. The best way to explain this is through metaphor; a sword is like a car today. Most people have one. Some cars are technological marvels of the road, while others are made for the common man to enjoy, to simply function as a car. All cars are relatively expensive when new and not many people buy a brand new vehicle. Most cars on the road have been sold second hand, some have been looked after—some have not—and others are closer to the scrap yard—more than most care to admit. Some newer cars are at the top end of the market and would cost a whole year's wages for some people. Other cars go beyond this and would take a whole lifetime of wages to be spent on acquiring one. Still there are cars beyond that—Formula One racing cars are even beyond the individual. Companies normally buy these racing cars because they are so far beyond an individual's spending power. Yet even with all of this in mind, almost everyone owns a car. This is exactly how Japanese swords should be understood. In old Japan there would be master-class swords on the "road;" there would be beat up "old bangers;" yet at the side of almost every man, there would be a blade, be it short or long. To travel without one would be risky.

A common occurrence in samurai manuals, and war chronicles, is the bending—and snapping—of swords. Some samurai sword schools teach to block an opponent's katana using the back and side of the blade. Plenty of chipped swords can be seen in museums. A primary aspect to understand about the Japanese sword is that it is not sharper than other swords; sharpness is not its special quality. The reason the Japanese sword is so well respected is because it is a blend of softer metal—which is found in the core of the blade—and harder metal used along the cutting edge. The katana is an optimum mix of the two. The result is a blade that is flexible and durable. However, this love of the katana was established before a proper interest in Western and Middle-Eastern weapons was developed, and promoted in the public image. The now infamous Damascus steel of the Middle East and "Viking" swords, such as the *Ulfberht* swords, easily compare to their Japanese counterpart. These other weapons, in fact, predate the katana—meaning that great swords have existed all over the world and are comparable to the Japanese sword. It was just that no one was told. That being said, a well-made katana was a superb weapon. Respect for its complex metallurgy should not diminish, whereas the fantasy of the Japanese "super sword" should be left behind.

Only Samurai Can Own Two Swords

A pair of swords in Japan consists of a katana long sword and the wakizashi short sword. Together they are known as *daisho*—"the big and the small." However chronology, region, and linguistic differences can complicate the argument. However, in short, There is a misconception that only samurai carry two swords. This is not entirely untrue, but it is only a half-truth. Before the late 1500s, everyone in Japan was allowed to carry a sword—or pair of swords—if they wished. At this point in history the wearing of two swords at their side did not mark out the samurai. However, "sword hunts" and weapon confiscations were soon enforced. This is the political move of disarming a conquered enemy, or the lower classes of a warlord's own province. By outlawing the wearing of swords (unless used during a journey for protection), a ruler could disarm the peasant class and secure a "peaceful" reign. These sword hunts were actually a hunt for all weapons found within a civilian population and were done so to remove any "teeth" from future rebellions. A key fact to remember is that in the late 1500s everyone could wear a sword but after this, in the age of peace, *only* the samurai wore a set of two swords. This created the now iconic image of the Japanese knight, an image that did not exist in the golden age of the samurai. So remember, before the late 1500s anyone could wear two swords, but after this it was only the samurai who could wear them.

Japan is the Land of the Samurai

Figures and statistics differ depending on which source is quoted, however, most figures agree that the ratio of the samurai class was between 5% and 10% of the entire Japanese population. For every ten people on the street, one would be a samurai at most. The rest fell into one of the other social classes. Therefore Japan was not the land of the samurai but the land where the samurai ruled, meaning that most people in modern Japan are descendants of farmers. In fact, it is hard to find people in Japan who are aware of their own family history, unless they are from a samurai family, in which case they are very proud of the fact (and rightly so).

Japan is the Greatest Race on the Planet—so Say the Japanese

The Japan of today is associated with an introverted attitude and non-hateful racism—i.e., other cultures and races are interesting but Japan is the greatest. They are also associated with an attitude of non-exploration and isolation. These attitudes cannot be denied fully but it is a modern approach. One crafted through the semi-self-imposed isolation of the peaceful period, an attitude reinforced by an early twentieth century imperialistic ideal. Ancient Japan in its Warring States (1467–1573) and Edo (1615–1868) periods at times held the belief that civilization, industry, and intellectual superiority were to be gained from mainland Asia. A samurai of the early period of Japanese warfare, even up until the Peaceful Period, would have looked overseas for artistic, military, and educational inspiration. With these inspirations came the desire to trade, explore, and invade other lands; even Western ideas were sought after and adopted. The idea of the Japanese nation's isolation came after this point, and even then it was not total isolation—meaning that at some points in Japanese history, the Japanese looked outside of Japan for inspiration, technology, trade, and interaction.

The Enemy of the Samurai is the Ninja

The enemy of a samurai is actually *other samurai*. Japan was a war-torn country under a feudal system; the very core of its nature was samurai fighting samurai. There was no separate social or warrior class known as "the ninja." The ninja did not hide in mountain villages out of the jurisdiction of the samurai overlords, developing skills to defeat the "evil samurai." The truth of the matter is that in different sections of Japanese history, the country has been united and has then fallen into warring clans—this happened more than once. The time Period we are interested in is predominantly around the middle of the 1400s to the start of the 1600s. At the start of this period, Japan was divided into factions and clan alliances, while central had government collapsed. This was the Sengoku Period (1467–1573), or Warring States era. If you run a slideshow of Japan's maps between these dates, giving each clan an allotted color, you will see that many colors disappear or merge into other colors—which seem to be taking over the board. By 1580 you will see a nation dominated by just a few colors with the Oda clan, led by warlord Oda Nobunaga, spilling over the picture. In the center of this spillage is a small section of land surrounded by mountains. This place is called Iga and has become the iconic, presumed homeland of the ninja. At this time the warlord Nobunaga was fighting on many fronts. One of those fronts was the invasion of Iga. The radical shift in the Japanese social structure at this point is that samurai clans that were once self-governing or automatous suddenly fell under the onslaught of ever growing, more powerful clans. Iga was one of the remaining self-governing collections of samurai clans. They are not peasant ninja hidden in the mountains nor is the invasion force only targeting them. They are simply in the way of the massive onslaught that is Nobunaga's war machine. Their freedom must be extinguished in the name of a unified Japan. The only difference is that these Iga samurai clans are exceptionally well versed in the skills of the ninja; skills which are called ninjutsu. The enemy of the samurai are other samurai or even warrior monks. Therefore ninja is not the identity of a social class, it is the identity of a military branch, a military position, and ninjutsu its set of skills.

Ninjutsu—The Arts of the Ninja

Ninjutsu is not a systematic form of hand-to-hand combat. There were no physical combat or martial arts techniques specific to the ninja. Ninjutsu is a set of skills used by the military, or "civilian" samurai. These skills were to infiltrate enemy positions, gain information, and even allow an agent to take revenge through deception and trickery. Put simply, ninjutsu is the way of espionage and of the commando.

The Difference Between Ninja and Shinobi

Until this point the terms "ninja" and "ninjutsu" have been used in the text; however, Japanese ideograms can be pronounced in multiple ways. The term *ninja* 忍者 is traditionally read as *shinobi no mono,* and the term *ninjutsu* 忍術 is traditionally read as *shinobi no jutsu.* It is not incorrect to say ninja or ninjutsu. Those readings are acceptable. However, the first phonetic use of ninja and ninjutsu come much later than the period when they were active and should be considered secondary. The term *shinobi no mono* ("person of stealth and endurance") is often shortened, or was in fact developed, from the word *shinobi.* Therefore for the remainder of this book the terms *shinobi, shinobi no mono* and *shinobi no jutsu* will take precedence.

So, for quick reference:

> *Ninja* was pronounced *shinobi no mono* or just *shinobi*
> *Ninjutsu* was pronounced as *shinobi no jutsu*

With most of the above myths starting to crumble, becoming wiped clean from the mind, a better understanding of the Japanese warrior class should begin to form. The next step is to clarify their identity and understand the variations in the identities of these warriors themselves.

Identity

Too often, individual identity becomes lost in the pages of history. Volumes are given to the outline and lives of rulers. Yet the masses may go unnoticed. It is easy to relegate the samurai and the *ashigaru* (foot soldiers) to the faceless rank-and-file figures that come from the "samurai factory." These faceless figures stood ready to fight, behind their leaders. Instead of this approach, we need to observe the samurai in three layers. First we need to see them as human beings, secondly as Japanese, and lastly as samurai. From this we will fill in the details of their lives. Each individual has strengths and weaknesses as a human, but what needs to be identified specifically is their personality, along with their skill sets. Personality inserts "color" into our picture of the Sengoku Period samurai. Skills help to fill in the "detailed lines." Each samurai was born into a world that has an established identity. Their individual identity was forged through personal experiences and the environment around them.

The basic elements of identity are as follows:

1. **Fundamental identity**—An individual has a basic identity. They are named and a self image is formed around that name. When their given name was spoken, the individual had a sense of himself or herself. Those looking upon that person formed an opinion in their mind—this name was their inner core.

2. **Identity of family**—Each person belongs to a family unit which has a name attached to it. The individual would have grown up within the social class and circumstances of that family, and their identity was shaped through a connection to the family and the lifestyle of that family.

3. **Identity through personality**—The emotions of a person and the nature they are born with, along with the influence of their society's ethics, would have formed into a part of that person's identity. A person may have been known as an angry person, a loving person, a wise person, or a cruel person, etc.

4. **Identity of position**—Occupation is a critical factor in developing identity. The role or function a person holds in society dictates how they are seen by others—and how they view themselves. This often determines their friendships and social class.

5. **Identity by personal interest**—Hobbies, likes, and interests form the periphery sections of a person. An individual's likes and dislikes added color to a forming and changing identity.

6. **Identity in connection to history**—A person's place in the thread of history dictate how they see themselves. Their place in history help form that

individual's identity. A person's country, culture, and religion also form a part of this identity.

7. **Identity through objectives**—With the other sections of identity in place, an objective and goal gave a person direction and purpose.

To illustrate this fact, separate fictional cases of three warriors from medieval Japan—each with their own identity—have been given below:

Samurai One

1. Fundamental identity—Resolved and quiet.

2. Identity by family—Born into a powerful family and son to a warlord, he has been groomed to lead men.

3. Identity through personality—A natural leader of men; however, prone to bursts of anger, refuses to apologize, lacks humility, does not appear sincere when admitting he is wrong.

4. Identity of position—Son to a powerful father, his position is based on name and family history; he is a warlord in training and therefore forever overshadowed by his father; always as a lesser in the eyes of his peers, his position always reminds him that he is second before another.

5. Identity by personal interest—Loves to shoot game birds over lakes and indulges in expensive clothes; however, has a generous side and gives benefits to religious orders.

6. Identity in connection to history—Born into a family that has a long and vast history, his understanding of it, and his place within it, is seen through the distorted lens of family agenda.

7. Identity through objectives—Wishes to best his father's legacy.

Samurai Two

1. Fundamental identity—Playful and kind hearted.

2. Identity of family—Born into a poorer samurai family, but never without food or shelter. His upbringing was in the shadow of richer samurai but he still underwent a solid samurai education. This has led him to push his abilities. His family are experts in the ways of shinobi and the identity of shinobi has formed within his mind.

3. Identity through personality—A warm and kind person with a happy countenance, he attracts others yet pushes them aside when there is hope of furthering his position.

4. Identity of position—Shinobi: as he was born in Iga, through his training and family arts he has gained employment as an *Iga mono*—a man of Iga, i.e., shinobi. He has been hired as an *In no shinobi*—"hidden agent." His cover is that of a low-ranking guardsman. Only the captain of the shinobi, other hidden agents, and the lord know his true role in the army. Often sent out undercover to perform missions for the lord, collect information, infiltrate the enemy, or set fires in a "black operations" strike team. Given the secondary role of rooting out enemy spies.

5. Identity by personal interest—Enjoys poetry and drinking songs, known to gamble but is considered a strongly stable character.

6. Identity in connection to history—Born in the Sengoku Period. His family, which are situated in Iga, are still at this time samurai class. Brought up in the Shingon sect of Buddhism, he also has an interest in the victories of those from Iga, attempting to remedy his lack of a notable family name.

7. Identity through objectives—His aim is to understand the deeper meanings of the Shingon texts and try to shift to a similar understanding of that of a "man of the cloth."

Ashigaru One

1. Fundamental identity—Strong willed and sly.

2. Identity of family—Born to servants within a farming family, he grew up in a rural area; his family are known to be shrewd, crafty, but honest. However, they are known for their strong family bonds and wild temper if one member is wronged.

3. Identity through personality—While crafty, he is not intelligent. Yet beside a lack of formal education he has "street wisdom" and understands well the working of the world. A jolly countenance with an eye for profit, he will steal monetarily from enemy targets that he has infiltrated.

4. Identity of position—An ashigaru foot soldier, he works the campaign months in the army and spends the rest of the year working his family farm. However, he has excellent shinobi infiltration skills obtained through years of stealing from rich mansions. He is often called upon to form up with shinobi night attack squads, helps identify routes, and find paths for the shinobi night attack teams. He was a very good advance infiltrator but in the last few years his body is getting older. Now he tends to find routes and position himself as a night signal coordinator, so that the teams work as one.

5. Identity by personal interest—Loves games, especially simple soldier games while in battle camps. Has a deft hand at carving. He often carves wooden religious figures for sale or barter.

6. Identity in connection to history—Has no connection to anyone of importance in history and believes that his family has farmed since ancient times. He thinks that his ancestors are part of the landscape of that area. He does not believe his family will ever move away. After he retires from active warfare he will probably never leave his town again.

7. Identity through objectives—Has saved up a secret stash of booty, gold, and silver in the hope of having a peaceful life; enjoying his time before he dies.

Having two shinobi in the three examples was done deliberately, as the use of these two examples show that shinobi can be from either the samurai class or the lower ashigaru foot soldier class. Their skills and expertise would be allotted to the task for which they were best suited.

So far, we have broken down many samurai myths and popular ideas. In the place of these misconceptions, we reformed the identity of the Eastern knight. A new character is starting to take shape. Japan is a world with a long history and full traditions. It has rituals and customs. It has a voice in the world all its own. It has live individuals, humans with names and family backgrounds. They have personalities, likes and dislikes. They have an ethical code shaped by the population's collective thinking (as all ethical codes are).

Part II

THE SAMURAI

The World of the
Samurai and the Shinobi

T o build this picture of the samurai and the shinobi, without stereotype, it is best to examine the world that they lived in. This includes the physical landscape, the social norms of the times, and the historical influences in the world into which they were born.

The Landscape and History of Japan

Japan is a mountainous country with a wide range of climate differences, from extremely cold in the northern parts to the hot climates of the islands of the south. A high percentage of the country is clad in mountains and forests, and much of the population dwell on the fertile plans and coastlines. The history of Japan can be divided into different eras, yet the world is primarily interested in a single thousand-year period—*the epoch of the samurai.* Before the samurai, Japan was a land heavily influenced by Chinese culture. This influence soaked into all areas of life. Much earlier, Japan moved through early "civilized" culture. It passed through its own stone ages, all of which were sophisticated in their own way. Around 800–900 AD—and taking a few hundred years to develop—the samurai started to form, adapting to a changing socio-political environment. Fast forward, they evolved into the now famous warrior culture known across the world, a culture that came to an end around the 1860s and 1870s.

Ignoring the rest of Japanese history, but without forgetting its existence, the age of the samurai can be broken up into sections. These are classifications that only exist here and are theoretical; their only purpose is to help form a visual understanding of the progress of samurai history. This timeline has been simplified for ease. Japanese history can be divided into many individual ages; however, this aid focuses on the samurai's development and the major changes that occurred.

Proto-Samurai

In the ninth and tenth centuries of the first millennium—that is, before 1000 AD—the samurai began to develop, moving from an obviously pre-samurai warrior template into a more identifiably Japanese form, the birth of the samurai.

The First Great Samurai

From around 1000 AD to 1450 AD comes the classical age of the samurai. This is the age of the samurai as the mounted warrior. His principle weapons include the bow and arrow; warfare is wider and more open. The Genpei War (1180–85) rages and the Kemmu Restoration (1333–1336) takes place. The land is at times in turmoil, heroes are created, and iconic images are crafted for future samurai to adore.

The Age of War

From around the 1400s to the early 1600s, Japan enters a fierce and bloody part of its history. The country is changed from collections of practically self-governing societies, under diffident warlords, to a unified country. A change achieved through consistent campaigning, in which military tactics are developed, classical samurai ideals are giving way to well-structured and formulated "modern" war-craft; gunnery is introduced and explosives gain a more solid foothold while warrior knights are supported by masses of foot soldiers. In a climactic clash at the battle of Sekigahara and the victories at the sieges of Osaka Castle, the Tokugawa family take control of the country and "peace" is restored to Japan.

The Age of Peace

From the early 1600s, "peace" was established in the country. "Peace" has been placed in quotation marks because it is wrongly considered a "peaceful" time. The start of the seventeenth century was full of rebellion and attempted coups, including the siege of Osaka Castle, the slaughter of the last Toyotomi members, the brutal murder of the Christian horde at the siege of Shimabara, and the attempted takeover led by Yui Shosetsu—possibly ordered by the Kishu domain. These are only a few examples of this bloody "peace." By 1650 the country had "calmed down" and the Tokugawa clan held an iron grip. "Peace" is provided through a feudal dictatorship and true power is held by the Shogun. All of the other clans are placed under the Sankin Kotai system, which means that each clan has to biannually move its chief personnel to the capital—at great cost. This was a measure designed to prevent anyone from rising in rebellion against the Tokugawa family. With the country under dictatorship and war at an end, the samurai class—in the main—moved towards bureaucracy, with less importance placed on combat efficiency. Armor and weapons become more decorative, ethics and the ideals of Confucianism take a stronger hold. Our idea of the perfectly honorable knight is shaped in this age, but in truth, the samurai declined in power and ability.*

The Modern Age
In the 1860s Japan once again became a land of war as the Meiji Restoration developed. The now weakened samurai class were outdated as a product of the old world. Modern society crashed into Japanese life. The samurai were disbanded, ending a thousand year rule of the shoguns, restoring the emperor to "power" under the guidance of a modern government.

The importance of a basic understanding of the above cannot be underestimated. Often these major divisions of the samurai age are mixed together and placed over each other. The ideas of honor, and a spiritual life that gained popularity in the "age of peace," are attached to the classical age—the "first great samurai." The warfare strategies of the "first great samurai" are mistakenly used to explain the "age of war." As a modern reader you must understand that these ages were divided by change—yet connected by the identity of the samurai. The role itself of these Eastern knights is a golden thread that runs through a millennium of change. However, remember that although the samurai were always samurai, they did change with time.

The *epoch of the samurai* can be expressed as a thousand year rule that starts with the emergence of a warrior class. This then moves from classical warfare, through the bloody years of unification, to the decline of practicality—the eventual fall of the warrior. Each part has its place in Japanese history and should not be mixed together nor mistaken as a single, continuous form.

History as the Samurai Saw It
History is ever changing. A modern understanding of history may not be the understanding that the samurai had. To the samurai and the shinobi, history, folklore, and legend existed in the same space. The Japanese considered their world created from the great Japanese gods in the Age of the Gods. They knew that China influenced Japanese culture. Yet they also knew that the ancestors had a hand in the making of their own history. Often a samurai school of war may have a divine origin and inspiration, meaning that their gods blessed their school. Most origin stories for samurai schools start with the founder leaving to undertake an episode of training in remote mountains. Here, after months of intense study, a god comes to them in the form of a spiritual or earthly creature that then gives the holy swordsman the secrets of the martial arts. This became the storied birth of their style. The

---

* This statement is an overview of the samurai class as a whole. In fact there were some fine examples of military samurai who studied the arts of war deeply and it is in this age that the samurai war arts were recorded for posterity. However, these individuals are a reflection of the Warring States Period and do not reflect the reality of the samurai as a whole in the period of peace.

origins and histories of samurai (and shinobi) schools can be put into three categories. Sometimes they include all three, and sometimes they only contain one or two of these elements:

1. The mythological element—A god or supernatural creature is the initial inspiration for the school and has conveyed divine wisdom and skills to that school.
2. The legendary element—A hero figure that may or may not have existed is factored into the school's history. The King Arthur or Robin Hood types of Japan include Kumasaka the famous thief, Yoshitsune the child warrior, and even Kusunoki Masashige, the famed but doomed hero figure; Real historical figures pushed into legend.
3. The historical element—A historical figure, episode, or fact that is without a doubt correct and that is considered true history.

The third is the only element that we now consider as proper history. However, it was not improper for a samurai to pass on the idea of the first two. As observers of history, we should not condemn samurai for taking this angle. Their schools were historically correct even with their origins being a mix of truth and legend, sometimes even claiming historical figures that had become famous.

Society in Japan

The concept of Shi-no-ko-sho—the four classes of feudal Japan—is well understood in the realm of samurai history. Below are some of the lesser-known aspects highlighted to create a balanced view.

The four main tiers:

1. 士 – Shi: The gentry or warrior class
2. 農 – Nojin or Nofu: The farmer
3. 工 – Ko or Shokunin: The artisan or craftsman
4. 商 – Shonin: The merchant

The above system is inherited from Chinese doctrine and influenced by Confucianism. It was not a solid practice until the beginning of the Edo Period, in the early seventeenth century. Most people are interested in periods of warfare when they contemplate samurai history. They tend to overlay this idea onto earlier times. Before the times of peace that came with the control of the Tokugawa family (after 1600), social mobility was more fluid. Lines between the classes were blurred—yet they still existed. The samurai were a social class with clearly developed identities; yet movement between or living on the border of two social classes was more common. A reader of history has to constantly avoid the "Disney Trap." This is the belief that a peasant is a poor creature who lives in a leaking hovel, a toothless grin reflecting the orange of a crackling fire. The lord is the opulent, fat, cruel dictator on a throne. The knight is the hero on the horse. The merchant is the jewel-encrusted, slimy fellow who rubs his hands together in anticipation of gold. The embedding of these images from childhood by countless mediums creates a thick coat of obscurity. It is paint that needs to be removed from an analytical mind. Peasants are not the lowest creatures. In most cases, slaves, outcasts, and the unseemly came below peasants. They weren't always poor. The merchant is not always affluent, and the ruler is not always all-powerful. Of course the knight is not always the hero. It is of great importance to identify your own cultural, opinionated distortions of class. Once they are identified, do the utmost to eradicate these falsely formulated ideas. Consider social class and the effects it has on the individual; see it as something fluid and in motion. From the standpoint of the person *in* history these things were fixed. From the standpoint of the historian these move with time—and for a historian, time can pass instantaneously. As students of history we can pass over 400 years in a moment, seeing an image of a nation change from static to fluid. Therefore, erase these social stereotypes, understand the basic principle: chronology and geography are factors that will determine the outcome of the image you create.

To paint a portrait in your mind: imagine that a given domain has a fair lord, who governs well. The state has satisfactory resources; a peasant may own two slaves and a small cottage in a rural area. A warrior family that rules fairly protects this area, yet they have a strict attitude. The cottage may be an extensive compound on the edge of the farmland that the occupants work, either for another or under their own control. They farm and spend surplus on luxury goods that are sold by the merchant class—an idyllic picture. This picture may be idyllic, yet it can also be realistic to a degree. On the other hand: another province may come under the control of a tyrant, taxes may be levied to unfair levels and the peasants may not even produce enough crops to feed themselves—let alone purchase luxury items. When civil war breaks out, the peasants (in classic horror movie fashion) march against the dictator with firebrands and pitchforks. Again, this is stylistic, yet realistic to a degree. In reality, most historical situations are somewhere between these two extreme examples. That does not mean that these two examples were never realities. Simple factors easily show truths of history. For example, if peasants—in the Japanese case, farmers—were hovel dwelling, disease ridden, skulking figures, then the merchant class would not exist. A merchant needs a customer base, and most of the population were peasant-farmers. Peasant-farmers fed the country, samurai ruled and defended the land, artisans crafted products, and merchants sold them across the islands. Finally, the outcasts perform the duties that the aforementioned will not undertake. Here, again, when imagining the social systems of Japan, do not fall into the "Disney Trap"—or have a blanket outlook. The blanket approach is filled with stereotypes and associated connotations. Instead, adopt the balanced approach of looking at Japanese history as a whole. Consider the merchant to be a hardworking shopkeeper, the craftsman to be the busy woodcarver or blacksmith. Consider the peasant to be a healthy farmer in the field. Consider the samurai a militarily trained landowner; a local power. Then, with this level playing field in place, investigate times and place. Learn how that at times the population became wealthier and life was easier; while at other times existence was harsh. Discover how these harsh times caused rebellion. It is *not until a date and a place is identified* that a correct understanding can be achieved—make sure to remember this.

Pop History and Academic History

It is important to understand the difference between popular history books and academic history books. Both—in *most* but *not all* cases—are well researched and are good representations of history. However, academic books bore the general public while popular history books become bestsellers. The difference is in extremes. An academic book tends to look even, middle-of-the-road and *to some* uninteresting—examples include *Crop Production in the Roman Republic* or *Pottery Placement in Iron Age Graves*, both of which can be found in university libraries. At the other end of the scale, popular history books are teaming with blood, sex, scandal, violence and war, all of which are extremes. It is without doubt that—most of the time—most people in history led very normal, very conventional lives. At certain points and in certain places, extreme events happen—and those extreme events end up being reported in popular books, films, and documentaries. They become a part of social identity and world history. This is *popular history* and is the basis of most people's understanding of the world. Just think; how many Latin or Japanese texts have you actually read in the original language, or translated? The answer is normally "few or none," therefore always check the source of your samurai or shinobi information (this applies to history in general). Not all pop history books carry factual information. Moreover, very few books on samurai or shinobi come under the banner of academic or true history.

To help understand medieval Japanese society, links can be made to the world around you—creating a picture that has understandable connotations.

- ◆ The samurai should be considered as army officers. Some are of extremely high rank and run military complexes, with hundreds of other officers below them, while some are standard officer stock. These men are still well educated, upper class, and affluent. Others are junior officers and have one foot in the lower class—poorer than the others. Yet by no means would they be considered poor by today's standard.

- ◆ The ashigaru foot soldiers are the basic army soldiers. They are the rank and file, the troops on the field. However, most of these army soldiers spend a high percentage of their time at home. Only when needed are they called to war. There were ashigaru foot soldiers that served professionally, full time, working all year round. These professionals were the exception, not the rule.
- ◆ The peasant-farmer can be divided into the many levels. They range from the wealthy to the semi-slave farmhand.
- ◆ Craftsmen can range from those who manufacture cheap commodities, to those who hand-stich leather gloves; these sell for extremely high prices.
- ◆ The merchant can be from the dilapidated old corner shop, selling cheap, outdated items. Or, he can be one of the extremely expensive shops in a big city somewhere.

Outcasts and Men of the Cloth

The aforementioned five classifications do not cover everyone in Japan. There is still a large section of the population that floats outside of this pyramid of power. The major external section is the "men of the cloth." That is, anyone who is in a religious order. It is commonly believed that men and women of religious denominations were outside of the secular structure. They are thought to exist purely in the "spiritual" realm of monasteries and hermitages. However, this was, of course, far from the truth. Monks and their monasteries held vast amounts of political power. Some of these places of worship were indescribably vast military complexes. Some monks were extremely militaristic. Also, the nobility—the emperor and the noble families—were outside of this system.

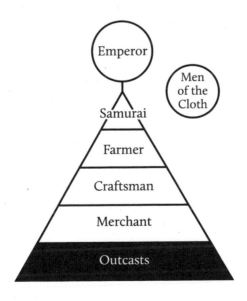

Outcasts were known by two basic names but the distinction is not always so clear.

1. The *Eta*—These were people who took on menial tasks such as cleaning and labor and also dealt with animal corpses and the dead.
2. The *Hinin*—These people also dealt with base tasks, but also were wandering entertainers and the like.

The Eta and Hinin classes were still in existence in the twentieth century. It is only now that Japan has almost, if not completely, shaken off the stigma of the Eta-Hinin background.

Ainu—The indigenous race of Japan were also not considered to be part of the four-tier system.

Prostitutes, courtesans and geisha—Pleasure girls and women in entertainment are also external to the system.

Slavery—The lowest of all were slaves. While the term "slave" is correct, it is better understood as a forced servant. The main difference being that a "standard servant" could leave and serve other people. Many masters could hire them during their lifetime. Slaves were taken during battle, and in raids where an enemy was defeated. The defeated warriors were taken captive, as were whole families. Their new owners used them in any way that they wished. Some were even sold abroad in the slave trade. It was in the late 1500s that people like Lord Hideyoshi put an end to slavery.

The Samurai and His Servants

A samurai will undoubtedly have servants to aid him; sandal holders, grooms, helm and spear bearers. The number depended on their social ranking. The following is the main structure of command:

1. Samurai—He acts as the master of the house.
2. Ashigaru—Foot soldiers, ashigaru can either be temporary or permanent and may be retained in large groups by wealthy lords.
3. Chugen—Direct servants to the samurai, these will place the shoes of the samurai ready for him to step into, help him with tasks and serve him in his daily activity.
4. Komono—Servants who do tasks around a samurai's house and deal with menial issues.

In a samurai household, the master is the head. His chugen will aid him and the komono will make the fires, cut wood, etc.

A point of interest: shinobi often infiltrated by moving into a house compound when the servants are performing their daily tasks. This was around dusk when it is difficult to see everyone's faces. The movement of the servants covered the shinobi's infiltration. They sometimes even acted as a servant in these twilight hours, such as carrying wood into the house, so that they could infiltrate without being noticed.

The Samurai and the Land

The samurai—and by default the shinobi—were heavily connected to the land and to farming in the first half of their thousand year history. The meaning of "feudal" is that overlords control farmland and men work it. The subclasses below an aristocratic or military rule would accept protection in exchange for working plots of land. This is not indigenous to Japan and is a worldwide phenomenon; however, this concept needs to be reapplied to the popular image of samurai life—the samurai were the knights and lords of their allotted land.

Japan was not always ruled by a central government. Throughout all of samurai history we see the land unified, then fall into collapse, only to be unified again. This cycle repeated itself. Therefore, depending on which point in history you are dealing with, the land and its produce may come under control of regional warlords. If we put the periods of unification aside for the moment, historical Japan can be seen as a "patchwork" of land. This is where each "patch" was a state (or province) owned by the leading warlord of that area. He was a baron of sorts. Below him were his commanders. Spread across his land were his knights (samurai)—who in this situation are his captains. They were full-time militarily capable warriors—the rest of the peasant population can be drawn upon as foot soldiers in times of need.

Focusing in on a single "patch," we move to a solitary samurai house, nestled in a landscape of green rice paddies. Peasant dwellings were relatively nearby the house (or house complex). The samurai was the master, his horse looked after in the stables by his groom. His squire (of sorts) looks after his armor. Servants make his food and look after his domestic tasks. Depending on the scope of his wealth he may have had many farms under his control, each of which produces stock for the area. This governing of the farmlands is what gave the samurai his wealth and income, as did the occasional levying of taxes on the people of the area. This was done to support his lifestyle and military equipment. In return for this control, he (as a samurai) had to be war-ready for the local warlord. In truth, the local warlord held power over all of his samurai and their land. He could take away the samurai's land and power if he wished. This is the very basis of a feudal system—that is until a stronger samurai came along and changed the balance.

With an understanding of the above, a divide between *samurai* and *jizamurai* can be explained. There is a basic rule of thumb—which is not true for every case, but which is a simplified overview. It is that in the first half of the epoch of the samurai, most samurai were landed gentry. Landed gentry were those men of good birth or standing—normally with a military background or a family history of military service. They were men who owned land and farms. They were considered a part of elite society. For a Westerner, consider the upper-class gentleman in his family manor house. With generations of antiques and family heirlooms, he looks out over his tracts of land. This was the primary situation for many, if not most, samurai in the first half of their age. However as history marched on, warlords controlled larger and larger areas of land. Their central powerbases became small cities. Samurai were encouraged to move from the land they oversaw, into towns and cities developed near their lords. This influx of samurai to towns and wards generated a new term, the *jizamurai*. The word jizamurai is made up of two ideograms, "ji" 地 (land/ground) and "samurai" 侍 and is translated as "samurai of the land" or "landed gentry." This term referred to those of the military class who owned land, lived on it, and controlled the farmers below them. As with all cultures, the town samurai perceived themselves as more cultured. They saw themselves as more refined than their samurai counterparts who are "up in them there hills." However, they are seen as equal in class and are without doubt samurai. When war beckoned, the town samurai rode out of the samurai district with banners in the sun. Drums and horns sounded in the countryside as the jizamurai rode out to war.

However, the story of the jizamurai takes on a sour twist. The land of the samurai was once a collection of fortified manor houses, mountain castles, and fortifications. These were spread across all the independent states. However, as the Sengoku Period progressed, more and more sections of this land came under a new ruler. The new conquering warlords changed the map of Japan to a land being predominantly ruled by a few powerful samurai. This had only one result. The jizamurai of each area were either defeated, their homes and lands taken from them, or they were absorbed into the armies. A new breed of war, on a national scale, spilled over the land. At the end of the Sengoku Period, when the Tokugawa family took control, almost all samurai were forced to leave their homes. They had to move to estates in the towns and cities nearer their lords. The mountain forts and castles were destroyed. The flatland castle was made a major center of all cities under the control of the defeated warlords—with the Tokugawa family sitting firmly at the top. This means that samurai left their natural habitat of independent lands and farming estates, and were now paid directly by the lord. They lived in luxury mansions in samurai districts next to flatland castles—the age of the country samurai manor came to an end.

The result of this depends on each individual case, but all of which fall into two main categories. Either the jizamurai became normal town samurai, or they were defeated. Their land was taken from them—dropping them outside of the samurai class system. However, as they are ex-samurai, their social position cannot be denied. They couldn't fit directly into the new samurai class. Therefore the term jizamurai took on a *new* meaning, it became "half-samurai." These ex-samurai became local leaders or took up other positions, with one foot in samurai life and the other foot in peasant life. It must be reinforced that *most* documentation from Japan is from the "age of peace." Therefore, the term jizamurai is sometimes used with derogatory overtones, meaning those who are no longer samurai—below the social status that their families once held. Most readers of Japanese history now consider the jizamurai to be the poor half-peasant with a sunburnt face; digging in the sunshine with the other toothless peasants. The image of the jizamurai being outside of the samurai class has set in. This is most problematic when we move to shinobi history.

The warriors of Iga and Koka can be described as jizamurai. This means that the above problem affects the story of the shinobi. The families of Iga and Koka (lands famous for shinobi) were considered jizamurai—landed gentry—before the invasions, and takeover, of Lord Nobunaga in the 1580s. These jizamurai families of Iga and Koka actually had no overlord and were independent. After the fall of Iga in the 1580s, with the surrender of Koka, these landed samurai fell from true jizamurai. They then came under the new definition of jizamurai—"half peasant half samurai;" or even straight peasants. However, this idea of the peasant in the field is simply not accurate. For example, the Yamanaka family of Koka were ex-samurai who were shinobi-trained. As a family, they owned land that was approximately one hundred meters square and had what we would consider a mansion complex and servants—not quite the financially struggling hovel-dweller that you would expect. However, there is without a doubt a financial shortfall. This is an inability to fund a military family or run a military clan, which train and retain full time warriors—who also practice the arts of the shinobi. This type of funding was not within the scope of the new jizamurai. Many attempts were made by the people of Koka to regain status and official employment. They wished to continue their military ways.

A simple way to remember this is that—from a broad perspective—the number of independent land-owning clans is *greater* at the start of samurai history and becomes *fewer* as time goes by. At the same time, the number of town samurai is *lower* at the start of samurai history but greatly *increases* as Japan is unified. The tipping of the balance resulted in jizamurai being displaced and pushed just outside of the samurai class. Remember, in early times most samurai were from small collections of families who owned areas of land. Later on most of these families moved to towns and cities to serve the new super-lords—like the Tokugawa family.

The Daimyo Warlords

Moving away from the general population of the samurai class, we will focus on the lords and warlords. All samurai were not created equal. Some samurai could have more interaction with the peasants that he ruled than with the lord he served.

Therefore the samurai class should be seen as an existing on a spectrum. The lowest are the poorer members of the samurai, barely affording to hold onto their military status. All the way to the shogun, who ruled the nation and was in essence an extremely rich king.

The Japanese term given to the lord of a province is *daimyo* which literally means "big name" 大名. The daimyo was comparable to a European baron, the lord-commander of the knights, the ruler of a domain. He was the final word in law and decision-making. While the country was at war the power of the daimyo amplified. He originally was second to no man, a lord in his own province, and wielder of total power. Many daimyo would enter into agreements and treaties, and marry into each other's families. They set up a system of hostages and loyalty. During Japan's history, the country has been unified a number of times under the emperor or the shogun. Which means that, at these times, the daimyo became second in command. His land was subject to the law of the shogun. However, when the country moved to war again, they generally formed independent coalitions—a country divided, where no one ruled above them.

The daimyo families can be *loosely* divided into three types according to the period.

1. *Shugo* (created pre-Sengoku Period by imperial decree)
2. Non-*shugo* (mainly rose to power in the Sengoku Period—known as Sengoku diamyo)
3. *Kinsei* (early modern, i.e., Edo Period).

A shugo family is a daimyo family that has been given official power—normally by imperial decree—and has authority to rule over the population. While the non-shugo families served in support, in the turmoil of war some non-shugo families formed uprisings against the higher clans and overthrew some of them. They became the most powerful families; especially in the Sengoku Period. The land became a mixture of ruling shugo and non-shugo families. The implications of this are that there was an undercurrent of thought on who had "the right to rule" and those who claimed "a right to rule through force." One reason for this reversal of power came from the way that non-shugo families were powerful families who usually resided in an area that was directly engaged in farm management. These clans were actually controlling and producing crops and food—the lifeblood of medieval Japan. The shugo families tended to be detached from direct interaction with these jizamurai families and used the non-shugo families as middlemen. When the wars came, the non-shugo families seized elements of power and the structure of Japan changed. The term used for this is *gekokujo* and means "those from below who take control and power." The term is still used in modern Japan.

One great example of this uprising and shift in power is the Tokugawa family, the family that took control of all of Japan. It is surprising to some to discover that the Tokugawa family were born from the Matsudaira family. Their lineage had to be adjusted to endorse their hold on Japan. This was because the Tokugawa family did not have the correct pedigree to have the right to rule—i.e., "proper samurai" should be linked to the Heike or Genji clans. They were not. Of course they had defeated all of Japan and unified the land, so there was nothing that could be done to challenge their unrivaled power. So instead, facts were changed to "allow" them to rule.

The image you should be developing is that of the samurai as a very stratified group. Even within their own ranks, there are pedigrees, hierarchies, and factors that need to be taken into account. A samurai could be at the bottom of the samurai ladder while a supreme ruler or lord of power sat at the top. However, that ladder could be climbed and people could fall off—some climbed from the bottom to the top. Some fell from great heights back to the ground—this is the reason that most wars were started. That is to say, most wars were started by clans that wanted to displace those in power.

Were the samurai aristocrats? I have tried to avoid using the words "aristocrat," "noble," and "blue-blooded." To term the samurai as aristocratic is difficult but not incorrect. Yet, on the other hand, this term is not wholly inaccurate. This is because the line between aristocrat and non-aristocrat is a difficult one to draw. In Europe the line is drawn at the level of a knight. The knight is sometimes considered an aristocrat, yet at other times and in different countries, they are not. Their position is just outside aristocratic, or at least straddling the line inbetween. This is similar for Japan. The true aristocrats of Japan have a connection to the imperial line and are offspring branches of royalty. *Some* samurai were not from that world, but they once served the aristocratic families. In the end though, the samurai formed an uprising; taking control of the country from these noble families. Thus, they slotted themselves into the position of "nobles." The complex connotations and difficulty in explaining the individual uses of these terms creates difficulty with using the word, "aristocrat." We should try to avoid calling samurai "aristocratic" or "noble," unless they are from a family of correct pedigree. Remember, some samurai had an aristocratic background and came from royal families; some did not.

Koku and Payment

The economy of medieval Japan was heavily based on its food production. For all the romanticism samurai hold, in truth, samurai history is a tale of those who owned the most farmland. Therefore, those who had the most produce had the most power. This makes the story of the samurai a story of the land and of rice.

Originally a samurai family would have owned their lands and, as farmer-warriors, they would have ruled over the farmers of that area. They would have distributed the wealth of that land appropriately. As is always the case when human culture moves to agriculture, a surplus of food develops, and individuals—normally to produce luxury goods—undertake skills and professions and then the population explodes. This population explosion means that the food, which once fed a nation, becomes insufficient. Warriors protect their land from raiding parties, living off any surplus, which exists for as long as they defend it. In short, a samurai had land, families banded together, and production kept the warrior class in their position of power. This gave the population of that area protection. After the wars had taken the country by storm, independent samurai communities were moved to cities and the day of the samurai as a farmer-overlord ended. *All* land belonged to the shogun, the Tokugawa family. From this high position they distributed the land between other major families—the smaller ones that were once the stock of Japan were absorbed.

The major samurai families distributed the land they were allowed to rule to their warriors, who were paid in "koku." Koku is a term of measurement that is equal to the amount of rice that feeds a person for one year. Samurai are paid in multiples of this amount—remembering that they have to redistribute this amount to any other samurai families that are under their patronage, at least to others under their control. A samurai of 10,000 koku was considered to be a daimyo warlord—some warlords earned more than 1,000,000 koku—while other samurai earned sums like 5000, 1000, 500, 300, 100, 25 koku, etc. This number is always representative of a part of land that produces that rice. Giving them the actual land that produces the amount could pay samurai, or instead they could be given pay equivalent to the cost of rice itself as an annual wage. To understand the samurai and his payment, imagine that at first, early samurai held their own land. This was in the service and protection of a higher lord, family head, or as independent samurai families. Then as land was swept up by mega-lords, this system was replaced with permission to run farmland or a salary was paid directly to them. In all cases, the samurai is tied to the land and wealth is not far removed from the agricultural world. Food is power. Control of more food gives someone more power. Remember, a samurai could own land that produced food and he would pay people below him with this food. A samurai could also live in a town and be given a salary that was measured by amounts of rice, but delivered to him in monetary form.

The Samurai Army

A samurai army is not a standing army *per se* in the true sense of the concept. It is more of a conglomerate of promises—but as always, this, too, changes depending on which time period you are looking at. Different samurai periods offer different attitudes and organization. For example, the Edo Period saw what could be considered the closest to a standing army, where samurai are made to live in towns, close to their lord, ready to go to war if they should be called upon. At the height of the Sengoku Period, armies could be said to be regular in use and formation, i.e., on the field and on campaign for extended periods. This resulted in long-standing forces, but this is also a period of defection and changing loyalties. At other times, a samurai army was made up of a *union of loyalty*; this was an amalgamation of oaths given and sides taken. Before the Edo Period, you must imagine samurai living across Japan, some close to centers of habitation. Imagine still vast numbers of samurai living in fortified manor houses and residences in rural areas, among mountains and farmlands. Those samurai would have sworn loyalty to a warlord, but would live away from any form of court life, managing their own land. These samurai may live in peace for a number of years, they may have skirmishes with other samurai; or even engage in family vendetta and blood feuds. When battle broached the horizon, orders to go to war would be given. The samurai, with equipment prepared, would leave his dwelling and make the journey to where the army was forming up. A knight with his hired (and maybe loyal) troop accompanied him. Together, he and his "squires" and servants would take up their position in the allied forces, under the leadership of a warlord. All of which is a system based on promises and land rights.

The following translations and statistics will help form a better visual understanding of such an army. This will help to solidify the idea of a mass of men coming together under the leadership of a prominent samurai.

Percentages of Distribution in a Samurai Army

A samurai army should not been seen as static. Some factors, such as size and technology, will greatly change. To form an understanding of ratios in military troops, two examples of army percentages are presented below. Remember that there are many varied roles in an army. The following statistics contain only the primary units.

The distribution of military personnel within the Hojo clan in 1572, in numerical order.

- ◆ 47% Spearmen
- ◆ 22% Mounted warriors
- ◆ 11% Samurai on foot
- ◆ 8% Flag bearers
- ◆ 6% Musketeers
- ◆ 3% Archers
- ◆ 3% Personal standard bearers

The following list is the distribution of military personnel found within the same clan in 1587. Notice the massive increase in the use of firearms, more than doubling in fifteen years.

- 27% Spearmen
- 19% Mounted warriors
- 19% Samurai on foot
- 14% Musketeers
- 14% Archers
- 6% Flag bearers
- 1% Personal standard bearers

Numbers Found Within a Samurai Army

It is impossible to answer the question, "How many men were in the average samurai army?" There was no common size and both situation and time period have an impact on the answer—it could range from a light skirmishing force of a few hundred samurai to the epic conflict of the Battle of Sekigahara, where more than 150,000 soldiers took to the field of battle. Remember that a battle can be a mixture of clans coming together and those armies were made up of coalitions of clans. The following example is taken from the Uesugi family and was recorded in 1575.

An army that is 5,135 men strong was divided thusly:

- Mounted warriors – 566
- Samurai on foot – 650
- Musketeers and archers – 320
- Pikemen – 3,519
- Short spears – 80

To get a better view of the samurai army, the question should be changed and should instead read: "What are the component parts of a samurai army?" Doing this shows the makeup of a military force in Japan. The following detailed list is taken from the Gunpo Jiyoshu military war manual of c.1612.

The Command Group
Musha Bugyo (samurai commander) – 1
Tactician – 1
Archers and musketeer commanders – 15
Flag commanders – 2
Foot soldier commanders – 4
Monomi scouts – 20

Secretaries – 3
Suppliers of weapons – 2
Drummer – 1
Bell ringer – 1
Conch shell blower – 1
Baton holders – 2
Spear commander – 1
Doctors – 4
Carpenter – 1
Total: 59

[Second group]
Standard bearers – 3
Flag bearers – 30
Archers – 100
Musketeers – 200
Shinobi [ninja] – 20
Non-mounted samurai – 60
Accountants – 5
Chefs – 2
Grooms – 30
Komono servants – 450
Laborers – 50
Spearmen – 130
Blacksmiths – 2
Arrow smith – 1
Bowyer – 1
Cordage maker – 1
Total: 1,085

Sword fittings of the warring periods and before tend to have less decoration and have a more robust look to them, with a more solid feel.

[Third group]
Mounted samurai – 80
Ponies – 15
Total: 95

Note: Fourteen people attend each mounted warrior and they are as follows.
Helmet bearer – 1
Footed soldier – 3
Spear bearers – 2
Sandal carrier – 1
Grooms – 3
Servants – 2

Laborers – 2
The above is the estimate for a warrior of 500 koku.

Total mounted warriors: 154
Total retainers: 2,156

Packhorses of the lord – 50
Packhorses of the retainers – 350
Grooms for the above horses – 400
Grand total for this army is 3,796

It is extremely interesting to note that in the list, shinobi appear as being twenty in number. This would mean that on average there would be one shinobi for every 180–200 men of the force. These were openly hired as shinobi and were allotted a section of the camp. They would sleep during the day and work the perimeter at night, lead night attack squads and hunt out enemy shinobi.

An even more detailed list can be found in the Giyoshu manual written in 1690. It clearly describes the people taken on campaign or those who follow military armies:

軍奉行 *Ikusa bugyō* – Commanding officer
旗奉行 *Hata bugyō* – Commanding officer of the flags
幕奉行 *Maku bugyō* – Commanding office for the war curtains
鉄砲大将 *Teppo daisho* – Musketeer captain
弓大将 *Yumi daisho* – Captain of the archers
鑓大将 *Yari daisho* – Captain of the spearmen
鉄砲奉行 *Teppo bugyō* – Commanding officer for the musketeers
弓奉行 *Yumi bugyō* – Commanding officer of the archers
鑓奉行 *Yari bugyō* – Commanding officer of the spearmen
御旗本衆 *On-Hatamoto shu* – Direct retainers to the shogun
近習衆 *Kinju shu* – Close retainers
小性衆 *Kosho shu* – Pages
歩行衆 *Kachi shu* – Foot soldiers
歩行頭 *Kachi gashira* – Head or captain of the foot soldiers
近習横目 *Kinju yokome* – Inspector of the close retainers
歩行横目 *Kachi yokome* – Inspector of footed soldiers
小横目 *Ko-yokome* – Secondary inspector
惣横目 *So yokome* – General inspector
貝ノ役 *Kai no yaku* – Conch shell blowers
鐘ノ役 *Kane no yaku* – Bell officer

太鼓ノ役 *Taiko no yaku* – Drummers

大物見 *O-Monomi* – Large scouting groups

中物見 *Chu-Monomi* – Medium scouting groups

小物見 *Ko-Monomi* – Small scouting groups

使番 *Tsukai ban* – The lord's messenger

軍者 *Gunsha* – Military strategist or military personnel*

御太刀奉行 *On-Tachi bugyō* – Protector of the lord's sword

馬奉行 *Uma bugyō* – Horse management

具足奉行 *Gusoku bugyō* – Armor management

小荷駄奉行 *Konida bugyō* – Baggage train management

金奉行 *Kane bugyō* – Accountant

納戸役 *Nando yaku* – Property keeper

扶持奉行 *Fuchi bugyō* – Treasurer

数鉄砲奉行 *Kazu Teppo bugyō* – Commanding officer to those who hold the
  lord's muskets

儒師 *Ju shi* – Master of Confucianism

目醫師 *Meishi* – Optician

外科付 *Geka* – Surgeon

金瘡 *Kinso* – Sword cut healer

易者 *Ekisha* – Diviner

能書 *Nojo* – Scrivener (scribe)

歌道者 *Kadosha* – Poet

伯楽 *Hakuraku* – Horse veterinarian

筭勘者 *Sankanja* – Mathematician

馬惣横目 *Uma so yokome* – General inspector of horses

雨用意役 *Ame yoi yaku* – Those who prepare for rain

忍者 *shinobi no mono* – Ninja

水奉行 *Mizu bugyō* – Water management

井堀 *Ido hori* – Well diggers

石切 *Ishi kiri* – Stone quarrymen

鉄砲張 *Teppo hari* – Gunsmiths

弓師 *Yumi sh I* – Bowyers

矢師 *Ya shi* – Fletchers

金堀 *Kane hori* – Miners

漏刻 *Rokoku* – Water clock maintainer

博士 *Hakase* – Scholar of Onmyodo magic, astrology, calendars, etc.

---

* Terminology varies in each province. The term "Gunposha" is used in different ways and can be a tactician, but can also be military personnel. Here it is considered to mean tactician because there are no others found in the list. However, Natori Sanjuro Masazumi in his writings states that even in his lifetime—which was at the same time that this manual was written—people were recording these terms incorrectly, which may be the case here.

兵法使 *Heiho tsukai* – Master of military skills
強力 *Goriki* – Load bearers
走態 *Sotai* – Runners
番匠棟梁 *Banjo Toryo* – Master builder
鍛冶 *Kaji* – Blacksmiths
惣賄人（マカナイ）*So Makanai* – Food supply manager
庖丁人 *Hocho nin* – Cooks
桶師 *Oke shi* – Wooden bucket makers
檜物師 *Himono shi-hinoki* – Cypress wood carvers
壁塗 *Kabe nuri* – Plasterers
猟師 *Ryo shi* – Hunters
鋳物師 *Imoji* – Metal casters
鎚屋 *Tsuchiya* – Hammer forger
具足屋 *Gusoku ya* – Armorer
瓦焼 *Kawara yaki* – Tile maker
屋葺 *Yane fuki* – Thatcher
舩奉行 *Funa bugyō* – Commanding officer of the naval forces
水主 *Kako* – Sailors
梶取 *Kaji tori* – Helmsmen
鷹匠 *Takajo* – Falconers
革屋 *Kawaya* – Leatherworkers
山伏 *Yamabushi* – Mountain priests
出家 *Shukke* – Monks
座頭 *Zato* – Musicians
繪師 *E shi* – Painters
白拍子 *Shirabyoshi* – Dancing girls
能太夫 *Nodayu* – Master of the Noh theater
塗師 *Nushi* – Lacquerer
紺屋 *Koya* – Dyers
油作 *Yusaku* – Oil makers
犬引 *Inu hiki* – Dog handlers
猿引 *Saru hiki* – Monkey trainers
舞〻 *Maimai* – Dancers
放下師 *Hoka shi* – Street entertainers
狂言師 *Kyogen shi* – Comical stage performers
磨屋 *Togi ya* – Craftsmen who sharpen blades
畳屋 *Tatami ya* – Tatami mat makers
百姓 *Hyakusho* – Farmers
町人 *Chonin* – Townspeople
商買人 *Shobainin* – Merchants
穢多 *Eta* – Outcasts

Some swords in the warring periods were "mass produced" and were of much lesser quality. These swords were exported.

The preceding lists bring the reality of the battle camp into the mind's eye. Servants and grooms attend each samurai. Carpenters and blacksmiths are at work; accountants are looking after the army treasure under guard. The command group is in the command tent and the cooks are stoking the fires. The soft grass is turning to mud and on the hill behind the camp, the *chi* masters are watching the enemy camp for auspicious signs. Dogs raid the perimeter, while prostitutes follow nearby. Merchants try to sell their wares in the daytime. Nighttime brings drinking and gambling, which are sometimes subdued or restricted by the command group. The army is a living, moving machine that is medieval life on the road. When on the road or taking up position, the army must erect a *jinsho*—a battle camp.

Battle Camps

Often a samurai army is depicted on the open ground, ashigaru to the front with shields in front of them. Banners wave in the wind as the lord-commander sits behind his closest samurai. However, the jinsho is seldom considered. This is a portable camp made up of huts constructed on site with local material. Fences are made from bamboo or wood, and internal divisions made from curtains or treated paper. Outside the camp, watch fires are built, guards are stationed, and shinobi are sent into the wilderness around. Strict guards are kept, identifying marks are needed, and passwords will gain a man entrance. In the center of the camp, the lord's command group meets to discuss strategy. On a nearby hill or at a relatively short distance away, the enemy are doing the same. Conch shells sound in the air, drums beat the time, gongs give signals. The chatter of men fills the air.

Aspects of a Battle Camp

There are basic items that will be familiar to those in these temporary camps and generally military manuals of the Edo Period display similar illustrations, giving us the basic elements that make up a campsite.

Watch Fires

In a typical watch fire, the walls are seven feet high, the fire front opens outwards so that light spills into the dark area away from the camp and allows the men behind the fire to remain in the shadows.

Fences

Fences are normally constructed of wood or bamboo in the fashions shown below. Sometimes double fences were constructed to stop infiltrators. Sometimes ditches were dug outside of the fences and filled with sand to show if any footprints had been left behind by shinobi.

Conch Shells

A common sound in a battle camp would be that of the conch shell. The system of use would change from camp to camp, but a samurai would expect that the camp would be awoken in a "call the hands" fashion, and then it would be "hands to breakfast" and "form divisions," etc. The conch shell would sound out and gain a response from the men of the camp, depending on the arrangements made.

Drums

The times of the day and the beat of the war march would sound out from the drum. Japanese hours are called *toki*, and the day is divided up into twelve toki. Each is 120* minutes long and has a name, such as hour of the Boar, hour of the Dog, etc.—thus drums are used to measure time in the camp and to keep men in step when marching.

---

* The number shifts as the seasons change and each hour can change in length. 120 minutes is the average.

Watch Towers

A soldier in a camp may have to spend his watch up a watchtower; these may be placed around the camps to observe the local area. As can be deduced from the illustration below, these towers can be dismantled and moved to a new location.

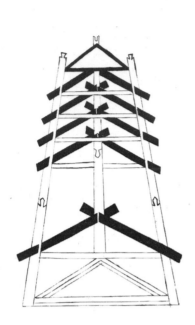

War Curtains

Large sections of cloth reinforced with rope would be pitched vertically and set up to make barriers. Here different groups would be sectioned off and conversations kept private. Shinobi would be looking for small viewing ports in the cloth for when they sneak into camps to try to observe the command group. War curtains also have various esoteric associations.

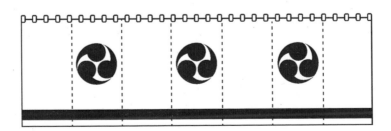

Fake Walls and Spiked Traps

There are various traps around the camp—these can be pitfall traps laden with spikes, stones hung from ropes, fake collapsing walls and tripwires. Consider the external perimeter of the camp to be a maze of bamboo shields, bamboo bundles, walls, wires and traps.

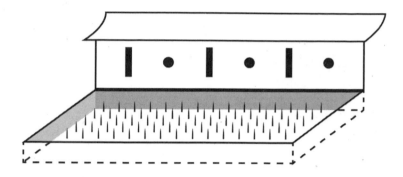

The Setup of a Fortified Battle Camp

One important item that can be gleaned from Japanese military manuals is that camps are seldom alike and the way a commander sets his camp is often a telltale indication of the workings of his mind. The following example and translation is one of many—this one taken from the Gunpo Jiyoshi manual—and it highlights the thinking behind troop placement. Things to note in the image on the following page are the bamboo fence around the perimeter, which appears like crosshatching, and the placement of shinobi directly next to the command tent.

1. Two units of mounted warriors with captains, one mounted scout, twenty messengers, one unit of archers and one unit of musketeers with captains
2. One unit of mounted warriors, one unit of archers and one unit of musketeers with captains
3. Two mounted warriors
4. One unit of archers and one unit of musketeers with captains
5. Flags and bannermen
6. One unit of mounted warriors with a captain
7. Three units of mounted warriors including those with conch shell and drums
8. Close retainers with captains
9. Two units of mounted warriors with captains, one mounted warrior scout, ashigaru foot soldiers
10. Musha bugyo—commander
11. One unit of archers, one unit of musketeers, two units of mounted warriors with captains

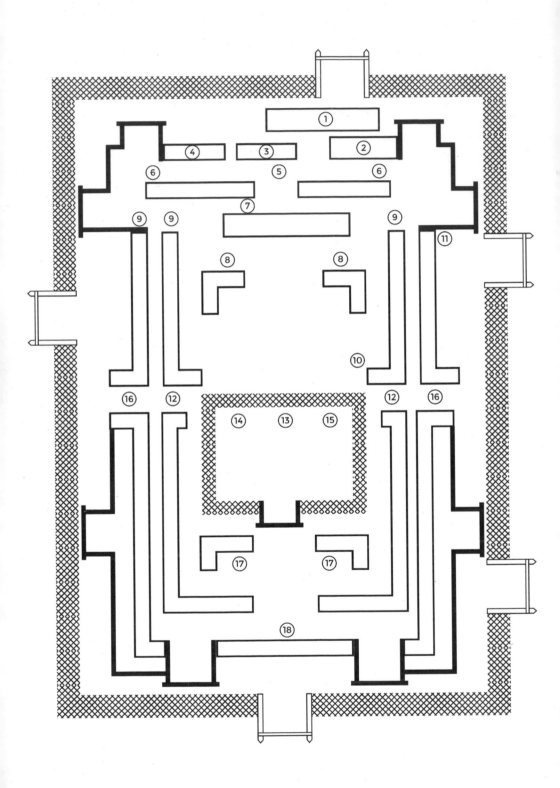

12. One unit of messengers, two units of spearmen with commanders, one unit of archers and one unit of musketeers with captains, two units of mounted warriors with captains

13. Headquarters

14. Doctors

15. Domestic staff

16. Two units of mounted warriors with captains, one unit of archers and one unit of musketeers with captains

17. Shinobi group (ninja)

18. One unit of archers and one unit of musketeers with captains

The *Yamaga-Ryu Bukyo Zensho* of the 1650s goes on to outline the people who should be put in their own quarters, those huts for people who share the same profession. It is here that we see that shinobi no mono get their own billets, due to the fact that they would have to work throughout the night.

When setting up a military camp, the following people should be billeted in huts:

1. Catering overseers
2. The quartermaster
3. Those who prepare the lord's meals
4. Doctors
5. Secretaries
6. Advisors
7. Monks
8. Carpenters
9. Craftsmen
10. Miners
11. Shinobi no mono (ninja)
12. Musicians
13. Swimmers
14. Cooks
15. Those who deal with supplies

The small area outside a castle wall just on top of the stone foundations is called the "dog run," while the same area on the inside of the wall is called the "warrior's run." If there is no wall on the top and it is just a raised mount then this is called a "horse's run."

According to Jinichi Kawakami, the following statement is found in Yoshitune-Ryu shinobi manuals and shows that shinobi, when they have time on their hands, should consider undertaking the following:

軍陣不断共謐時は、心を一入れ、強く張り詰め、物人数の上を遠目
に見て、油断透間を勘へ心懸る可き事

*When you are in a battle camp and things are quiet, keep your mind
attentive and observe your army from a distant position and consider
the gaps and openings within.*

The image of the Japanese battle camp should be one of a working community
on the move. The smell of the latrines is thick in the air. The food is cooking, and
the fire smoke rises. Huts and shelters would be in neat formations (if the commander is experienced) while the fences would be erected on soil banks. Signals
and drums would sound out and orders would be given. Nearby a merchant train
with gambling and prostitution would follow. Entry in and out of the camp would
only be permitted with strict permission; and with the use of identifying mark-
ers/passwords. Fear of night raids would be constant and the sound of the war cry
before a raid would be dreaded. As night falls, fires and braziers would flare up.
Guardsmen would change the watch. Shinobi or secret scouts would be sent into
the area around them. They would smell the air for fuses and odors that give away
ambushes; or listen for sounds of the enemy—as enemy shinobi move through the
bush and forests. A samurai may be taking part in a night raid. They may be wet-
ting paper and wrapping it around anything that jangles. They may also be tying
up the horses tongue with string soaked in blood, ready to make them silent for
the raid. All the while the enemy shinobi are watching; listening to this so that they
can report back to their own allies. The military battle camp of Japan was a dirty,
odor-filled environment, normally with strict laws and protocols in place. It was a
society in its own right. Men within it, be they ashigaru foot soldiers, servants, or
samurai could be away for months at a time.

The Samurai Castle

In the popular imagination, a European castle is dark and cold. It smells, and is
set against the backdrop of a cliff above raging seas; while the rain and lightning
crash down upon it. In contrast the Japanese castle is considered clean, quiet, whitewashed and is always set against a hot Japanese summer. Originally, Japanese castles
were much smaller and many were set on clifftops and hills. Many were actually
black in color. They were similar to their European counterpart in that they were
filled with the normalities of castle life. This included horse muck, smoke from
cooking fires, and the trappings of medieval life. So to correctly picture the Japanese castle: imagine an even blend between the gothic stone citadel on the hill and
the pristine white palace-castle. At the end of the Sengoku Period, and into the
start of the Edo Period, castle technology advanced greatly. This means that the
castles of the generation before, those that were at the center of the wars, were different from the ones that people picture and visit today. The result is that we often

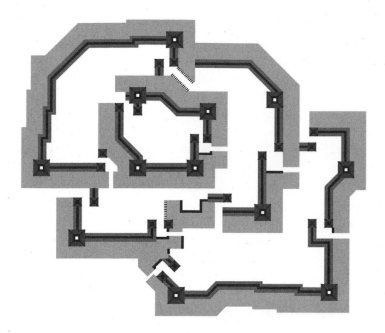

place the wrong castle in the wrong time frame. The rule of thumb is that in the Sengoku Period there existed a greater number of castles, fortified manor houses, and building complexes. This includes temporary fortifications, mountain retreats, and heavily fortified monasteries. As the Sengoku Period was reaching its height in the later 1500s, castle technology made a massive leap. Castles became much bigger and more complex. Then, in the Edo Period, the shogun had the mountain and outlying castles destroyed. He forced all samurai to leave their ancestral fortified manor houses and move into castle towns—most of which were flatland castles. He removed any natural advantage of position, leaving us with the image of the grand castle with whitewashed walls in the center of major cities. This was not the norm in the warring periods. In the Warring States Period, castles would have been smaller than we know them now, and fortified houses and monasteries would have been bigger than the ones visited by tourists today.

The Areas and Fortifications of the Castle

The following is a short description of the major parts of a castle and their functions. While castle technology and the story of the Japanese castle stretches way beyond this description, the basics can be found here, providing an understanding and sense of Japanese fortresses.

天守
The Tenshu

The *tenshu* is the main keep of the castle, the fortified tower at the center.

本丸

The Honmaru

The *honmaru* is the primary enclosure, which surrounds the Tenshukaku keep; sometimes the main tower can also be described as a Honmaru.

二の丸

The Nimaru

The *nimaru* is the secondary enclosure, which makes a second outer ring in the castle.

三の丸

The Sanmaru

The *sanmaru* is the third enclosure, which surrounds the castle; this can be the final wall, but castles with more enclosures did exist.

大手門

The Otemon

The *otemon* is the main gate of a castle; it is considered the primary entrance and exit.

鐘楼

The Shoro

The *shoro* is a bell tower.

矢倉

The Yagura

A *yagura* is a form of turret or building on top of a castle wall. The wall normally consists of a stone foundation and then a plaster and wooden wall on top of this foundation. On the top of this wall is a room-like building from which troops can shoot—this is the yagura turret. Shinobi manuals often talk about fire-setting skills that bring about the destruction of yagura turret houses.

石落

Ishiotoshi

An *ishiotoshi* is a section or hole where stones and rocks can be dropped. As enemy troops climb up the outside of the walls, debris is dropped on them from these relatively small areas.

逆茂木

Sakamogi

Sakamogi are thorny branches and spiky sections that are positioned to keep invaders from attempting to infiltrate.

忍返
Shinobi-gaeshi

These are more permanent spikes that are erected along the edges of walls. They are there to keep shinobi from climbing over. However, the shinobi have various ways to deal with this issue—for example, the Bansenshukai shinobi manual says that they should be hooked with rope and ripped down.

堀
The Hori

The *hori* is the moat that surrounds the castle. Shinobi would have to measure these and wade their way across them in the dark.

馬出
The Umadashi

The *umadashi* is a fortified exit. Walls are positioned outside of the exit so that a direct charge cannot be made against it. These can be "horseshoe" shaped walls just outside of the outlet.

縄張
The Nawabari

The term *nawabari* means the overall layout of the castle, the ground plan or the birds-eye view. The term originated from stretching rope (*nawa*) used to map out the ground of a castle site.

The Japanese castle was a complex system of defense with its own kill zones and tricks to keep enemies out. In this new image of the samurai that is being built as you read, the castle must start to be seen as a complex part of samurai warfare—similar to the complexities of its Western counterpart. And of course, if there are castles, there must be sieges.

Siege Warfare

Japanese castles were adapted to siege warfare. Again the similarities between Western and Eastern warfare are evident and the sophistication of Japanese siegecraft is obvious.

If a samurai is on the defending force, the following items are things he would be familiar with as he moved in and around the castle.

Arrow and Gun Ports

Inset into the walls of castle defenses are small holes—they are normally rectangular, circular or triangular. Positioned at different heights, the defenders use them to shoot out over the field of battle. However, shinobi creep up to these apertures and fire burning arrows and flash arrows through them into the interior of the castle grounds to discover details about the interior layout. In addition to this, they would throw in hand grenades to kill those shooting out at the opposition.

Stanchions, Walkways and Shields

Along the inside of castle walls, wooden stanchions and frames would support multiple levels of walkways—similar to modern day scaffolding. Samurai would use these levels from which to shoot outward, either through arrow and gun ports or over the tops of castle battlements from between shields. In addition to this, bridges that could be retracted were set up at various positions; if the enemy breached the defenses these walkways could be retracted, allowing defending samurai to kill the enemy from the opposite side.

Killing Zones

Walls, turrets and enclosures were created to form killing grounds and zones, where the defending army could attack the enemy with crossfire and pin them into a corner and halt movement.

Turrets and Palisades

As discussed before, the castles of the early Sengoku Period and before were generally smaller; walls could be protected by turret towers, wooden shields and semi-permanent buildings that were made of wood and were built along the tops of walls. Shinobi had various mixtures that would set fire to these, fires that would be difficult to extinguish, helping to break through the castle defenses.

Allied Help

A defending castle could set up a series of fire beacons and send messenger relays to request allied forces to counter the siege. Sometimes the relieving force could surround the besiegers, forcing them to defend their own rear and fight on two fronts.

Sallies and Sorties

The castle would send out night raids and attacks when they thought that the time was right. They may even evacuate a castle from an non-besieged section—if any—through gates and ports. Shinobi were trained to watch the smoke rising from castles. If the smoke from cooking fires and kitchens was too much, too little, or later than normal, a shinobi would know that the enemy had either started to evacuate or that they were preparing extra food for those going on night raids or that the food stores were diminishing. All of which was information the shinobi would pass on to his commander.

Those who were attacking the castle had certain weapons and tools to help degrade the height and protection advantages of the defenders.

Trench Warfare

Trenches at their smallest were three feet deep with an earth mound on the top of around two feet; this total of five feet covered the average height of a samurai. The closer to the castle the trench lines were the deeper they had to be dug, as arrows could be shot into the defenses from such an angle.

Towers and Constructed Turrets

As discussed previously, the enemy battle camp had collapsible turrets and towers; these were erected to see enemy troop movements and shinobi.

Battering Rams

Covered rams on wheels were used to take down castle doors and break open sections of defenses.

Shields and Walls on Wheels

Small platforms were placed on low carts with walls erected on the front. These walls had shooting ports and would be rolled into place, and from here attacking samurai could shoot at the enemy. This included walls mounted on arms that could be raised so that samurai could shoot out from below them and other such contraptions.

Shields, Bamboo Fences and Bundles

Human-sized wooden shields that stood erect with the help of a hinged single leg would protect samurai. In addition to this, bamboo was tied in large bundles and shooting ports were cut out of the middle. These bundles could be leaned against waist-height temporary fences so that samurai could shoot from behind cover.

Cannon and Fire

Cannon were used to launch fire and incendiary weapons and shot. *Kajutsu*— "the skills of fire"—included long-range rockets, flares and anything that causes flames in the enemy camp. Some shinobi were essentially agents who moved into the enemy castle and made sure that fires were set from within. One shinobi trick was to set a fire away from the main target to distract the defenders from the actual target and then to move on with their initial aim of setting fire to more important things like the main compound.

Tunneling

Tunneling was undertaken to undermine the enemy defenses. If done in secret and not on a war front, the tunnel had to start far from the target, or start from inside a nearby house. To discover if tunneling was taking place, empty barrels would be set into the ground to listen for mining below.

A samurai may have to leave his lord to undertake a mission of vengeance. This may make him a rōnin for the duration of that mission, which could last years.

Moat Crossing Skills

Portable bridges and temporary structures were used to cross rivers and bridges. The shinobi's task was to discover the length, width and depth of a moat and report the dimensions, or to cross it in secret at night.

On the whole, the samurai castle was a place of residence and the target of a siege. The samurai would defend and attack castles with ingenious tricks and tactics and shinobi on both sides would come and go, stealing information or setting fires to things, something that was quite normal in life as a samurai.

Life as a Samurai

The world of the samurai has formed and has now taken shape within your mind; the idea of the castles that they manned and the battle camps they erected is now firm within this new image. The next step is to form an idea of the life that the samurai and shinobi led.

Bunbu—The Brush and the Sword

The samurai were not just "butchers of men" and were not purely fighting machines—and I do not wish to give the impression that they were just ruthless killers. Quite the opposite; they were educated poet-warriors (to varying degrees). Samurai tried to adhere to the concept of *bunbu*, a concept that translates as "literature and the military," or in Japanese, "the brush and sword." A samurai was required to follow two ways: *the way of the soldier* and also the *way of education and literature*.

The first part, the military, is the way of the soldier. The way of the soldier means the arts of war, the equipment used and knowledge of conflict. A Natori-Ryu manual from the early Edo Period states the following about the martial arts that are to be used by the samurai:

武藝者之品々之事
Bugeisha no Shinajina no Koto
The types of martial artists
A samurai serves through good martial arts; also, samurai are skilled in various paths that have been transmitted to them. The following are the kinds of arts in which samurai should train themselves:

1. *Yumi* – archery
2. *Uma* – horsemanship
3. *Kenjutsu* – swordsmanship
4. *Sōjutsu* – spearsmanship
5. *Gunjutsu* – the skills of war
6. *Yawara Jutoritei* – wrestling and grappling
7. *Teppō* – marksmanship
8. *Suiren* – Aquatic training

There are a myriad of other styles; however, they are offshoots from the above and all have benefits. Study each of these arts from someone who is skilled in that way.

The second part—literature, study and education, including the flowing topics—would also be in the samurai curriculum. Remember that subjects came into and moved out of fashion. This list covers the whole age of the samurai and may be added to:

1. Chinese literary classics
2. Chinese warfare classics
3. Etiquette
4. Japanese and Chinese grammar and written language
5. Calligraphy
6. Shinto
7. Buddhism
8. Confucianism and Neo-confucianism
9. *Omyodo* esoteric magic
10. Esoteric cosmology
11. Astronomy and astrology
12. Poetry
13. Ballads
14. Dance
15. Tea ceremony
16. Ritual magic
17. *Chi* (with connection to warfare)
18. Command and leadership
19. Hunting and falconry
20. Ritual and ceremony of various smaller forms

Education in the Warring States Period focused on practical military ability. In the times of peace it centered on bureaucratic and artistic subjects. The level of attention to each of the above shifted, depending on each situation, but in the main the samurai were the educated warriors of their day. The samurai were not brute raiders and fighters alone, but comprised of educated upper middle class gentry who could involve themselves in deeds of warfare and bloodshed. Overall, the best among them were well educated and very dangerous; the thinking officer.

The Samurai and Shinobi Schools

For approximately half of the history of the samurai—that being the latter half—samurai formed themselves into "schools" and "traditions." Starting around the fourteenth century but gaining popularity in the fifteenth century, they started to form organizations that collected under a single title.

They added the suffix "Ryu" to their names. Examples of these are Tenshin Katori Shinto-Ryu, and Shinkage-Ryu. The term "Ryu" can be translated in two ways that are not separate; first it is translated as "school" and second as "flow of tradition." Therefore, Sekiguchi-Ryu means the "flow of traditions from in the Sekiguchi family." However, this of course still holds the connotations of the codified school.

The school can either start with a family name or can adopt a name that the founder finds appropriate to his style. The following show both examples:

Natori-Ryu—Named after the Natori family, they also adopted the name Shin-Kusunoki-Ryu as a secondary title due to their integration with Kusunoki tactics. Natori-Ryu is a school of Gungaku military study and concentrates on the higher tasks of warfare, such as tactics and warfare strategy. This school includes *shinobi no jutsu*—"the arts of the ninja." Another example is Sekiguchi-Ryu, which is also based on a family name.

Mubyoshi-Ryu—Literally "no rhythm school" was most likely named to show the elite nature of the founder. Started by Hagiwara Juzo in the 1600s—he took many teachings from Shinjin-Ryu—the name Mubyoshi is correctly translated as "the school without any discernible rhythm," i.e., an enemy cannot predict their tactics. The school is a comprehensive martial arts school which includes martial arts of various forms, ritual magic, weapons training, criminal capture, martial philosophy and shinobi no jutsu—the arts of the shinobi.

Generally a school is founded by a single man who has a moment of divine inspiration, such as a god who came to them as they diligently trained in the mountains for a number of weeks or months. At this point a god or spirit gave them the secrets that their school was based on. In addition to this a school may also include a famous name from history, a great general, or famous fighter to help attract students. This was done to give a prestige to their image. Often examples such as Kusunoki and Takeda (including Koshu where the great general was from) are used to add that bit of extra appeal. Likewise for shinobi related schools—names such as Yoshitune were used for the same reason. People famed for their expertise in guerrilla warfare may have been added to a school's background. These backgrounds may have been given because schools would be formed by a swordsman studying other arts, combining them to form a "new style." Therefore they needed an anchor point in history. Founders may pick a god to establish the school, and maybe add a famous person from history that was well known; or at least highlighted during the founder's lifetime. For example, the founder might use a person long dead, but whose name was known to give prestige to the school. But this was not always the case.

Generally a school has a central building that it uses as a headquarters, where the master will teach. It may have branches in certain areas. Each building will normally have a "kan" name, the ideogram "kan" 館 means "building" or "construction." It is the name given to the place where that branch studies—for example, the previously mentioned Mubyoshi-Ryu had its headquarters in Kaga domain. Their training hall or group were called "Keibukan" 経武館, meaning "To pursue the way of Samurai," and of course any other branch was entitled to have their own "kan" name, while remaining under the overall banner of the school. It did not always have to follow this "kan" format. For example, the headquarters of Ichizen-Ryu, which was run by a samurai named Chikamatsu Shigenori in the 1700s in Nagoya castle, was called Rempeido.

To enter a samurai school a warrior normally had to make an oath to confirm that he would not reveal the school's secrets to anyone. Often this would take the form of *keppan*—a blood oath. This was normally an oath to the gods with a small offering of blood to seal the vow between the student and the gods, not the instructor. A student could leave a samurai school if they wished, it was not a lifetime commitment. Upon formally leaving a school the samurai may have to give back any scrolls they had received or copied, and they would then be free to join another school. Samurai could train in multiple schools at the same time. This was not an issue. Some samurai would use a martial arts school to study combat and other schools to study military arts, ceremony and other facets of samurai life.

The following is a keppan from the school Oishi Shinkage-Ryu that was signed in 1837 or 1838.

The texts can be summed up as follows:

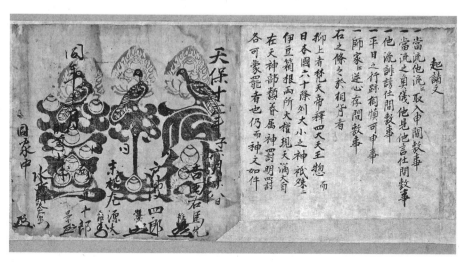

- Those of our school should not enter combat with people of other schools
- Do not give away the secrets of our school to others
- Do not speak ill of other schools
- Be reserved in your manner
- Do not transgress against our master

After this there is a list of gods to whom the student had to swear an oath.

Qualifications in samurai schools were also varied in format, but the most famous is the concept of *menkyo*—"licence." The black belt is a modern invention. Proper samurai schools would be divided into students, both high and new, then instructors. At the top of all these were master teachers at the head of the school. Students on entering a school would move through a very limited selection of positions, ranks, or levels until they had mastered the style enough to be awarded menkyo, henceforth being recognized as a teacher of the art. The next and final step was to achieve the kaiden level, making them *menkyo kaiden*—"master teacher." This was an extremely high position and required decades of training with a full knowledge of the school and all of its secrets. The level of training and skill to acquire this position must not be underestimated. For example, the above mentioned war master Chikamatsu Shigenori was a student of Naganuma-Ryu (considered an extremely prestigious samurai school) and out of around one thousand students at the time, only ten were awarded menkyo kaiden. Chikamatsu Shigenori was one of them—meaning his skills should have been exceptional.

A sample of a Naganuma-Ryu manual, all of which is in mock Chinese.

Teachings inside a school could be divided into many different formats and normally followed a rising pattern of levels; there are multiple ways to divide the inner teachings of a school, so the following is a sampler to get the feel of how it would work.

The shinobi arts of Yoshitune-Ryu are divided into the following levels or gradients:

1. 法 *Ho*
2. 配 *Hai*
3. 術 *Jutsu*

Some of the shinobi arts that were transmitted by Chikamatsu Shigenori are not divided into sections; instead, each individual skill is divided into three, starting with the most basic teachings of that skill and moving to the highest level of achievement in that *specific* skill:

1. 初 *Sho*
2. 中 *Chu*
3. 後 *Go*

A similar concept is to have skills divided into three levels known as *shuhari*:

1. 守 *Shu* – The form, the structure of a skill, and to follow the basics.
2. 破 *Ha* – To break from the form, to start to allow the form to fall away, and the teaching to be used freely.
3. 離 *Ri* – To be free of the form and to create using principles.

Remember, we must not imagine that the samurai is simply a brute, yet we must not see him as incapable of horrific acts; so to help to show the complexities of samurai thinking the following are examples of just how deep samurai thought could be:

本末

The concept of Honmatsu

Hon 本—Meaning "source" or "origin," this is the root of things, the focus and the center; an analogy would be the trunk of a tree and could be seen as internal.

Matsu 末—Meaning "secondary," this is the surface of all things, the outside; an analogy would be the leaves of a tree and it could be seen as things external.

The concept of *honmatsu* is to identify and discern between that which is an internal truth and the periphery, the reality of what is happening on the inside of a situation and that which is external—i.e., to identify if information is directly from the source or if it is secondhand, or to know a person's true feelings above the feelings that they display publicly.

利 & 道理

Ri and Dori

Ri 利 – Constructed logic

Dori 道理 – Truth

A samurai and shinobi need to identify that which is a *truth* and that which is *constructed logic*. Ri is the false, the man-made information and the arguments constructed with an agenda, while Dori is the truth of a matter, the reality.

虚実

Kyojitsu

Kyo 虚 – Insubstantial

Jitsu 実 – Substantial

This term is heavily used in samurai and shinobi records; it is equated to *solid and weak, presence and the illusion of presence, a true attack or a feint.* The idea is that in warfare a strategic move is either a real and serious move or it is a feint. This is found in all warfare: the movement of troops, the positioning of forces, the outward structure of a fortress, etc. One of the main tasks of the shinobi is to discover if something is *kyo* or if it is *jitsu,* i.e., if it is fake or true.

There are numerous examples like the above, but only a few have been outlined here to show that the samurai followed the intellectual and the philosophical—yet at the same time, their primary aim was war.

Samurai and Shinobi Scrolls

When the period of the great wars came to an end, the samurai were concerned with the skills of their schools becoming useless and a massive increase in written scrolls erupted with the aim to preserve their teachings. At a basic level, samurai manuals are written to preserve the teachings when those teachings cannot be tested in warfare.

Samurai and shinobi skills are often given names and are collated together. This has led to the belief that samurai and shinobi scrolls are written in code, which is erroneous. Normally the name of a skill is poetic or has a visual trigger and the contents are taught by word of mouth—*kuden.* This means that often some samurai and shinobi scrolls are in the format of a *mokuroku*—a list. This list is unintelligible to a normal reader, not because it is in code, but because it is a list of skill *names* that the reader has not had the opportunity to have explained to them. For example, the *Bansenshukai ninja* scroll—*The Book of Ninja* in English—lists the following skills:

- Six points on preparations
- Three points of *Katsuraotoko no jutsu* (planting an undercover agent within a possible enemy)
- Three points of *Jokei jutsu* (planning an undercover attack in a tense or urgent situation)
- Two points of *Kunoichi no jutsu* when using *Kunoichi* (female agents)
- Two points of *Satobito no jutsu* (utilizing local people)
- Two point of *Minomushi no jutsu* (making a spy out of a local inhabitant)
- Two points on *Fukurogaeshi no jutsu—the skill of reversing a bag* (serving the enemy and then betraying them in the end)
- Three points on *Hotarubi no jutsu—the skill of fireflies* (the skill of writing a false letter to make an enemy's retainer look like a betrayer)
- Two points on *Tenda no jutsu—spitting with your face skyward* (making the enemy shinobi convert to your side)
- Two points on *Shikyu no jutsu—the skill of relaxing a bowstring* (falsely defecting to the enemy's side when you have been captured but in truth betraying them in the end)
- Two points on *Yamabiko no jutsu—the skill of echoes* (the relation between the commander and the *shinobi* and how they should have a good accord)
- Three points of *Mukaeire no jutsu* (infiltrating into the enemy long before they get close)
- Two points of *Bakemono jutsu* (disguise and transformation)
- Three points of *Katatagae no jutsu* (infiltrating the enemy when they attack at night)
- Three points of *Minazuki no jutsu* (infiltrating the enemy when they retreat from a night attack)
- Five points on the skill of *Taniiri no jutsu* (infiltrating the enemy sporadically)
- Two points on *Ryohen no jutsu* (using a prisoner)
- Two points on *Fukurogaeshi no jutsu* (making the enemy's commander or retainer look like a betrayer by forging letters to his family or relatives)

The above skill list has had explanations added in brackets, but the original terms still remain poetic or cryptic. For example, the skill *Bakemono jutsu* means "the skill of the shape-shifter" and includes the idea of a ghost shape-shifter, making the skill sound supernatural to the uninitiated. This is while *Fukurogaeshi no jutsu* means "the skill of reversing a bag." As can be seen, if there was no explanation to these teachings, it would be impossible to decipher what the skills actually were, some of which are extremely ambiguous. Of course, if the scroll is simply a mokuroku, or list, then the teachings are missing. Yet it is extremely important to understand that many scrolls were written down to capture and record these skills.

For example, the above skills are all explained in detail in the actual *Bansenshukai* manual. Therefore, the first question when looking at a scroll is if it contains a full explanation or simply a list.

Something that is very much a staple part of Japanese life is to make a "Way" out of a subject, to give it an identity. Inside that identity the Japanese love to give names to skills. These names have various suffixes attached to them; the following is a selection of the most common, with their respective translations. However, these are normally considered less strong than the intention of the English word. It sometimes can be generally seen as "things to do with X" or "points and items to discuss about X." So you often find that the Japanese themselves will swap between them even within the same manual:

- ⋯ノ傳 – *no Tsutae* can be translated as "Tradition of"
- ⋯之事 – *no Koto* can be translated as "Art of"
- ⋯大事 – *no Daiji* can be translated as "Principle of"
- ⋯ノ術 – *no Jutsu* can be translated as "Skill of"

The schools of the shinobi are much harder to pinpoint than straight samurai schools. There is an extremely difficult line to identify between a samurai school with a shinobi syllabus and a pure shinobi school, if such a thing ever existed. There are of course samurai schools with zero shinobi skill sets. However, many of them have some form of shinobi teachings. For example, Sekiguchi-Ryu Battojutsu— headed by the seventeenth inheritor Yamada Toshiyasu—have scrolls with a small selection of points on shinobi ways. These include poisons, sleeping powders, and shinobi torches. Even while smaller than other schools, they still are shinobi related.

Yamada Toshiyasu, the seventeenth inheritor of Sekiguchi-Ryu Battojutsu.

Other schools, such as Chikamatsu Shigenori's Ichizen-Ryu and Natori-Masazumi's Natori-Ryu, contained high levels of shinobi arts. Yet schools like Fujibayashi-Ryu,* Iga-Ryu, and Koka-Ryu appear to have taught only, or predominantly, shinobi arts. However, in the main, military schools have a headquarters with a lineage that connects their students to the past. The two schools that seem to fall outside of this theme are predominantly shinobi schools, which only add to the confusion. Iga-Ryu and Koka-Ryu are famous for being shi-

---

* The author of the *Bansenshukai* named Fujibayashi never states the name of his school and only uses "To-Ryu" ("our school"); therefore I have simply named it after his family, but the school name may have been different.

nobi schools; however, they have no central organization and no unified direct lineage. They do not share the same teachings between their incarnations. That means that the terms Iga-Ryu and Koka-Ryu appear to be used in the literal sense, that is, they are considered "flows of tradition from Iga and from Koka." In most cases their teachings are passed on from master to student and attached to another school of military arts. It is likely that a samurai would study a "standard" school and then study the teachings of Iga and Koka, which would add shinobi expertise to their skill set. These two schools have varying lineages and histories, and appear to be branches of Iga and Koka shinobi skill sets.

People in Samurai Life

Samurai is a generic term for a thousand years of history and a very stratified social system. When dealing with samurai history there are certain words that continue to appear and certain subsections start to form. The classification of samurai and samurai life is a vast subject; therefore, the following is a basic outline of some of the elements found within it. Each title can have many variations depending on dialect and the ideograms used, and even the geographical location, but most importantly, chronology has a drastic effect on samurai terminology—therefore not all terms existed at the same time.

侍
Samurai
Generic term for the warrior class.

武士
Bushi
Alternative name for samurai.

武者
Musha
A term used to mean warriors in general.

武士
Mononofu
Alternative name for samurai used in poetry.

大将
Taisho
The lord-commander, or commander-in-chief, of a state or army.

旗本
Hatamoto
A samurai group around the lord. Normally sons from *fudai* families, which have served the same clan for generations, securing loyalty. However, the use of Hatomoto does have variations throughout history but should be seen as the command group or inner circle around a samurai lord.

母衣武者
Horomusha
High-ranking samurai who wear a *horo,* which is a form of arrow-catching cape; they are normally mounted.

軍法者
Gunposha
A samurai trained in military strategy.

軍配者
Gunbaisha
A samurai trained in astrology, divination, the observation of *chi* and auspicious dates and days.

騎馬武者
Kibamusha
A mounted samurai.

徒士武者
Kachizamurai
A samurai on foot.

譜代
Fudai
A fudai family is a family that has served the same clan for generations, giving loyalty generation after generation.

外様
Tozama
A *tozama* is a samurai or family who is "new" to service, i.e. they have less than one generation of service to a lord. They may have served for an entire lifetime, or they may have served for only a short time; the issue is that they do not have a record of generational service and are therefore considered "outside" the "trust" of the lord, even though they may be loyal in actuality.

小姓

Kosho

A kosho is a form of page or squire who serves a lord. The concept of squire is difficult to place in Japan. Samurai are born into the samurai class or are promoted through deeds of arms; there is no need for promotion from squire to knight as in the West and pages may be of any age, even though they are normally younger boys. They normally do not serve samurai themselves, mainly lords.

浪人／牢人

Rōnin

A displaced samurai yet still of the samurai class. They are samurai without land or fief and have no official employment. Considered vagabonds, however, the story of the rōnin is deep and interesting and shall be discussed later.

用心棒

Yojimbo

A personal bodyguard hired in times of peace to give close and personal protection.

渡り侍

Watari Zamurai

Wandering mercenaries, a form of rōnin for hire who would rent their services to different sides in times of conflict.

地侍

Jizamurai

Landed gentry as previously described, who later became half samurai.

土豪

Dogo

The dogo class are similar to the jizamurai, being land-owning families. In the Edo Period these were half samurai, and according to Charles J. Dunn in his book *Everyday Life in Traditional Japan*, they wore a single sword, a jacket and had bare legs and served within the cities.

徒膚者

Suhadamono

Half-dressed warriors, normally warriors on the field of battle who had bare legs and light armor.

無足人

Musokunin

A term from the Edo Period given to ex-samurai who had fallen from samurai status yet who had been given the title of Musokunin, so as to differentiate them from the peasant class.

古士

Koshi

Ex-samurai, similar to the above.

野武士

Nobushi, Yamadachi, and *Sanzoku*

Bandit samurai, groups of bandits who lived from pillaging but yet are considered warriors.

足軽

Ashigaru

Foot soldiers, just below samurai class but still considered military personnel.

忍

Shinobi

A commando-spy employed by the military to act in covert operations; also known as shinobi no mono and ninja.

間者

Kanja

A spy. The term is often interchangeable with shinobi no mono but has slight differences depending on the primary source used.

Oda Nobunaga had the heads of three men cut off—one was his brother-in-law—and had their skulls lacquered and sprinkled with gold dust and presented at a party.

盗人

Nusubito

A thief.

盗賊

Tozoku

Thieves, normally in gangs, who break into property in organized teams but can be solitary; the term is often interchangeable with nusubito.

The Rōnin

By definition, a samurai either needed to be an independent landowner or employed by a lord. If the samurai were to lose either of these he would either drop in social class or become a rōnin. The term rōnin is thought to originally derive from *furonin*, which literally translates as "float-wave person." This should be understood as "those people who float on the wave," i.e., they have no fixed position. A different origin and use of ideogram has the same pronunciation as rōnin, but has the meaning of "imprisoned person."

Remembering that samurai status in the pre-Edo Period was transient and that people could flow between the samurai and non-samurai class; this meant that becoming a rōnin was not career threatening. However, in the late 1500s laws were passed that stopped rōnin from gaining employment without the permission of their last employer. This created a dangerous mass of wandering rōnin who could not find employment for their military skills. In the Warring States Period, rōnin could hire their skills out to the next lord. However, on agreement of employment they would stop being a rōnin and become a samurai retainer—this means that a samurai was only a rōnin for the period he was not employed for. However, in the early Edo Period, a samurai had to remain as rōnin without the blessing of his previous lord. To make matters worse, in the early Edo Period some of the larger samurai clans fell and had their lands possessed, adding to the growing rōnin problem. From this emerged attempted coups, rebellions and incidents where the rōnin tried to force political matters and change. Eventually the ban on the re-hiring of rōnin was lifted and they could serve once more as samurai.

To imagine the rōnin and place him in the overall spectrum of the samurai, think of the Warring States period and of a samurai who was dissatisfied with his lord, or of a lord dissatisfied with his vassal, or even that the lord had died. This samurai would take to the road, move in samurai circles and present his credentials to new lords where he may find new employment and join the ranks of a samurai army once more. As peace came over the horizon, the re-hiring of rōnin became rigidly controlled and masses of rōnin start appearing on the map of Japan. They started causing trouble and became a force unto themselves. In response, the Tokugawa shogunate relaxed the rules and they were reabsorbed into society—the story of the rōnin has given birth to the iconic wandering samurai of modern cinema, the vagabond killer.

Kabukimono

The dandy of old Japan, this figure was a subculture of the samurai. At the end of the Warring States Period and the start of the era of peace came libertine-style dandies. They were warriors who dressed with flamboyance, were loud and caused a ruckus. They wore extravagant sword fittings, sometimes even female clothes, and bright colors, moved in bands and generally caused ample trouble.

The Knight Errant

A *Musha shugyo* is a samurai pilgrimage, where a warrior will wander the country in search of other combatants to test their skills against; pitting themselves in duels to the death and challenges to other schools, the most famous of these is Miyamoto Musashi—the legendary sword saint.

The Tools of the Samurai

Is the samurai sword the soul of the samurai? Well, not quite. The katana has been given a central place in the image of the samurai; however, as mentioned previously, the spear and the bow also have a claim to be the samurai's principle weapon. The heightened glory of the sword is a factor from an era of peace, when armor was stowed away and spears were put to rest; but the samurai kept the sword. A samurai was a warrior and each could pick his own weapons. One samurai may favor the chain and sickle, another the bow and the next a long sword. If a samurai knows his opponent has a specialty with a specific weapon, then it is best to defend against that samurai by forcing him to fight with a different weapon, or alternatively to create distance between the enemy and to hit them with projectiles. A samurai may not carry his bow or spear but they must *always* have their swords.

To understand the samurai and his tools, consider the following list of weapons used by the samurai—they have been placed together according to their range capabilities:

- Fire rockets
- Bows: including fire arrows and gas attacks
- Muskets
- Hand-thrown projectile weapons and grenades
- Long chain weapons
- The spear and other pole-arms, including quarterstaffs
- Shorter chain weapons
- Long swords
- Short swords
- Daggers and dirks
- Truncheons, knuckle dusters and grappling tools

Samurai would have to utilize whichever tool or weapon that situation demanded and have proficiency in most, if not all, with the additional constraint or having to own and maintain most of the above. Many modern cinema adaptions from Japan would have the modern reader believe that poor samurai wandered the land, having to sell their sword blades or work as evil bodyguards to save their ailing wife. However, while it cannot be disputed that some samurai were poor, this image has been portrayed because of the audience's love of the "underdog" story. In truth, a samurai who has been retained by a lord has lodgings or a house; they are furnished with a salary proportionate to their abilities or social status, and they themselves retain servants. The concept of the "poor samurai" image is heavily associated with the end of the period of peace. Peace had been in Japan for over two centuries and land grabbing through war was no longer an option. Samurai being hereditary positions in this period meant that land and income could be divided between sons—or given to the eldest—and over the generations retainer fees become smaller and smaller. The pressure of this reduction in monetary power was increased with the rise in wealth of the merchant class, and together they saw many samurai fall into poverty.

However, this was only *one* period of samurai history, the end. The actual periods of interest are in the warring years when a samurai could make a fortune, and fortunes were made and land and vast incomes were competed for. In these times the samurai supported a house complex, possibly horses, an array of martial weapons and armor, food stocks, slaves and servants. A retained samurai could afford these things—with only the horse being out of reach of some samurai—therefore it was not a case of "if they could afford a sword, etc.," but was more of a case of what level of sword they could afford. Samurai would pass down family heirlooms; however, at times they would also have to purchase their own arsenal or add to their stocks and both a market for secondhand and new items existed. Remember, a samurai had an arsenal and in the main a samurai had a good life by the standards of the day and the katana was only a small part of that; and while some samurai fell on hard times it is not an image you should maintain as your primary image of the samurai.

A samurai called Arisawa Nagasada (1638–1715) from Kaga domain wrote about samurai arts and equipment in the seventeenth century in a manual called *Heiho Nukigaki Hippu no Sho*. His writings were made to educate other samurai. The following is a reduced list of topics from the manual:

- ◆ Concerning lightweight armor
- ◆ Understanding outfits
- ◆ Knowing which tools are appropriate to status
- ◆ Concerning high and low status as a warrior
- ◆ Concerning decoration
- ◆ Understanding the equipment that you excel in and the mindset to have
- ◆ Of advantages and disadvantages
- ◆ Preparation of armor

The clothes a samurai needs:

- Headband
- Under-jacket
- Undergarments—for both summer and winter
- The outer belt
- Underwear and loin cloth
- Leggings
- Outer trousers
- Straw sandals
- Straw boots

Gear for battle:

- Armor containers
- The helmet rest
- The banner holder
- The battle hat
- Rainproof gear

The basic parts of armor:

- The breast plate
- The helmet
- The face mask
- Gauntlets and arm protection
- Thigh plates
- Greaves

The Shoka no Hyojo manual says that most people should be captured if they are roaming around where they should not be on a battlefield or around battle camps, but if they resist then they should be killed. It goes on to say that it is best to capture shinobi that are sneaking around and not to kill them.

Arisawa continues with some hints and advice on tools and equipment that lower samurai should focus on—the headings are given here:

- The banner
- Small flags
- Flag attachments and poles
- Decoration on flag poles
- Short swords and daggers
- Identification marks
- War swords
- Sword handles—both long and short
- Issues on the length of the sword handle

- Hilt fittings
- Sword rivets—to hold the sword in place
- Concerning the "mouth" of the scabbard
- The hilt washer
- Hair arranger—a small blunt spike on the side of the sword [shinobi use these to climb]
- The sword cord
- The cord to tie the sword to the wrist
- The sword belt
- The different forms of daisho—long and short swords

The manual continues on the topic of spears:

- The fittings used on our own spears
- The advantages and disadvantages of spear length, especially in night raids
- Pikes and pole-arms
- The three types of spear haft
- The parts of the spear—blade, haft, butt with socket, iron bands on the haft and rings attached
- The size of spear scabbards

The above gives an understanding of the complexity of samurai equipment and offers only a brief overview of the samurai arsenal. The sword is not given a place of prestige: what is important is that a samurai maintain gear for war and be ready to move to battle at short notice, with all of the equipment needed.

Having understood that the sword is not the only weapon of the samurai, the following list is that which a samurai should take to help him in day-to-day life during military campaigns. Lists contained within original Japanese documents do differ; therefore the following items have been compiled from multiple sources and are things a samurai should carry in his portable box:

- Comb
- Scissors
- Tweezers
- Rolls of cloth—including a three feet cloth band
- Razor
- Whetstone
- Powdered makeup (white)
- Mirror
- Magnet or compass
- Needle and thread

- Glue
- Dried bonito
- Dried abalone
- Strong paper strings
- Torches
- Hooks and rings
- Digging tools
- Drills
- Saws
- Ropes of different lengths and thickness
- Hammer and nails
- Ink and ink stone (black and red)
- Paper
- Leather thongs
- Warning clappers (two blocks on a string to clap together to give signals)

The Sword of the Samurai

Now that it has been established that the sword is not in the exalted position of the single focus of the samurai, it has to be reinforced that it was still of high importance and is a constant companion in his life. One thing that must be clear is that *a* sword is of vital importance and *not* that a *certain* sword is of importance. A samurai may have his sword stolen, the blades taken or snapped by shinobi; a temporary servant may steal them and sell the swords on the market at Edo so that he can go off gambling; street thieves may take the samurai's sword by force; a samurai may lend his sword to a man in a duel; or a sword can even be taken home by the wrong person after a drinking party. The main issue of samurai honor is to have and be seen *with* a sword, it does not necessarily have to be the *same* sword. In addition, a samurai will always carry his short sword at his side unless he is forced to remove it by a higher-ranking person. Normally, long swords are left in allotted rooms or put into storage when visiting others or when a guest in another's house—the samurai can also put his sword next to him on the floor.

Sword Typology

The study of the sword is a deep and well-researched subject, and experts in both Japan and the rest of the world have dedicated their lives to the beauty and craftsmanship of the Japanese sword. Therefore, here I will give a brief overview of the evolution of the sword. Being a specialist subject, I have turned to Mr Paul Martin, a specialist on Japanese swords who has kindly provided the following chronology. The descriptions are heavy with terminology; however, Mr. Martin provides a full glossary of terms on his website www.thejapanesesword.com.

Mr Paul Martin at work in Japan. His work can be seen on social media sites under the name *The Japanese Sword* or at his website of the same name (www.thejapanesesword.com).

Paul Martin's sword chronology:

1. Late Heian to Early Kamakura

   From the late Heian Period and the early Kamakura Period (1185–1333) we can see the Japanese sword as we know it: *shinogi-zukuri* (ridgeline) construction, with a wide base, narrowing acutely towards the small point section (*ko-kissaki*). They are quite slender blades with the curvature concentrated between the handle and base. This shape is called *koshi-zori*. From midway towards the point there is very little curvature. These blades are usually around 2.5–6 shaku in length (75.8–78.8 cm).

2. Mid-Kamakura

   At the zenith of the warrior class's power during the Kamakura Period, the blade's *kasane* becomes thick, the *mihaba* becomes wide, and they take on magnificent *tachi* shape. There is not much difference between the size of the *moto-haba* and the *saki-haba*. The blade still has *koshi-zori*, but the center of the curvature has moved further along the blade. The *kissaki* has become a compact *chu-kissaki* (*ikubi*). The hamon has developed into a flowing gorgeous *choji-midare*. Also around this time, *tanto* production appears.

3. Late Kamakura

   Tachi at the end of the Kamakura Period have developed into magnificent blades. There are two types: one is wide throughout its length and the point section is the same as mid-Kamakura period *kissaki*, but slightly extended. The other is quite slender and similar in appearance to the late Heian, early Kamakura shapes. However, when you look further along the blade the shape has changed; the curvature has moved further along the blade. During this period *notare-gunome hamon* appeared. It is said that in Sagami province Goro Nyudo Masamune perfected the production of *nie-deki* blades.

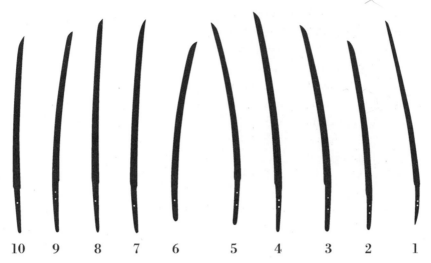

10   9   8   7   6   5   4   3   2   1

The numbers on the image coincide with the numbers in the text on the opposite page and below.

4. Nanbokucho

   During the Nanbokucho Period many long blades of three shaku (90.9 cm) and other long *tachi* were made. *Tanto* of large proportions were also produced. *Tachi* were majestic, wide, and proportionally long. Among these were some over 90 cm in length and worn over the back. These types of blade are called *no-dachi* and *o-dachi*. They were rather thin in construction to decrease the weight. Additionally, many have a *bo-hi* (groove) cut into the *shinogi-ji* area in order to lighten the blade. Many *tachi* from this period are *o-suriage* (shortened in later periods as they were difficult to wield). Consequently, many extant blades from the Nanbokucho Period are unsigned.

5. Early Muromachi

   Blades of the early part of the Muromachi Period are reminiscent in construction to the blades of the early Kamakura Period. When compared to the shape of the Nanbokucho Period, the shape has completely changed and no longer includes *o-kissaki*. At around 2.4–5 shaku (72.7–75.7 cm) in length, they are quite narrow and deeply curved, with a medium-sized point section. At first glance they may appear somewhat similar to Kamakura Period blades, but on closer inspection they are *saki-zori* character.

6. Late Muromachi

   By the late Muromachi Period, samurai fighting methods had changed from cavalry to mass infantry-style warfare. *Uchigatana*, worn with the cutting edge uppermost thrust through the sash, had become popular. After the Onin War, conflicts broke out in many places and *kazu-uchi mono* began to appear (mass-produced blades inferior in quality to regular Japanese blades). However, specially ordered blades of excellent quality (*chumon-uchi*) were also produced at this time. Bizen (Okayama prefecture) and Mino (Gifu prefecture) were the major places of production. Many blades produced in this period are around 2.1 shaku (63.6 cm) in length. They are slightly wider than the standard width, with either a *chu-kissaki* or an extended *chu-kissaki* and strong *saki-zori*. The *nakago* are short, intended for one-handed use.

7. Azuchi-Momoyama

Swords produced up to the Keicho era (1596–1614) are classified as *kotō* ("old blades"). Blades made during and after this era are classified as *shintō* ("new swords"). When Japan entered the Azuchi-Momoyama Period, many smiths moved to Edo or Kyoto, or gathered in castle towns of various influential daimyo. Additionally, developments in transportation brought about experimentation with materials, and foreign-made steel (known as *nanbantetsu*) was utilized. The blade's shape from around this period mirrors that of shortened Nanbokucho blades. They are generally wide, with little or no difference between the *moto* and *saki-haba*. Many have an extended *chu-kissaki*, while some have *o-kissaki*, with a thick *kasane* and are usually around 2.4–5 shaku (72.7–75.8 cm) in length.

8. Mid-Edo

Swords of the mid-Edo Period are of standard width. The *saki-haba* is relatively narrow when compared to the *moto-haba*. The curvature is noticeably shallow with a small to medium-sized point section. They are usually around 2.3 shaku (69.7 cm) in length. This particular type of construction was generally produced around the middle of the Kanbun (1661–73) and Enpo (1673–81) eras, and is usually referred to as Kanbun-shintō.

9. Edo Period, Genroku era

The change in shape of Japanese swords between the Jokyo (1684–88) and Genroku (1688–1704) eras reflects the transition of shape from Kanbun-shintō blades to the beginning of the Shin-shintō period of sword manufacture. As it was a very peaceful period in Japanese history, rather flamboyant *hamon* appear, and as opposed to that of Kanbun-shintō blades, the curvature is quite deep.

10. Edo Period, Bakamatsu era

Blades made after the Bunka (1804–18) and Bunsei (1818–30) eras are referred to as *fukko-shintō* (revival swords). Pioneers of the revival movement include Suishinshi Masahide and Nankai Taro Tomotaka. Taikei Naotane was among Masahide's students. Minamoto Kiyomaro led a revival aimed at *soshu-den* and

Mino-Shizu workmanship. Bakumatsu blades are shallow in curvature, have a wide *haba* with not much difference in width between the *saki* and *moto-haba*, and are around 2.5–6 shaku (75.7–78.7 cm) in length, with an *o-kissaki* and thick *kasane*.

Testing the sword

Test cutting on bamboo and rolled straw is now a staple of the samurai image; however, it does have a darker side. The use of convicted criminals or the corpses of dead criminals was done to test the efficiency of a blade. In addition to this, there was also the criminal activity of *tsujigiri*—"testing swords on passers-by at night."

Cleaning and sharpening the sword

If you have held an original samurai sword it is likely that it was in a dim museum room or antique collectors shop. You will have been passed the sword, blade upright with the back of the blade towards your face. Then you probably rested the blade on the sleeve of your jacket and commented on the beauty of the object, before you passed it back in the same manner, white gloves grasping the black hilt. In contrast, a samurai would grab it in a flash, draw it and hack a man's head off with it or open up his belly, spilling his guts; then if it was bent he would try and hammer it back into shape—not quite the same treatment. Also, if you have ever seen a sword polished and cleaned, the whole affair is a delicate art and the sword is not allowed to be breathed on in some circles (a factor that one of my friends was unaware of when he was politely told by the head teacher of Katori Shinto Ryu, when we were having tea and biscuits with him one day, and the friend had happened to breath all over the sword). In contrast, a samurai, after he had removed the blade from the head of his victim, would normally pick up horse droppings, or gravel, fold it inside some paper and scratch the blade as he cleaned the slopping red liquid off the sword. This means that in modern and some high-class circles of samurai days, swords were regarded as elegant works of art, but for the common samurai his sword was a vicious tool. It must be stressed that you have to be careful not to sway too far from the image that is already present and know that in fact a samurai would take good care of his sword. They would have it cleaned and polished if needed, they would give another samurai's sword respect—a respect for the samurai owner which was transferred through the sword. The sword was held as a valuable weapon and a thing of beauty, but it was also a practical weapon. Therefore a middle view is required: a sword was the racecar of its day, a high performance instrument that was to be cared for but was also an object that could be destroyed in the heat of the moment. Remember, a samurai may have many swords or just a single pair; he would keep it clean and look after it, but the idea of highly polished swords that are passed around in whispers is a modern idea as samurai often came to blows in drinking parties—complaints about bent and broken swords are not few in number.

The *Shoka no Hyojo* manual from the first two decades of the 1600s gives great examples of this less professional approach to sharpening and cleaning a blade.

Hayanetaba no Koto
Quick Sharpening
The following recipe is taken from a secret text from within a tradition of swords-manship:
Use a skin of a toad: Skin a toad in the hour of the Cockerel on the fifteenth day of the eighth month and dry it in the shade. Carry this with you and when you wipe your sword with it, you will find that your sword can even cut through iron or stone. This is also known as *Netaba no Daiji*: this is an oral tradition.

Nori wo Otosu Kusuri no Koto
A recipe to wipe clean coagulated blood [from the blade of a sword]
This recipe is also taken from the writing of the above swordsmanship school:
Skin a mole and dry the skin in the shade, sprinkle powdered *boseki* stone on the fur side and carry this to wipe the blade after you have killed someone. This will remove the blood extremely well. There is more on this in oral traditions.

The above two skills are *haya-waza*—ad hoc skills.

The above shows that the idea of a samurai "flicking the blood" from his sword in a swift motion is a romantic idea and most of the time, paper, horse manure, mole and toad skins and the like were used—a much less romantic image. Of course a samurai would then have to clean the swords properly at the next convenient time to stop them from rusting, but simply flicking the blood off a blade should be considered more ceremonial. This leads us to consider idealistic notions of the samurai in battle and samurai warfare.

The Reality of Battle

Warfare in Japan, like warfare around the world, moved through stages of development and while the veneer of the samurai image overlays all of samurai history, the skills of samurai warfare adapted and changed. Up until this point, the image of the samurai has been developing in your mind's eye. The castle of the samurai looms on hilltops and in flatland defensive positions while the military and portable battle camp, with its spiked defenses and ditches overlooked by watchtowers, sits against the gray skyline. Enemy trenches and huts surround fortifications and war curtains have been erected, signal fires and beacons are on hilltops and mountain crests, horns blare, bells chime and drums beat on the wind, passing their hidden and open messages to the troops. Above all, columns of thin smoke tell of a signal being manned in the distance. Outside of these fortifications, samurai armies move through valleys—but never over the crests of hills—and through ancient forests, forming up on battlefields, displaying the substantial or the insubstantial. Two or more armies join on the field of battle after a game of "cat and mouse," all done to acquire the best positioning, ranks form up and get ready to clash. The cavalry will try to outflank the divisions and fleets will blockade escape routes or other troops from landing. The drums beat the approach and the ashigaru march forward, arrows nocked and muskets primed; they move together or in open formation so that the samurai can charge through, each looking to be the first spear of the battle or even to achieve *ichibankubi—to capture the first head*. While a change in battle tactics, the use of foot soldiers over samurai, the introduction of guns, the decline of mounted warfare and modernization are all important factors to take into account, the main issue to understand and accept is that samurai warfare develops and cannot be pinned down to a single style—also that it has variations between clans, and that evolution and regression have their part to play. At the heart of all this is a military trained, soldier-warrior who has religious determination, who is trained in the ways of weapons and of tactics, with a hardened edge that comes with having taken human life. Standing on the field of battle, his "tribe" with him, his crest splashed across his banner pole, with headband keeping the sweat back, he can see the enemy massed before him. The question is what will kill him first?

The Most Common Killer of Samurai

There have been various examinations of battle wounds and archaeological reports on the frequency of wounds given by Japanese weapons and while some of the statistics differ slightly, a general theme emerges. It has to be taken into account that weapons technology developed greatly, so the following list is a general overview—if you wish to examine a specific time then the position of each may shift.

Most samurai deaths were caused by:

1. Arrows
2. Bullets (this becomes the most common cause towards the end of the Warring States Period)
3. Pole-arms
4. Swords
5. Rocks and stones

The most common killer of samurai is projectile weapons and killing at a distance, followed by the clash of spears and then, lastly, the melee of swords. The idea of the samurai facing off in a sword fight as the world battles around him is a romantic notion and in truth he would have to pass the great volleys of arrows and later on arrows and bullets mixed. Generally a battle consists of the following components:

1. Initial duels or contests (if any)
2. Arrows and gunshot when in range
3. The approach and clash of both sides with spears
4. The general melee
5. The retreat, victory or stand-off

Samurai warfare is complex and many factors contribute to a victory—cavalry charges, deceptive movements, fire attacks, etc.—but in the main, a samurai should worry more about deadly projectiles coming from the sky or the bow of a samurai on horseback than an armed opponent charging them with a sword. But all of the above do kill.

War Cries

War cries can be divided into four basic types:

Before Battle

A single person cries out "Ei, Ei" (this is pronounced "A-A"); after this everyone cries out "Ou" (pronounced "O"), making the war cry "A-A-O" (as said in the alphabet).

Upon Victory

The victors move to the area where the enemy once stood to display dominance; from there they perform the same war cry as above.

A samurai war cry is "Ei Ei O," this is said "A, A, O," as if you were saying them from the alphabet.

After Capturing a Castle

When a castle has been captured, the victors cry out together "A-A-O, A-A-O." The first one is made by a single man who says "A-A-O" and then everyone cries back "A-A-O."

At a Head Inspection

When the head inspection has finished, normally the lord will start the war cry—this is probably just the "A-A" section and the company around him should finish with "O."

The above was taken from an Ohara family document and shows that different war cries were used for different situations.

Guaranteeing a Kill

A field of battle could stretch out over a long distance and war campaigns can reach across states, therefore the need for proof of kills is required. At the center of this requirement for proof is the headhunting cult of the samurai—this is because a head is undeniable proof of a kill. The problem is that at times there may be no time to take a head, a samurai may not have space to carry a head or additional heads or he may even be a shinobi or a member of a night raid, ordered not to take heads because the night raid has to move fast to have the advantage of surprise or momentum. To counter this, samurai had several ways to prove their kill without actually taking a head.

Taking the nose and top lip—In place of a head, a samurai or foot soldier could cut off the nose of the dead. However both the nose and the top lip were needed, this is because the top lip would have stubble or a moustache and therefore proves that a man has been killed and not a woman in place of a man. Sometimes the nose was taken along with the upper part of the skin of the face, including the section with the eyebrows, in essence ripping off the face. In addition the bottom lip and skin of the chin could be taken.

Hidden cloth—A samurai or shinobi could write his name on a cloth and screw it up, then when he has killed an enemy he pushes the cloth or paper to the back of the throat of the dead man. If the head is stolen by battlefield scavengers before the samurai or shinobi can come back to claim it, they could identify which was theirs by checking the back of the throat for their paper or cloth.

Wooden pegs—Samurai or shinobi may write their names on sharpened wooden pegs and as they move through on a night raid they would make a kill and then stab the wooden peg into the body to prove that they had been the one to make the kill if the head was later stolen.

Named arrows—Thin strips of paper with a samurai's name can be threaded through the fletching; in an exchange of arrows, a samurai could identify which of his arrows killed which enemy.

Vows and promises—If on a battlefield a samurai had made a kill and there was time to spare but the head could not be taken, then the man who made the kill would ask a samurai near him to swear to the kill. As a reminder of this, the samurai would rip out a small section of cloth from his armor or helmet and give the other samurai a tag with his name on it; then if both lived until the end of the battle, the two would join again and match the cloth to the helmet and in this way the other samurai—whose word was considered solid—would testify to the kill.

The reason that a samurai may not be able to carry more heads is because he would normally attach the heads to the horns or rings of his saddle on both sides, or he would use a *kubibukuro*, a head-carrying sack—this was a bag of wide netting, not unlike a grandmothers' shopping bag, where heads were placed to be carried back to the battle camp. However, if a samurai killed a *horomusha* ("samurai of the cape"), which is someone of high status, then he would wrap the head in that cape.

Mist, Wind, Rain, and the Sun
The samurai had a few tricks on the field of battle concerning the weather:

Mist—If there is a mist or a fog or even a smoke screen from burning vegetation, such as pine needles, etc., then a samurai or force will try to have their face to the wind. This is because the fog will move to the leeward, which means that the enemy will become the first to be visible—this is because the wind will bring them into the open before the samurai on the leeward side. This principle also applies to illumination at night. Wherever a light source will appear first is where the enemy should be and the defending samurai should not be.

Wind and rain—Rain will follow the direction of the wind. The general rule in most cases is that the rain and the wind must come over a samurai's right shoulder—this is where his attack will come from, meaning that his enemy must look into the wind and the rain, while the samurai's vision is shielded from them.

Sun and the moon—This is the same as the above.

Battles and Rivers
To move an army over a river, shinobi and long distance scouts were used to check the situation ahead. Then a landing position was set up on the opposite bank and troops would move over in stages and not all at once. Bridges may be built or lifelines put in place. The first troops over the river would set up defensively and leave room for the rest of the army to land. Then in stages the army would cross. If the army did not take these precautions and an enemy force was on the other side, the enemy army would let half of the army cross and then attack, making the fleeing troops collide with the crossing troops, drowning many in the process.

Troops can cross water using the following: bridges, with life-lines, by moving in teams and moving across together, by using life jackets, or by moving in teams holding on to horses.

The image on the facing page is an Edo Period block print and shows the now infamous "floating shoes." The Japanese term is *Ukigutsu* and translates literally as "floating" and "shoe;" however, a more fitting translation would be "water platform," and as can be seen, they do not go on the feet as a shoe but act as a plat-

form to move through the water. Other types consist of floats held in cloth and tied around the body.

A samurai army on the move from field of battle to field of battle would invariably cross water. This created a need for water training to be used in battle and on campaign—this became quite a serious and technical affair.

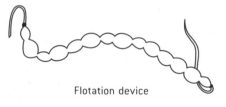

Flotation device

Samurai Swimming

Suiren is a term best translated as "aquatic skills" or "aquatic training." These were collections of skills to help a samurai or foot soldier when swimming in a military capacity. One of the last surviving schools still in existence today is Nojima-Ryu and the following is a selection of their skills, which were written by Tada Ichiro Yoshinao in the late 1800s from a lecture concerning their school's swimming skills:

平泳

Hira oyogi

Breaststroke

This is a basic swimming stroke of our school. This is the most simple and easiest way of swimming. In this stroke you are required to have a full view of both the right and left sides while facing the enemy in the water—just as if you were walking on the ground—and if needs arise to swim wearing your armor and swords. That is why this stroke is designated as a fundamental skill.

抜手
Nukite
Withdrawing hand
Use this when you swim facing the wind and waves or when crossing the tide. In this style your body naturally leans obliquely [in the water], which allows you to cut through the waves with your shoulder and to avoid the waves foaming against your face. This enables you to swim at a higher speed.

水入
Suiri
Diving under water
A method of moving under water.

底息
Sokoiki
Holding your breath
A method to hold your breath for longer periods in water.

捨浮
Suteuki
Floating body
A method of floating on the surface of the sea to rest when you are tired.

枯木流シ
Kareki nagashi
Flowing like a stick
Method used when you get leg cramps while swimming.

筏流
Ikada nagashi
Flowing raft
A method in which people, or even tens of people, perform the above skill of *kareki nagashi* in a united form.

輕石流シ
Karuishi nagashi
Flowing pumice stone
A method of floating on the water without using hands and feet—done in a similar way as pumice stone floats on the water.

安坐

Anza

Floating in a cross-legged sitting position

A method of floating in a cross-legged sitting position in the water.

鷗形

Kamome gata

Form of the seagull

A method used to observe the state of the river/seabed or to search for something sunk on the water bottom in shallower areas.

Note: Feet are most important for both swimming skills and the soldier himself. If you are wounded on the foot, it will significantly reduce your capacity for activity; therefore it is important to observe the bed of the water you are in when you are about to land on an unknown land.

飛込ミ

Tobikomi

Diving into the water

A method of diving into water from a high position.

鰹落シ

Katsuo otoshi

Bonito diving

A method used to dive into shallow water and to swim swiftly away after entering the water.

中轉リ

Chugaeri

To turn in water

A method used when you do not know how deep the water is or if there is the possibility of stepping in a muddy floor.

立泳

Tachioyogi

Treading water

Use this when you have to raise both of your hands out of the water to use them for some purpose or other.

Everyone imagines the samurai with the now famous topknot–this is called a *chonmage*– but in the warring periods when samurai went into battle they would let thei hair down so that it would fit into their helmets–this is called *owarawa*.

水書
Suisho
Writing when in the water
This is an interesting skill where you can write or draw something while treading water.

水歩
Suiho
Water walking
This is one kind of treading water and you should apply this when you need to know the depth.

鯔飛
Inatobi
Gray mullet "jumping" (sinking below the water)
When you are swimming using breaststroke use this for avoiding floating waterweeds and any flotsam that is drifting towards you.

水入鯔飛
Suiri inatobi
"Jumping" like gray mullet below the water (swimming below the waves)
Use this when scouting the state of the enemy's camp, or when you go under the water for a while to conceal your wake, or when you need to search for something on the bed of the water you are in, or even when you want to use water tools.

掻分
Kakiwake
Paddle aside
This is a variation of the skill above, named *inatobi*, and is used to avoid continuous waves.

傳馬形
Tenmagata
Float like a flat-bottomed barge
This is a skill used to come on shore when there is something dangerous close to the shore.

鯱泳
Shachi oyogi*
Shachi swimming
A method used when you cannot swim and is used in a pond, marsh and so on, where debris is floating and a normal way of swimming cannot be used or you cannot walk.

手足搦
Shusoku garami
Bound hands and feet
A method of swimming with your arms and legs bound together.

竹具足術
Take Gusokujutsu
The skill of bamboo armor
This is a preliminary skill to be practiced for swimming with armor.

二ツ搔
Futatsu kaki
Twin paddles
A skill used when you need to keep a "correct posture" during swimming.

瓜剥
Uri muki
Peeling the gourd
Skill of peeling a gourd [with a knife] while treading water.

操銃及弓術
Souju oyobi kyujutsu
Shooting guns and bows while swimming
A method of using muskets or bows when treading water.

水馬
Suiba
Crossing water with a horse
The skill of leading a horse into water and crossing over to the other side with it.

---

* *Shachi*—a mythical carp with the head of a lion and the body of a fish and auspicious protectors of well-being. Pairs are traditionally used to decorate the roof ridges of Japanese castles.

煙花船
Enkasen
"Signal fire ship"
This means to hide yourself immediately, this is a skill for avoiding danger.

免許術
Menkyo Jutsu
The following are skills for those with a teaching license:

甲冑泳
Kacchu oyogi
Swimming in armor
To swim wearing armor and a sword.

軍貝音入
Gunkai neire
Signaling with a conch shell
The skill of blowing a conch shell while treading water—use this as a signal for going ahead or exiting.

秘傳術
The following are secret skills:

浮沓
Ukigutsu
Floating aids
From ancient times the following information has been given to those who receive it by the use of a written oath. When you put this tool around your waist, you tread water without using your hands and legs. Also it is useful as lifesaving equipment, and can be used as a water bottle on dry land. When not in use, fold and stow it away in your kimono.

畳三船竝継船
Tatami-bune narabini Tsugi-fune
Military boat and jointed boat*
The first boat is for three people. It should be sized so that one person can carry this on his back. It should be constructed with materials available at hand and the oar should be of two parts and jointed. This boat has often brought benefits to Nojima-Ryu. [The second vessel, the jointed boat] can be used as a flat-bottomed version

---

* This last section has been heavily edited.

with a few boats [sections] joined together; also, each boat can be used separately according to the situation. The directions for use and structure are given through written oath and this has been the way from ancient times.

Fighting and Men-at-Arms

The Western term "man-at-arms" can be described as an armored fighting man who is sometimes on horseback and is considered a professional warrior. In this section, I shall consider a man-at-arms to not be of the knightly class but to be a professional soldier in a medieval army, meaning that while many people on a battlefield look like knights, they may not be, because "knight" is a social class—so remember, just because a man may be on a samurai battlefield wearing two swords, they may not actually be a samurai.

Taking the samurai to be the knight, we could consider the ashigaru foot soldiers, or even at a stretch some servants, to be men-at-arms and in addition to this we could also consider samurai mercenaries to fall into the same bracket, but here we shall concentrate on support fighters only. Armored and equipped for war, they were soldiers on foot who could support other samurai, including mounted samurai, or fight alone. Normally they were full-time employees of a samurai or lord or were taken from the general population in times of war. However, we must avoid the "Disney Trap" and not consider these as inexperienced peasants dragged into the conflicts of the nobles. While some may have been uneducated, inexperienced or even useless in war, some were full-time professional fighters, in the constant presence of a samurai. This man-at-arms would be well versed in the setting up of camp, of getting fires ignited, or maintaining weapons and armor, and also of fighting alongside a samurai master. Remember, not all warriors on a Japanese battlefield are samurai—there were many trained and sometimes well-armed non-samurai who would also fight and take heads.

Head Hunting

Head hunting is one of *the* core activities of the samurai. Their purpose was to cut the heads from fallen warriors, thrust them on to spears or the ends of their swords and cry out in triumph to the gods of war—the samurai were a head cult. This section will look at the samurai and the head of the enemy and the ritual that surrounds the taking of the ultimate human trophy. A much-overlooked factor is the requirement of the samurai to gain heads and as modern readers we rarely—if ever—observe the samurai from this perspective. For a samurai, honor in battle, the death and destruction of the enemy, and the elevation of prowess through the display of decapitated human heads is the main track that their lives are geared towards.

Cutting off the Head

In the main, a man does not like having his head cut from his neck, and seldom did a man sit there and allow this to happen in the heat of battle. To stop a victim from struggling free, the samurai would pin the victim's right arm under his leg, pull back the peak of his helmet and make a cut across the throat or put the knife behind the windpipe and cut outwards, then he would reverse the grip and start to saw and cut away at the man's neck until it separated from his body. Some samurai may carry a specific knife for this task. Prior to this, a samurai may give a *coup de grâce* in one of the following areas:

1. A cut along the throat
2. A stab to the heart
3. A cut to an artery in the leg

Chimatsuri—the Blood Sacrifice

Chimatsui, literally "blood-festival," was the act of dedicating the first head taken in a battle to specific gods of war. The following quote is taken from the *Gunpo Jiyoshu* manual and explains the concept—after the quote the gods and directions will be explained.

> *Chimatsuri is to offer the first head gained in battle to the ninety-eight thousands gods of war, with your hands joined in prayer, chanting the following:*
>
> *"Namu* Marishisonten† and to all the other gods of war, you gave us this head today, it is all thanks to your gratifying wonderful will, we pray for our continued luck in battle."*
>
> *The above must be said in the direction of Tomobiki [while offering this head] to the eight demons serving the four Devas, who guard Buddha, also offer this head to the nine devil gods, saying:*
>
> *"Give us a victory, our continued luck in battle and save us, Kyu Kyu Nyonitsuryo."‡*
>
> *When you do this you should not face in the direction of Hagun.*

---

* A common word used in praying in Buddhism meaning "I sincerely believe" or "Save us."

† Usually pronounced "Marishiten."

‡ A ritualistic phrase used in Japanese magic, also used in the *Shoninki* ninja manual.

The nighty-eight thousand gods of war is not literal, it means innumerable number of gods; also the goddess Marishiten (the common pronunciation) is a goddess of war, the direction of Tomobiki and Hagun change daily and must be identified before the ritual is performed.

Displaying Heads

The displaying of heads is highly ritualized and formulated. The idea is that a lord should observe and inspect the decapitated heads of the enemy. There are multiple historical sources on the different types of inspection, but most revolve around the lord being protected from the enemy ghosts by chants and spells, at which point the heads are displayed, confirmed and recorded to then be gibbeted elsewhere. For a full translation of a head inspection ritual see *Samurai War Stories*.

The *Gunpo Jiyoshu* manual states the following:

The head inspection was conducted for the purpose of distribution of honors of the warriors by inspecting and deciding who they killed and how.

The *Gunpo Jiyoshu* continues with an instruction for when only one head is taken in battle:

Hitotsukubi—the one head

Though the Hitotsukubi is usually not shown to the lord, it is sometimes shown to those lords who have understanding about these things. When having it inspected by the lord, its hair should be tied in a style called *Sakawage*—into two top knots, with a pin made from the *shrubby althaea tree;* the pin is then penetrated through these knots. Next, put the head on a white cloth with the cut end [of the head pointing] down and wrap it so that the face is covered; finish by tying it up at the top of the head. If the person was an archer, you should show [the head] with a bow before the lord. The lord should first cut the nine *kuji* lines in the air, then open three folds of his war fan and look at the head through the fan itself. At this point chant the following verse three times:

をのがとがを あづさにかけて いる時は おもひかへすな あびらうんけん
Wonogatoka wo azusani kakete iru toki wa omoi kaesuna abirakenun
"When calling a spirit of a dead person, do not think back on your faults, abirakenun!"

The manual continues with:

Decapitated heads with special requirements:
Heads with a special reason for submission and which are put forward for the lord's inspection should have the one who killed the victim between

the head and the lord and armed with a bow, the string closest to the lord. Otherwise, the lord should block the view of the head with his sleeve, details to be orally transmitted.

Generally, the heads of samurai should not be carried in one hand. Those with a terrible look, such as throwing up of the eyes, sticking out of the tongue, etc., should not be offered up for the lord's inspection.

Sometimes incense is burned and the helmet is passed over it—this is a courtesy for the enemy who has to deal with a samurai's head. Alternatively a samurai would wear incense so that his odor was agreeable in death. The same manual continues:

Before the inspection [of decapitated heads] women applied makeup and arranged the hair of the heads; also they applied tooth-blacking dye. Warriors were careful about their appearance; they prepared to die with the knowledge that their heads were to be inspected. Makeup and the wearing of fragrance and incense are considered proper. If [the head] has scars, conceal them with rice powder.

The Five Types of Heads

The decapitated head of a victim normally falls into one of five categories. However some heads—those that are grotesque and evil-looking—are considered as malevolent.

右眼
Ugan
Right-eyed
The eyes of the dead stare to the right.

左眼
Sagan
Left-eyed
The eyes of the dead stare to the left.

天眼
Tengan
Heaven-eyed
The eyes of the dead stare up at the heavens.

地眼

Jigan

Earth-eyed

The eyes of the dead stare down to the earth.

仏眼

Butsugan

Buddha-eyed

The eyes of the dead are half closed in a Buddha-like position.

Divination and Heads of Evil

Being a head cult, the samurai had rituals prescribed for the heads they collected. This included divination through heads and the exorcism of those that were deemed evil.

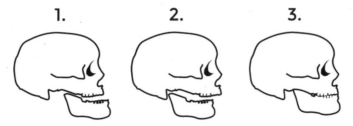

To divine the future through a decapitated head the samurai would look at the mouth by lifting the upper lip:

1. If the lower jaw protruded forward past the upper teeth, then it was good luck for the side who had taken the head.
2. If the upper teeth protruded past the lower jaw then it was bad luck for the side which had taken the head.
3. If the teeth were flush together then the result of the situation would be a stalemate or end in an agreement of peace.

Respect had to be shown to this head—if it was an auspicious head then a monk would chant the correct formula to appease the soul of the dead, and if a head of evil intent the correct exorcism would be performed.

If a head (see image on the following page) has its eyes wide open, its teeth exposed, and the hair along the side of the face and sideburns sticking out and upward, then it is an evil head. This head should not be shown to a lord-commander. The man who killed this enemy and took the head must undergo an exorcism—people should be respectful around the head and it should be treated properly. The

ideogram as seen in the image should be written on the head and then it should be taken to a place where it is to be buried. The direction that it should be buried is the "direction of inviting death" while the person burying it should stand in the "direction of life." The man performing this rite must stand with hands together in prayer and incant a specific spell seven times, then holding his left hand on his chest and his index finger of the right hand pointing to the sky, he should move to write the following ideograms on the ground:

They must next cut the kuji grid of protection in the air with their finger and take seven steps backwards and then trace the following Sanskrit mark in the air:

The person who should deal with this head does not have to be the person who killed; this should be done by a person of great skill, a technician.

Gibbeting the Heads

A samurai, with head in hand who has finished presenting it to the lord and has received his reward, has to dispose of the trophy. Unlike some other head cultures, the samurai do not keep the heads as a normal rule, but tend to return them to the families of the fallen warrior; or they gibbet them on wooden beams that have spikes to hold them firmly in place.

These stands—being made of the correct wood—are erected and the heads are placed upon the spikes and left to rot in the wind. Sometimes the heads are wrapped in cloth—normally in an arrow cape if it is an important warrior—or they are returned to the family. If they are returned then they are presented in a box container with the correct spells and prayers provided.

Head-taking was not only a factor of the warring periods but also in times of peace. It would not be unheard of to see a man on a mission of vengeance and a duel between the pursuer and the pursued as they battled in the streets or fields of peacetime Japan. The result would be the victor walking down the street with a bloody head in his hands while the authorities tried to discover if the killing was legal or not. Overall, the samurai is a taker of heads; his victory count, prestige and employment often depend upon the heads taken in battle.

Chi and Magic

Samurai life was medieval and at the same time that the samurai existed, in Europe there were the Crusades, the Renaissance, the witch trials, and many other medieval movements. Crime was detected by defeat in combat through the judgement of god, spells were used for many facets of life, charms and rituals were performed and medicine was in its infancy. What we see as "black magic" or connote as evil arts or ridiculous practices are not far removed from our own history. As a Christian knight would wear the cross, so a samurai would wear a divine talisman.

Chi

In Japanese, the Chinese word *chi* becomes *ki*. It is the idea of an internal spirit and energy that is found in the living world, in each person and in the air, and is understood by most people. In an army the gunbaisha's task was to identify chi in the sky or the chi of the opposite army—they would observe shapes in the clouds and air to identify and divine future events or the feel of an enemy. Defeat, victory, fires, illness and an array of many other things were "predicted" through chi.

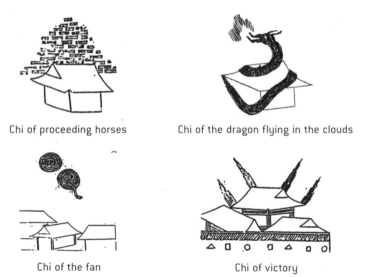

Chi of proceeding horses   Chi of the dragon flying in the clouds

Chi of the fan   Chi of victory

The teachings of chi are in depth and very detailed, with multiple variations, including differences in color and direction. A master would be skilled in chi and they would give their findings to the lord-commander.

Magic, Divination and Auspicious Dates

Magic in the world of the samurai normally consisted of talismans of protection and divine ritual magic that brings about a desired result or again, protection and even invisibility.

Magic

Magic is too loose a term to cover samurai arts of this nature. Some have foundations in Buddhism, others Shinto and others in shamanism. The subject is vast and potentially a limitless investigation. Shinobi and samurai would both use the now famous kuji-in, a form of self-protection normally formed by drawing a grid in the sky, projecting their will into the universe to bring about change and protection. In addition to this is the making of talismans, normally through some form of animal sacrifice, such as killing mating dogs or birds, turtles, etc., and other forms of what we would consider "magic," i.e., practices that alter nature or bring about change through supernatural ways.

Samurai performing kuji-in

Auspicious directions and dates

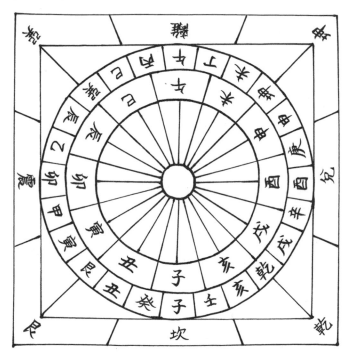

The cardinal points and associations

Samurai warfare, especially in earlier times, would focus on the calculation of auspicious dates and directions. Deciding a date in this way is called *hidori* while deciding the direction is *katadori*. The general idea is to use ancient and sometimes secret systems of identifying which hour, day or year was auspicious for a samurai's forces, yet ill-fated for the enemy. Different schools of thought grew around this concept and multiple elements were considered to discover the correct time. Three major factors played their part in this decision:

1. 十干 The Ten Celestial Stems—A ten day cycle and record.
2. 十二支 The Twelve Heavenly Bodies (also symbols, earthly branches, animals or zodiac)—The Japanese zodiac.
3. 五行 The Five Elements—Normally in connection with the direction that the army faced or the birth element of the lord, etc.

A master astrologer would use the above and have to take the following points into account to decide if an hour, day, year, direction or chi formation was beneficial for the allies but hostile for the enemy. They would consider:

♦ The direction the army are facing
♦ The day they left for war
♦ The day of the battle
♦ The hour of the battle
♦ The element of the year in reference to other factors
♦ The element of the allied and enemy lords
♦ The year of birth for the allied and enemy lords
♦ The position of evil directions in relation to the army, including evil stars in the night sky and the position of the gods at that time
♦ The movement of birds and animals
♦ The movement of flags and banners and how they act in the wind
♦ The types and color of chi visible in the sky
♦ The types and color of chi rising from an allied or enemy army
♦ The results of divination through such things as burning turtle shells

After consulting the teachings and skills of that school, the master astrologer would give his advice to the lord, who would match it to the advice of his more practical tacticians and make a decision on an army's next move.

The shinobi also had to perform divination when they were to move out to attack or venture on a secret mission; the following elements are found in the shinobi curriculum:

♦ Divination by torches, to throw up to three torches—with spikes on the bottom—around an enemy target. The fumes from the sulphur and gunpowder mixtures would force an enemy to surrender, or at least be incapacitated; the torch that made the enemy surrender, be it number one, two, or three, would be used to divine a future attack.

- The sound of birds and the movement of birds in the sky
- The direction that the shinobi left home from
- The hour and day on which the shinobi left for his mission
- Before a shinobi infiltrated a position they would pick the most auspicious direction for that hour or day and in response defenders would defend those directions
- Divination through the observation of incense smoke would tell a shinobi if a mission was to be ill-fated or not
- The use of protective amulets to avert the eyes of the enemy and render the shinobi invisible

Samurai Vengeance Attacks

With the samurai being a knightly warrior class, honor and family are important central elements of a samurai's being. The blood feud is a common factor in Western history and literature and family feuds, such as the infamous Campbells versus McDonalds of Scotland, have become the symbols of this form of warfare. Like the rest of the world, Japan has its fair share of family vendettas.

This form of conflict is called *adauchi*, and can be broken down into 仇 "grudge," and 討 "killing" or "strike," allowing it to be rendered as "grudge-strike" or "revenge-killing." The idea of family feuds or revenge killings stretches back into samurai history. However for the main part, revenge killings and feuds become lost and mixed in with the turbulent war years—of which there are many in samurai history when most wars were feuds between clans—so therefore I will concentrate on the "peaceful" Edo Period. If a fight was initiated between samurai, and if one of them was killed, then this would start the legal procedure of "official murder." The man to take up the act of revenge would report to his lord and ask for a leave of absence while he tracked down the enemy in question and attempted to kill him. If given permission and if the man was in his own domain, then a game of cat-and-mouse would start—deception, infiltration, street fights and blood would start to flow. However, if the enemy was in another province then the samurai would have to travel there as a rōnin, where he would have to report to the local magistrate and obtain permission to kill his target. The problem this caused is that, when officially registered the enemy knew that his pursuer was in town. If permission was granted, then the pursuer would hunt down his enemy and vengeance was unleashed. Having killed the enemy, the head of his opponent was his to take and vengeance was complete.

The difference with Edo Period revenge attacks is that once a vengeance killing had taken place then the family of the now dead samurai could not take further vengeance and the matter was considered closed, halting any escalating family wars. However, keeping to the rules was not always the path that some samurai took and samurai would sometimes not get authorization for the killing; this made the vengeance attack an act of true murder. If the pursuing samurai had committed an unlawful killing then he may be captured and killed as a murderer or released without charge—the latter because samurai had a tendency to support acts of filial devotion—but also and most likely, the samurai would go on the run, trying to reach the safety of his own province. Alternatively, the samurai may not be successful in the murder; they may spend years on the road, go into poverty and starvation and may even have to hire themselves out to another clan to fund their death mission. Furthermore, even if he finds his enemy, the enemy may outmatch him in skill and win the combat; this is called *kaeriuchi*, and this is a man who is on a vengeance killing but has been killed by his own target.

His lord may stop a samurai from leaving for a mission of vengeance; however, the common understanding in Edo Period Japan was that if a member of a family dies through ill measure, then vengeance must be undertaken. Furthermore, it happened at times that if the head of the family has been killed then the inheritor might not inherit the family lands and income until they had killed the enemy of their father/leader.

In the mid to late 1600s, Natori-Ryu lists the following skills as requirements for a mission of vengeance:

- Swordsmanship
- Sword quick-drawing
- Capturing and binding skills
- Fast-travel skills
- Concealed chainmail
- Traveling as a rōnin
- Understanding how to accumulate money to cover expenses
- Constructing plans and tactics
- Spying
- The arts of the shinobi

The three most famous vengeance stories in Japan are:

1. *Ako-jiken* 1702—the 47 Rōnin
2. *Igagoe no Adauchi* 1634—Vengeance in Iga
3. *Soga Kyodai Aduchi* 1193—The Vengeance of the Soga Brothers

The *Bansenshukai* shinobi manual of 1676 gives the following episode as an example of vengeance:

In older days, someone from another province killed his colleague and ran to Edo. He sought shelter with a hatamoto *warrior, and the warrior carefully hid him. The victim's son came to Edo to look for his father's killer and searched for a few years. However, the enemy was securely protected and there was no way to kill him. After all the years, he eventually worked out a plan, in which he wrote a letter saying: "Though I have sought after my enemy for years, I have had no luck and have no clue where he is. As all of my effort has come to nothing, I am bitterly disappointed and therefore I will kill myself by disembowelment." He then sent this letter, together with his short sword, to his mother, wife and children. Then he hid himself while his mother, wife and children grieved deeply, a fact that became known. This resulted in a message from the enemy family being sent to the killer in Edo; he did not doubt the validity of the letter and that it might be a stratagem and thus fully allowed his guard to slip, going out here and about. This then ended with the son killing him without difficulty.*

This is an example of making the enemy become less attentive and taking advantage of the gap. Learning from such an example, you can think of a countless number of ways to make the enemy drop their guard. The deepest principle of ninjutsu is to avoid where the enemy is attentive and strike where they are negligent.

Law officially banned the way of Adauchi in 1873 as Japan entered into the modern era.

Honor and bushido

The first thing to understand is that the term bushido 武士道 is made up of two parts, *bushi* 武士, military person or warrior, and *do* 道, the "Way," which results in the now common translation, "the way of the warrior," or "the way of the samurai." The ideograms can be broken down thus:

武

Bu

Military

Originally this ideogram was made up of two parts, 止 and 戈, and meant to "go to war with a halberd." Later changed to "to stop a halberd" this has come about because the ideogram 止 now means "to stop" in Japanese. However, the original Chinese was "to go to war with weapons," a warrior. The change from "to go to war with weapons" to "to stop a weapon" was made in later times.

士

Shi

Originally it represented a type of battle-ax, and came to mean those men in a proper position as to have a battle-ax.

道

Do

A path or "way," as in the Way of Eastern philosophy.

A major misconception around this subject is that bushido was first developed in 1900, when Inazo Nitobe wrote the bestseller, *Bushido: the Soul of Japan*. The book was originally written in English and later translated into Japanese and was not the first use of the term "bushido." The term bushido is much older and is a staple of samurai culture. While fine details may change on the interpretation of the matter by the samurai themselves, it was understood as following the ethics of samurai life, even if those ethics changed with the times; this meant that as long as the actions of a samurai fell inside the ethics of his time and his actions served the lord, he was following bushido.

In the West, the term "chivalry" has an accurate association with bushido but both Western chivalry and Japanese bushido are misrepresented by a connection to the word "honor." The reason for this misguided and popular misunderstanding of honor and its connection to chivalry is an overshoot from Victorian romance.

The Oxford English dictionary states that honor is "the quality of knowing and doing what is morally right." The problem with this is that what is considered moral or morally correct differs from country to country and between times. What was morally acceptable to a samurai is not that which is morally acceptable to us as modern people. Ethics and morals change with time and the Victorian need for high moral standards (often more of an ideal than a reality) was superimposed on medieval chivalry and in turn the term bushido was translated as chivalry, giving us a romantic idea of what chivalry should be but not what it actually was. Because of this, both chivalry and samurai bushido have been romanticized—the knight fights off evil in the land and the samurai is bound to the elevation of correct moral conduct. The problem is that the "evil in the land" may be the non tax-paying peasant class or the people over the hill who are led by a rival and thus are considered immoral. This has led to a position where some samurai ethics and morals are now considered honorable while others are most certainly not. A feudal network by its very nature is a hierarchy and those people below others in such a system are sometimes considered subhuman, or at least not entitled to the same ethical considerations as other more elite humans.

A samurai was concerned with honor, very much so, but this may not gel with our concept of honor. For example, it is considered acceptable for a samurai to kill someone who has been declared an enemy—for almost any reason, simply because the lord wishes it so—they may also take the "spoils of war" after the massacre of a village who are in league with the enemy, yet it is a dishonorable act to sneak in and steal the same property in a stealthy manner. This means that while the motivation may be as small as plain dislike, it was honorable to kill the enemy and steal from him, yet to leave him alive and steal from him without him knowing and in a stealthy manner was not. Yet, if that same samurai was trained as a shinobi and his lord so wished, it was a honorable act for him to infiltrate and take that which was "needed." Also, for him to lie and construct vicious plans was considered a form of loyalty if it was done in the service of a lord, while if done for personal greed, then again this was an unspeakable act—meaning that ethics, chivalry and honor change with the *intent* of the action and that the action itself is neither chivalrous or honorable.

War was also under the scrutiny of what *was* and what *was not* honorable. Thomas Cleary in his book *Training the Samurai Mind* translates the writings of the samurai Naganuma Muneyoshi (1635–90) who talks about the classification and justification of wars. Naganuma states that war can be divided into the following, but that only wars of justice are acceptable for samurai:

Wars of Justice
These can be divided into seven types:

1. A war against a tyrant
2. To quell a rebellion against a truly just lord
3. To go to war against treacherous retainers who have killed their lord
4. To fight retainers who have taken power from their lord
5. When the land is still under the rule of a lord but is in chaos
6. To undertake an act of revenge for the killings of a samurai's family
7. When a state is without a ruler

Wars of Prestige
These are unjustified wars and are when samurai use the idea of honor to establish a war that is based on a display or contest of prestige.

Wars of Greed
These are unjustified wars and occur when samurai are motivated to war for personal gain.

Do not be mistaken, a samurai was fully concerned with personal honor and chivalry, but it was not what we imagine, i.e., it was not to fight fairly, to share peace and the word of Buddhism, or to defend the helpless—and while examples of this may be found in history, most samurai were concerned with the following:

♦ To have a formidable reputation

- To gain an escalation in pay
- To be seen as morally correct by his peers
- To serve his lord with services required of him (some of which we would not deem ethical)
- To move up the ladder of hierarchy (which for some could means moving to a different lord)

Acts that are considered dishonorable:

- Claiming that a head is not who it is named as
- Stealing a head
- Killing an ally to use his head to falsely claim a kill in battle
- Stealing by stealth
- Lying
- Commanding an inexperienced and younger samurai to perform an act that will get them killed so that his body can be used for cover from projectiles
- To kill women, take their nose and claim it was a man killed in combat
- To die a dog's death, i.e., in a natural disaster or by something less heroic than battle
- Giving aid to a man who has been targeted for vengeance due to a family dispute
- Banditry, murder (the killing of someone in a non-acceptable way) and robbery
- Some forms of theater and entertainment

Acts that are considered honorable, loyal or have no connotations of negativity:

- Leading enemies into traps
- Ambushes performed by samurai on smaller enemy groups
- Deception in warfare and combat (something which was hailed as superior)
- To kill from a distance
- Infiltration in stealth—the deeper a samurai infiltrates the more prestige he gains
- Torture
- Decapitating a man while he is still alive by having him pinned down and sawing through his neck with a sword
- Giving aid to a stranger to help kill someone who has been targeted for vengeance
- For many to fight against one

- ◆ Ritual suicide
- ◆ Homosexuality
- ◆ Pedophilia (which had no negative or legal connotations)

Samurai honor must remain understood as *honor*, but the factors of moral and ethical shift must be applied. What a samurai considered honorable, or to be without shame is not what we as modern Western people consider honorable, and while some elements of moral conduct are universal to all, some elements of ethics normally shift in time. Therefore, a samurai *is* on a quest of honor but the idea of honor may change with the time and situation. As a modern reader of samurai history, consider the samurai as a man with a core of personal honor that each individual would try to promote; this could be done from behind the scenes by acting as a shinobi, it could be in the height of battle, banners snapping at the front lines of an army, but in most if not *all* cases, samurai honor came at the destruction of an enemy—an enemy who were other samurai like him, trying to gain honor. Remember, the enemy of the samurai is another samurai.

That being said, if a samurai did transgress against the current moral code there was one sure way to regain honor—ritual suicide.

Suicide and Seppuku

Ritual suicide is an iconic image which has become a hallmark of the samurai. However, again the romantic element has allowed to flourish and truth has been obscured leaving the topic as not fully explored. The following section will give an insight into the ritual and meaning; however, for a more comprehensive read on this subject see *Seppuku* by Andrew Rankin.

Ritual suicide is called by many names and while most revolve around terms to cut open the stomach, the most popular two in today's world are *Seppuku* and *Hari-kiri*. The basic idea is to open the stomach and to expose the guts and innards to the world so that a samurai may take control of his own death instead of letting another take his life. This is done when all else has failed and the enemy may capture them; it is also done to correct a mistake that other actions will not correct. Ritual suicide was not a static ritual and forms changed depending on the time. According to the work of Rankin, the older forms of seppuku appear to be more spontaneous and in battlefield situations, examples such as samurai opening their stomachs on castle walls while the fortress burns around them or sitting down, still bloody from a battle, a samurai writes a death poem and opens up his stomach. Then as time progresses a fixed ritual takes place, drinks are offered to the condemned, small but sombre parties are held, poems may be written and measurements for the ceremony are mapped out as food is laid on thin wooden sheets placed upon small tables. Our image of the seppuku ceremony is altogether quite correct; the main issue is the darker side of the story, the fact that many men did not wish to commit suicide and that an unknown percentage were forced into the act. What cannot be known is how many people willingly opened up their stomachs to kill themselves for the loss of a lord or to atone for a "crime" and how many were forced into the act because their families and their future line were under threat. Therefore a middle lane approach must be taken again and the idea that sometimes, some samurai could be heroic and romantic and that they did in fact die for their lords and they did commit this ritual with the proper intent; while at the other end of the scale it must be remembered that there were many who did not wish to perform suicide and that the regulations of the ceremony itself were constructed to stop a person from striking out at those who had commanded such a death.

The following points are used in seppuku to stop the victim from taking control:

Paper around the wakizashi short sword

A short sword is placed on a tray for the victims to use to disembowel themselves with. The handle is removed and the tang of the blade is wrapped in thick paper, and only the end section of the tip of the blade is left exposed. This is done so that the victim cannot take up the short sword and kill those around them and escape.

The distance between the examiner and the victim

The examining official should sit approximately eleven-and-a-half feet (three-and-a-half meters) away from the victim. This is so that the victim cannot jump up and take the sword of the sitting official and kill those around him.

The Second should observe the attitude of the victim and adjust to fit.

The Second is the man that decapitates the victim. There are three basic positions that a Second can adopt or move through (see the illustration on the opposite page). Their task is to observe the feeling and actions of the victim, and they may have to kill the supplicant before the ceremony starts if they think that action is required:

1. They should kneel down about five feet (one-and-a-half meters) from the victim with one knee up, ready to pounce and kill the victim if he looks like he is about to move to an offensive action.
2. If the victim looks like they are going to commit suicide without incident then the Second moves to stand to the victim's left, the big toe of his right foot in line with the victim's hip.
3. If the victim looks agitated or the Second gets the feeling that the victim is going to move on the offensive just before the moment that they should cut open their own stomach, then the Second will move in close and position themselves almost central and behind them. The Second will place the sword blade on the back of their left hand, with the tip pointing towards the center of the back of the victim. If the victim makes a move then the Second will stab with the tip through the back of their ribs, killing them.

The victim should face the sun or moon.

The victim should always have the sun, moon or illumination to their front. This is so that they cannot see the shadow of the executioner and his sword swing.

Seppuku is an intriguing part of samurai culture, yet at times it should be considered oppression and forced suicide, making it *execution* and *not* suicide. A samurai may be forced to commit suicide so that their "crimes" do not fall on their families. It has to be remembered that entire samurai families may be eradicated because of one person's "crimes." Alongside this, the above methods of defending against a victim of seppuku and their possible attack are all sure signs that some people who were forced to commit suicide clearly did not wish to and could and did attack officials—making the history of ritual suicide in Japan one of forced execution, heroic deeds and last-ditch attempts at life. Seppuku must be seen as a blood ritual that elevated the honorable, killed the innocent and was used as a tool to take control. However, Japan had a long tradition of warriors following their lords in death, rituals that existed before the samurai, and this fact should not be ignored. And it should be remembered that countless individuals killed themselves to journey to the afterlife and accompany their lord in death, so much so that the act of killing yourself to follow your lord to the afterlife was banned in Japan in the Edo Period; while some samurai would not die by their own hand, many willingly did.

The Major Players

The history of Japan and of the "major players" in its development is vast, expansive, political and complex. In the West we generally focus on a few of the main characters from samurai history and tend to have a limited understanding of the intricacies of the "story" itself (which is understandable as it is vastly complex). Therefore, the following list is a short description of those people commonly discussed and where they fit into the story of the samurai—this will help you to understand the basics of a "samurai narrative" and at least start to form a structure in your mind of the overview of the samurai story. More samurai profiles and outlines can be found at the back of *Samurai War Stories*.

The 1100s

Minamoto no Yoritomo was a member of the Genji clan and the victor of one of Japan's most famous wars, the Genji versus the Heike clan.

Minamoto no Yoshitsune was of the same family and time as the above; he is also often connected to the origin of shinobi or covert tactics.

Ise no Saburo Yoshimori was a general under the above Minamoto no Yoshitsune and is thought to be connected with the origin and history of the shinobi—he is the supposed author of the 100 ninja poems.

Taira no Kiyomori was a member of the above-mentioned Heike clan that flourished under him; he died of disease.

The 1300s

Kusunoki Masashige served the Emperor of Japan against the rise of the Ashikaga clan. Kusunoki is considered one of the greatest Japanese generals of all time and is a paragon of loyalty, allowing himself to die due to a bad command given by his lord, even though he knew it meant his death. He is also mentioned in shinobi literature as being connected to the ninja, not as a shinobi himself but as an unconventional tactician.

The 1500s

The sixteenth century included the Warring States Period and was a time of blood, fire, and destruction. It was filled with treaties, broken treaties, political moves and shifts and should be understood as a highly complex time in Japanese history filled with war but which lead to an era of peace. Many samurai changed allegiance, formed new pacts and the country was in a state of turmoil. The people below are the main players of that time and are followed by the location they are most associated with.

Takeda Shingen in Kai, considered to be one of the greatest warlords in Japanese history, died of disease before his military campaigns ended.

Uesugi Kenshin in Echigo, he engaged in many battles and is famous for his battles with Takeda Shingen.

Oda Nobunaga in Owari and Gifu, the first of the great unifiers of Japan, united Japan towards the end of the Sengoku Period but died due to a rebellion within his ranks.

Toyotomi Hideyoshi in Osaka, followed on after Nobunaga and continued to hold a unified Japan and then invaded Korea.

Ishida Mitsunari in Omi, protector and regent to the son of the above Hideyoshi, he went to battle with and lost against Tokugawa Ieyasu at the Battle of Sekigahara, ending the Sengoku Period.

Tokugawa Ieyasu in Edo, after the death of Hideyoshi he took the country by force, which culminated at the Battle of Sekigahara where he defeated the last of his opposition and started the golden "age of peace."

Samurai and Shinobi Literature

While there are thousands of volumes of samurai literature left to the world, they are of course in Japanese and "lost" in vast collections; therefore the following list is of those documents which are available in English. It must be remembered that it is often the case that documents are chosen for publication for different reasons and that published samurai documents predominantly focus on ethics and not war. The reason for this is that essays on ethics fit in more with our modern mind-set as the reality of samurai battle is sometimes too harsh to consider. The aim of my team—the Historical Ninjutsu Research Team—is to bring about a new line of published work that exposes the truth and a more balanced view of what was being written in samurai times, a work in progress. Often the date of writing and stance of the author can affect the feeling of the history of the samurai, so as a reader you must take care as to when the document was written and why. Remember that the slices of English translations that are available can skew our understanding of the world of the samurai, giving us tunnel vision and a localized view of what samurai thought and did.

Epic samurai stories and poems translated into English:
Heike Monogatari—The Tale of Heike
Hogen Monogatari—Tale of the Disorder in Hogen
Taiheiki War Chronicle—The war chronicle in which Kusunoki Masashige appears

Samurai military and practical manuals in English:
Yoshimori's 100 shinobi poems
A collection of shinobi poems attributed to Ise no Saburo Yoshimori, a general under the Minamoto family; these have been translated in *Secret Traditions of the Shinobi*.

The Shinobi Hiden
A ninja manual said to be written by Hattori Hanzo in 1560, the date of which has been contested by some but is still a topic of debate, translated in *Secret Traditions of the Shinobi*.

The shinobi scrolls of the Gunpo Jiyoshu
The collected skills of the shinobi written in around 1612 by Ogasawara Saku'un, translated in *Secret Traditions of the Shinobi*.

The Gorin no Sho
The famous treatise on swordsmanship by Miyamoto Musashi in the 1600s, it is oftern translated as the *Book of Five Rings*—the title should be understood as "the universal writing."

The writings of Yagyu Munenori
In the first half of the 1600s, Yagyu Munenori wrote on the way of the sword and his family tradition, published as the *Life Giving Sword*. A further work that is heavily connected to the above man and to Zen are the writings published in English as the *Unfettered Mind*.

Heiho Hidensho
A martial arts manual with some military study, attributed to Yamamoto Kanusuke but most likely written by a later student in or around the mid 1600s, published as *Secrets of the Japanese Art of Warfare*.

The Zohyo Monogatari and the Musha Monogatari
Two manuals, one written to train foot soldiers and the other written to collect heroic stories of the past, both from the mid 1600s and published as *Samurai War Stories*.

The Bansenshukai
Written in 1676 by Fujibayashi Yasutake, it is considered *the* comprehensive text on ninjutsu published as the *Book of Ninja,* with further writings under the title *Book of Samurai*.

The Shoninki
Written in 1681 by Natori Sanjuro Masazumi who was a prolific writer and chronicler of ancient Japanese ways, the *Shoninki* is one of the secret shinobi documents of Natori-Ryu, a school of military tactics and branch school of Kusunoki-Ryu and is published as *True Path of the Ninja*.

The writings of Yamaga Soko
Yamaga Soko was a prolific writer on multiple subjects. While he produced a colossal manual on military warfare, translators have concentrated on his philosophical stance; five of his texts are published in *Samurai Wisdom*.

The Yojokun
A samurai doctor, Kaibara Ekiken wrote in the second half of the 1600s; his work was devoted to health and healthy living, published as the *Yojokun*.

The Hagakure
Written by Yamamoto Tsunetomo around 1716, the *Hagakure* is a record of sayings and teachings, partly published as *Hagakure: The Book of the Samurai*.

The shinobi scrolls of Chikamatsu Shigenori
In 1719 a samurai called Chikamatsu Shigenori recorded the shinobi teachings

of both Iga and Koka—places famous for shinobi no jutsu—in the hope of keeping the secrets alive for future generations, published as *Iga and Koka Ninja Skills*.

The writings of Issai Chozanshi

In the first half of the 1700s Issai Chozanshi wrote a collection of narratives on the art of swordsmanship and Zen in a supernatural setting, published as *The Demon's Sermon on the Martial Arts*.

In addition to the above, the book *Ideals of the Samurai* and *Training the Samurai Mind* both have collections of samurai works within them.

This list of literature concludes the first half of this book that has painted the basic picture of the samurai. The image of the holy-warrior sword-saint with a devotion to death and honor should now be replaced with a more realistic and brutal image of the professional soldier-warrior, a man of principles that were shaped by the barbaric times of medieval warfare yet tightly wrapped up in educated philosophy and ritual. The samurai was an independent warrior, armed and prepared for battle, ready to be called upon in times of war. They may have changed sides, acted in deception or have been loyal for generations, but above all they were real humans with all the complexities that accompany human society and affairs—making the story of the samurai a complex and human one. While there are ample truths found in the righteous image of the samurai, there is also the other side of the coin, the art of deception and the way of the shinobi.

Part III

THE SHINOBI

Concerning Shinobi no Mono

Concerning how to utilize shinobi no mono—although it is not definite as to where you should send them, the first place should be enemy territory or the enemy's camp. They should infiltrate such places to observe and to provide information on their defenses and to burn down the enemy position. Also, they should report the advantages and disadvantages of the topography around the enemy camp and while you and the enemy are confronting each other. Shinobi should infiltrate and listen to glean information on if the enemy are preparing for battle or if they are commencing a night attack—these are the things that they should report back. When your allies are going to give a night attack, shinobi should guide these forces with torches and when the allies retreat, shinobi stay close by and identify if there are enemy forces in hiding, waiting to attack—this is also what shinobi report. Furthermore, shinobi should work as liaison officers between ambushes and guards and pass information between them. On the day before a battle, shinobi should go out in the early evening as distance scouts or they should close in on the sleeping quarters and observe the area—these are the skills of the shinobi.

Someone who is righteous and has the above skills is called a **Yoto** ヨトウ, *it is essential to spare him from regular duties [and less important tasks] and you should grant him a fief. Even if you have only one Yoto [in command] it will result in you gaining more advanced shinobi and also, if you have young and inexperienced [shinobi], they will become efficient and excellent at their task. Therefore, those who are only competent at shinobi skills are called shinobi no mono and excellent practitioners are titled with the term,* Yoto-mono ヨトウ者, *but some people call them Kumi-gashira—"group captains." In the "language used by shinobi" this Yoto* 與頭 *is classed as the head of a shinobi no mono group; however, you must understand that it is not the same as Yato* 夜盗—*that is, they are not night thieves.*

Concerning the outfit 装束 *used by this captain at night—if his master gives him the appropriate outfit, [then he] should have one prepared for himself immediately.*

The Iike Gunki Military Manual

Hopefully, by now the image of the samurai in popular culture has been fully taken away. A more realistic, yet colorful, representation has been put in its place. This image shown now should be of a samurai leaving the castle area, or their farmland home; or fortified manor house in the rural areas of his province. The call to battle has been given and the clans are on the march. Following the horns of war, coming together to form an army, the samurai came out of the hills, the plains, and from the towns. Some old feuds will erupt and new alliances will be forged. One thing is for sure; the blood of the enemy is on the horizon and heads will be taken. For a few of these samurai and ashigaru troops, there is a further level to contemplate: these few are the shinobi who will fight a different type of war.

As was shown earlier, the ratio of one to every two hundred men is a fair approximation for those who *officially* hold the position of shinobi within an army. However, the number of shinobi-trained personnel unofficially listed in the army is unknown. It can be assured that some of the "standard" samurai in the force have performed as shinobi, though they are not recorded in army listings. The knowledge that they did in fact possess shinobi skills is now lost. Both of the aforementioned official and unofficial shinobi-trained men can be divided into various subsections.

Military and Civilian Roles

The first of these divides is a modern divide. By that I mean the shinobi themselves did not identify such a partition. It does not exist as a label in historical documentation. However analysis leads to a clear divide. Two terms have been picked to show this theoretical split, *military* and *civilian*. Samurai are not technically within the realm of military at all times, so to clarify the use of these two, consider the terms as:

1. *Military*—to mean when samurai are actively on military campaign, a call to war has been given and orders for war have been issued and the army has taken form.
2. *Civilian*—covers samurai who are not at war and are either at home or traveling on personal business or for pleasure in a time of peace.

Shinobi information often takes the side of either of these above and while they are never fully divided, a theme can be identified in most cases. Both modes have a shared but broad goal, the defeat of the enemy through deceptive arts, but can be identified in the two following lists:

Military:

- The establishment of spy networks
- The gathering of large scale information from multiple agents
- The personal profiling of key members of the enemy
- To secure influence
- Topographical information about enemy territory
- The search for converted spy candidates
- The planting of long-term agents
- The distribution of disinformation and propaganda
- To gather information from clandestine operations
- To take the role of captains of night attack squads
- To act as guides through enemy territory
- The infiltration of enemy castles and battle camps
- To commit arson
- The assassination of military targets (with no personal motive)
- Destruction of enemy supplies
- Signaling and secret messages
- To be used as incineration and explosive experts
- Ritual and divine "magic" to enhance performance in stealth or to hinder the enemy
- Defense against all of the above

Civilian:

- The infiltration of domestic dwellings for personal reasons that are not theft
- For domestic use against people of their own province with the authorization of the lord
- To perform skills that allow the discovery of a personal enemy
- Collective shinobi skills that aid in the assassination of an enemy on a mission of personal revenge
- To gain an advantage in an upcoming combat
- For personal defense while at home
- For personal defense while traveling
- To defend against thieves
- To hide from an enemy after a personal kill has been made
- To hide if being pursued for other reasons

While not always a rule, most *civilian* shinobi arts are found attached to samurai sword schools. Examples are Shinjin-Ryu, Mubyoshi-Ryu and Tenshin Katori-Ryu. It must be stated that it is without doubt that the *military* aspects of the shinobi arts far outnumber the *civilian* versions. However, there is enough of a divide to show that a theoretical separation exists. The result is that shinobi arts are primarily *military* arts; yet they can be transferred to *civilian* life. In addition to this, *civilian* shinobi arts can easily stray into banditry and thievery.

Public and Hidden Shinobi

A separation that *was* recorded in medieval Japan was that of shinobi who were hidden and shinobi that were presented to the public. A lord would hire the amount of shinobi he could afford and place them in one of two categories. They would either become:

1. Public shinobi—shinobi hired in the open to defend the lord or his castle; or to go to war in a shinobi group
2. Hidden shinobi—shinobi hired in secret who either stay in their home province or work under a hidden identity in the lord's army; or in the army of the enemy

The Japanese terms are *Yo no shinobi* and *In no shinobi*, terms which originate from the Chinese concept of yin-yang:

1. *Yo*—public (In the light)
2. *In*—hidden (In the dark)

Yo no shinobi are shinobi who are "exposed to the light." They are hired by a clan to fill the role of shinobi. They are then billeted in the castle, or local area, as a shinobi in full view of the public (and enemy spies). The purpose of having these shinobi in public view is twofold. First it displays a lord's use of shinobi to his enemies, which gives the message that a lord is well-informed, that he is well-defended and that, should issues arise, there are personnel in place to deal with such matters. This is also a standard practice among clans. Secondly, public shinobi are used openly in teams during military campaigns as was discussed previously. Therefore others know their identity. Further to this, these shinobi in the public eye are vital contact points for enemy shinobi—a subject that will be discussed later. Interaction between shinobi, no matter which side they appear to be working for, did exist.

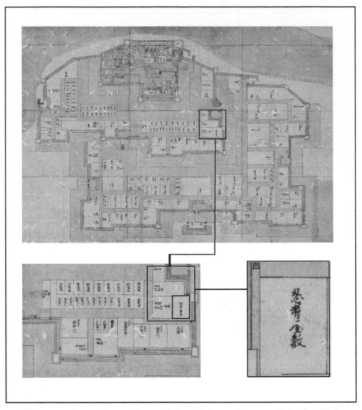

The map above shows the position of the residence of the "public" shinobi no mono in Okayama Castle.

The jacket used by "public" shinobi no mono in the Ikeda clan.
"They wear a blue sleeveless haori jacket with a silver crest on the rear.
Their helmet should be of the zunari shape, be lacquered in black with a *hinomaru*—gold circle. Other crests are not allowed."

The quote and image on the opposite page were recorded in Okayama and show the "uniform" that the public shinobi would wear in and around the castle during the Edo period.

In no shinobi are those shinobi that are not displayed openly and are hidden. These could already be in position within the enemy ranks. According to Chikamatsu Shigenori, an early eighteenth century shinobi chronicler, they could be hidden among the castle's own troops. Troops would be unaware that a certain number among them are actually hired for their shinobi skills, not their appointed jobs. Also, these shinobi could be agents still living in their own province, paid as a full retainer. All this is with the arrangements and transactions being clandestine. If these shinobi are needed for a mission of espionage, the "public" shinobi—who will be under the watchful eye of the enemy shinobi—appear to be doing nothing. Yet unknown to the enemy, the hidden shinobi are on the move. In essence, it is sleight of hand and misdirection with people.

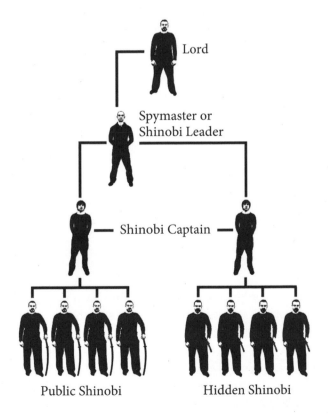

As illustrated above, an ideal situation for the deployment of shinobi is that the lord will support the use of shinobi and appoint one of his close retainers or trusted followers to the task of spymaster. The term "spymaster" is used here but it is not a translation, it is a modern term; normally these are considered to be shinobi leaders or shinobi commanders. The spymaster will hire "public" shinobi and from these he will elect a leader. Depending on how many shinobi a lord retains there could be various captains running multiple but probably independent teams of agents, with the lower end of the chain being filled with shinobi ashigaru, those of the foot soldier class. Parallel to this a hidden shinobi team will be in place, or at least hidden shinobi individuals. The same spymaster will hire and allot tasks to these hidden shinobi who undertake missions of espionage or will infiltrate the enemy in advance. The Bansenshukai shinobi manual of 1676 warns shinobi not to attempt to gain fame for their skills—something which apparently was an issue—as the more well-known an agent becomes due to his expert skills, the greater the chance of being detected by the enemy. Remembering, of course, that movement between lords and political alliances was fluid in the Warring States Period and that often in this period shinobi from the same family could be hired out across the country. This means that others may have known faces and detection was a real issue. However, later, writers such as Chikamatsu Shigenori through his master Kimura of Koka state that some lords of the Edo Period did not fully understand how to utilize the shinobi and that many lords did not fully understand the correct procedures for running shinobi teams—there seems to be a running complaint about the mismanagement of shinobi and shinobi teams. This means that during the Warring States Period, hidden shinobi had the real issue of being detected by other shinobi who may recognize them, especially if they had family connections or if they had let it be known they were shinobi, and that in the Edo Period some lords were so disconnected from the reality of war that they were unaware of the methods and benefits of using shinobi.

The Two Divisions of Military Shinobi

The military function of the shinobi can be further broken down into two main areas:

First section:
Before a war has even erupted, it is the task of the shinobi captain and strategists to identify potential enemies. Therefore advance shinobi are sent to perform the following tasks, or adopt the following positions.

1. To have lived in the enemy province for an extended period beforehand. This is so that when war erupts, and highways and communication routes are closed; they are already on the "correct side of the fence." As rōnin, or samurai living in that area, they gain employment for the upcoming war. However, they will of course work as shinobi for their original lord.
2. They have approached the enemy side, stating that they are shinobi and

have asked to be employed. The enemy has employed them but keeps them under observation. This being so as to identify if they are mercenary shinobi, or if they have a hidden agenda. It must be remembered that shinobi were hired out across Japan. It was not uncommon to hire a stranger as a shinobi. However it was a dangerous gamble, because both shinobi and their adversaries had ways of discovering the true plans of the other.

3. To have positioned themselves—probably in groups or working as individuals—within the enemy castle town or camp; spreading misinformation, rumors and accusations among the enemy. Discord within an enemy camp was a vital key in a military campaign, and the goal was to divide an army. For an army was made up of a coalition of clans. They sought to sow distrust between a lord and his best tacticians. Disinformation must not be underestimated; the aim was to achieve a summary execution of expert tacticians. This was by the use of rumors and fake letters; through the copying of handwriting and seals. Months if not years of planning can be invested in the discrediting of an experienced general. Like a key piece in chess, if he is "taken off the board" during the most important phases of the battle, an army may be defeated.

4. To infiltrate allied forces. Tokugawa Ieyasu was known for his use of shinobi against his own forces. This was to understand the nature of the minds of his "allies." Samurai warfare was a shifting political arena. Notions of loyalty at high levels are not adhered to when great amounts of power and gold are in play. Therefore, lords would have shinobi infiltrate their own army or allied forces; especially if an army was a coalition of the clans. This way he could identify if betrayal was in the air or not.

Second section:
Those shinobi that are not sent in advance will march with the army as highlighted previously. They are identifiable as shinobi and are billeted separately. They work outside of the camp routines and regulations. Their tasks include:

1. Scouting ahead of the army—They must identify "choke points," potential ambush sites, camp positions, topography, water sources and enemy troop movements. They must also investigate mountain tops, valleys and suspicious forests and woodlands.

2. They must scout close to the enemy and obtain numbers of troops, banners, crests, and famous samurai in attendance.* They must also identify weapons stores, army routes, and support troops in the area.

3. Defense and safety—The camp perimeter is guarded by regular samu-

---

* i.e., skilled and experienced generals.

rai and foot soldiers. However, beyond the light of the watch fires, shinobi hide in the bushes and forests. They listen and smell for night attack squads or other shinobi.

4. Attack squad captains—Shinobi allotted to the army will sleep during the day but then lead attack squads at nighttime. Their task is to identify the best way to attack the enemy. Once established they lead regular samurai on night raids.

5. Communications systems—Shinobi tend to run communications networks. Examples are: horse relay systems, running messengers, messenger relay teams, light and fire signals—including fire rockets and smoke. Also flag signals were used as well as signals on the wind, i.e., coded messages sent through sounding flutes, drums and conch shells.

6. Bodyguards—Part of a shinobi's task is to protect the lord. Normally loyal and trusted retainers are close to the lord. The lord will have a personal group of older loyal samurai around him. Some of those samurai may be shinobi-trained. Those who are trusted will protect the lord's perimeter when he travels. If he stays in lodgings, the shinobi will check the area and position, securing the safety of the environment. Their task is to identify and protect weak points in a lord's defense, such as keeping watch below the flooring of houses. Housing is raised off the ground. If the lord is on the ground floor then a shinobi will be positioned below his bed chamber while he sleeps.

7. Fire skills and gunnery—Shinobi are trained in the use of firearms and gunnery. While they are not the only ones, their tasks will include the manufacture of gunpowder weapons. This included landmines, hand grenades and rockets; poisonous-gas-filled projectiles, and "Greek fire" style devices.

8. Infiltration into enemy camps and castles—A primary task for the shinobi is to gain entrance into enemy castles and camps. This was used during sieges to gain information, or to work in unison with a besieging force. The shionobi burns down castle keeps and buildings while the regular forces attack. This creates a two-pronged attack.

This basic outline highlights tasks and positions that a shinobi would undertake during wartime. In a time of peace, shinobi still under government employment would have traveled the land, infiltrating the enemy. Their priority was constant data collection. Through spy networks they would feed information to the spymaster, or sometimes directly to the lord. This data would then be analyzed and cross-referenced. The material would then be fed back to the lord and his council so that correct decisions could be made.

The Difference Between In-nin and Yo-nin

The same ideograms used for *In no shinobi* and *Yo no shinobi* as described previously are also used in a different way. The individual skills and arts of the shinobi can be roughly divided into two further sections and this division is heavily referenced in the shinobi manual, *Bansenshukai*.

1. *In-nin*—"Dark shinobi," the arts of creeping in darkness or to be out of sight of the enemy. This can also be during the daytime, the main factor is that the enemy do not see the agent; this is classic shinobi infiltration.
2. *Yo-nin*—"Light shinobi," the arts of disguise and moving through the enemy in the open, having a false identity and being visually observable, but ignored or perceived as something that they are not.

To avoid confusion between the two types of shinobi, the ideograms will always be defined as:

♦ *In no shinobi* 陰ノ忍 – hidden shinobi; to be hired in secret
♦ *Yo no shinobi* 陽ノ忍 – public shinobi; to be hired in the open
♦ *In-nin* 陰忍 – dark shinobi; infiltration through stealth
♦ *Yo-nin* 陽忍 – light shinobi; open infiltration and disguise

Now that an understanding of the tasks and aims of the shinobi have been identified, a more detailed look into the arts of the shinobi will be explored. Up until this point, environment, identity and the skills of the samurai—and foot soldier—have been discussed. A broad view of the Japanese "knight" has become a solid character. The basic tasks of the shinobi have been highlighted. Now, let us take that image and examine it through specialized training. Let's see the development of the shinobi appear.

A Shinobi Curriculum

Upon reading a shinobi scroll, looking at the various translations the Historical Ninjutsu Research Team have made public, readers are sometimes left with a hole in the overall sketch of the shinobi. There seems to be no fixed place to lay these skills in the outline of the world they inhabited, it can be almost disappointing—seemingly ethereal and without an "anchor."

It needs to be understood that the element that is always missing from any translated Japanese scroll is the *human*. It is the physical human being that holds these as practical skills. When the actual samurai is placed in the picture, with the skills and knowledge of war fixed on a human; our understanding of the scrolls comes to life.

As a reader you have to fully imagine the world of the samurai–and the shinobi–in place with all of its details: The rules, customs, geography, and political climate. Then apply the shinobi skills to the already-accomplished warrior. What makes the shinobi popular in our image is that they moved beyond the normal ways of the samurai. They acquired a very special set of skills that elevated them to a new level. This is why the shinobi are compared to the special forces of today. They are sometimes officers, sometimes rank-and-file soldiers who have been trained outside of conventional arts. They perfected what we would see as "black ops" (with a hint of magic). Therefore, when you add this "special training" to the skill set of the samurai, the skills of the shinobi find their place and no longer float without meaning.

The following original ninja scroll is a complete list—and only a list—of the shinobi arts found in the Akutagawa family, and are skills that are added to conventional military training. *Only* the titles are recorded here and I have given a brief explanation of the skills indicated [inside brackets]. They are broad and they expand *beyond* the contents of the original scroll. This is so that a general understanding of all shinobi arts can be gained. This is to show you, the reader, the makeup of a real shinobi system. This also allows for a better understanding with further information. The original manual is titled *Akutagawa Kaden* 芥川家伝, that is, *Akutagawa Family Traditions*. It is translated with kind permission from Jin'ichi Kawakami.

The text:
Fundamental Teachings
忍術門入起證文
The Shinobi-Jutsu Oath
[A shinobi, having being chosen to train as such or who has been born into a family which specializes in shinobi no jutsu, will first make promises and oaths, maybe even exchange a hostage, giving a wife or child into the care of the lord to ensure trusty service. They must also understand the origins of their art and in the case of the Akutagawa, understand that the art is divine and was inherited from the gods.]

忍術来由
Shinobi-jutsu origin
Transmitted from the Akutagawa to the Kimura Family of Koka
[The Akutagawa family consider their skills to be given through the divinity of the gods to humans, who then passed them down the generations until they ended up in the area of Koka, with the Akutagawa Clan.]

Menkyo Level

[The first step for a shinobi is to master the basics. As a warrior they can fight; they have various levels of education and have been brought up in a medieval world where blood and death are not separated from life. The first part of their training consists of tools and the fundamental building blocks requiring mastery, before they progress further. From here the skills increase and move towards the more difficult. Sometimes the same skills are expanded upon.]

天之巻
Ten no maki
The Scroll of Heaven

入用道具之事
The Tools Needed

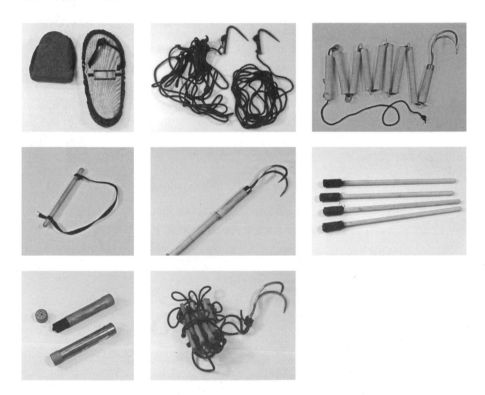

[Shinobi must be proficient in tools that allow them to infiltrate enemy mansions and castles. Ladders, climbing spikes, saws, nails, drills, lock picks, etc., are all manufactured and used when a shinobi needs to enter an enemy position.]

起臥ヲ知ル事

The Art of Knowing if Someone is Asleep or Awake

[Once inside an enemy position, the shinobi has to know if the enemy is asleep
or awake. Sometimes this is done before the final infiltration, i.e., the shinobi has
moved into the grounds of the target complex but has yet to reach the inner quarters and is listening to those "asleep" in the room. In Akutagawa-Ryu this is a mixture of folklore and skill and also appears in other schools. A string is tied to a roof
beam and a rock or weight is hung from the string, allowing this weight to hang
close to the ground. When the stone hits the floor (which is most likely when the
roof beams have contracted in the coldest part of the night) the shinobi will enter,
believing all inside to be asleep. This also has a religious element and a shinobi will
pray for sleep to come over those inside.]

手火之事

The Art of Palm Fire

[Once inside a house the shinobi need to see
where they are going. The use of small lights—often with a
bluish flame—allows the shinobi to see inside. The "fire within
the palm" is a popular torch among the shinobi and consists of
small flammable mixtures, either rolled into a ball or applied to
a small splint of wood. When the shinobi fears detection, they
simply close their hand to extinguish the light.]

塀乗之事

The Art Climbing Fences and Walls

[The walls of samurai houses are set at around seven feet or more with the average Japanese man of the medieval period measuring only five feet in height. Cas-

Left, Gabriel Rossa with
the Cloud Ladder from the
Bansenshukai manual and
(below) a two-pronged
grapple and rope ladder.

tle walls are of course much larger. The shinobi have various skills for climbing, including sets of spikes for placing into cracks in a wall, grapples and ropes, and even pulley systems.]

菱ヲ知事
The Art of Understanding Caltrops

[Caltrops are small objects thrown on the ground that will always stand with one point in the air; they are spread to stop people from giving chase. These are not normally scattered at random but are positioned where the shinobi feels they will be most effective. They are also attached to strings so that they can trail behind the shinobi, catching the feet of anyone in pursuit. They may be scattered while on the run if an emergency arises.]

堀ノ浅深ヲ知事
The Art of Knowing the Depth or Shallowness of a Moat

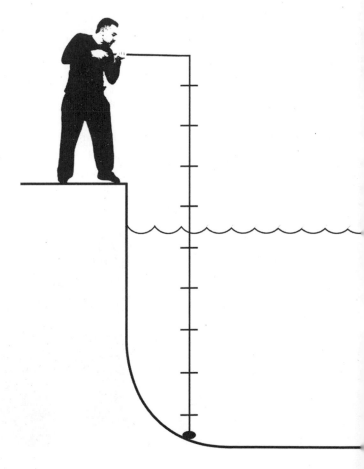

[Knowing the depth of the moat is a key factor when the shinobi is infiltrating a mansion or a castle. This is also done for information gathering for a lord who wishes to attack a castle. Normally depth is measured by a lead weight and a rope, while distances and heights are worked out with mathematical equations. The science of measuring is an art in itself.]

堅キ物ヲ切ル事
The Art of Cutting Through Hard Objects

[Without doubt, on most missions a shinobi will have to cut through a wall, fence or door, etc. There are various traditions on helping the agent cut through these objects, most deal with a form of lubrication that will muffle the sound of a hand drill turning or a saw cutting.]

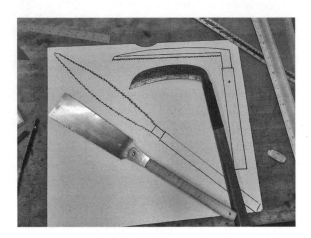

咳仕様之事
The Art of Coughing

[To date, this art has been found in Akutagawa-Ryu and Mubyoshi-Ryu and consists of using a bamboo tube to cough into. The aim is to either suffocate the cough to stop the sound from reaching the enemy that they are about to infiltrate and therefore not giving away the shinobi's position; or it can also be used to give the illusion that the sound of the cough is at a distance, at which the guards will hear

the cough, but because the sound is "small and light" they will look beyond where the shinobi actually is.]

続松之事
The Art of the Torch

[Torches should not be underestimated in value nor should they be considered simple. Shinobi torches are varied and numerous, with many alternative mixtures for different opportunities. A selection of torches and gunpowder skills are required to be mastered by shinobi and torch construction is fundamental to the shinobi arts. One of their primary tasks is to lead people through the dark of no-man's-land in war—which could stretch for miles—and also to journey in harsh weather conditions across many leagues; therefore, torches need to be strong, weatherproof and long-lasting.]

巾着火之事
The Art of Kinchakubi—
Fire in Drawstring Leather Purse

[To ignite the above torches and to commit arson, a shinobi needs fire time and time again; manuals continually state the importance of fire. Even with the aid of modern fire-lighting equipment it is difficult to start fires in wet conditions, and for the medieval person without modern aids it could be an extremely difficult task. The shinobi developed many recipes that allowed them to maintain hot embers for extended periods of time and they also developed many methods of carrying them. These could range from metal cylinders to the example here, a *kinchaku*, which is a leather drawstring purse; this version would have the insides treated so that hot embers could be carried on the shinobi, either in his kimono or on his belt—these were often kept in the sleeve.]

眠薬之事
The Art of Sleeping Powder

[Sleeping powder is normally a mixture of a charred creature, such as slugs or intestinal worms which have been ground to powder and then wrapped in cloth tablets, or alternatively they can be coated on paper soaked in blood. A shinobi would place this tablet or paper into a closed room and its effects are said to cause those in the room to fall asleep, or those who are already asleep will fall into a deeper slumber. To prevent the shinobi from succumbing to their own weapon, they would stuff grass up their nose or inhale pepper so that their nose became blocked.]

無言薬之事

The Art of the Speechless Powder

[This theme tends to come in two versions. Once a shinobi is passing those who are asleep, they will sprinkle or lightly dust this powder on to the face of the enemy. If their enemy should wake, disturb the powder and breathe in then they will inhale it and their voice will be rough and their throat sticky. The second version is that of blinding powders, as displayed in Natori-Ryu, where ground burnt tadpoles are sprinkled on the eyes of a sleeping person—then when they awake and open their eyes the powder will act as an irritant.]

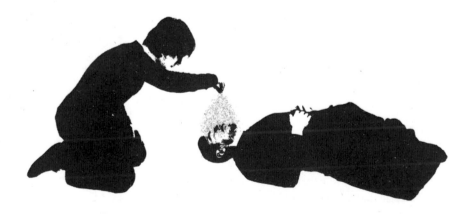

道二不迷之事
The Art of Not Losing Your Way in a House

[One tool that shinobi carry is a long cord that was attached to a doorway or exit—after a shinobi had cut out a section of a wall the cord was reeled out behind the agent. In the dark of the house with only a small amount of light they may lose their way; then if an emergency arises or if the mission has finished and they need to leave in stealth or in haste, they can simply follow the cord back to the opening and escape into the night.]

闇所ニテ人ヲ見ル事
The Art of Observing People in the Dark

[Once in the main rooms of the house, with people sleeping in quarters, the shinobi will need to identify who is there and how many are present. This can be done in many ways; most involve the use of small lights and fire. One method from the *Bansenshukai* ninja manual is to blow a dart from a blowpipe into a wall. The dart has a very small charge of gunpowder; with a slight hiss, it ignites. This illuminates the inside of a room for a second. Another way is to test with light on the end of a

stick, pushing it through gaps while another shinobi looks into the room. In addition to this, directional lights can be used.]

地之巻
Chi no Maki
The Scroll of Earth

忍物語口傳書
Shinobi Monogatari Kudensho
Secret Shinobi Sagas that have been Orally Transmitted
[The second stage in Akutagawa-Ryu is to understand the deeds of shinobi that have gone before them: the tales of ancient masters. Often such stories are included in ninja scrolls to encourage students to aspire to the heights of previous shinobi. The tales often return to events in China, or of famous ninja who helped achieve a great victory, either by burning down a castle or succeeding in killing someone who was well protected—naturally all of these tales hold keys to the arts of the shinobi. These also hold applicability and correctly concentrate the mind.]

人之巻
Jin no maki
The Scroll of Man
[This scroll repeats from the first scroll; this is due to differing degrees of learning. The repeat skills have been left in place so that the full scroll-list is available; however no further explanations are given, they simply go into greater detail.]

空立火之事
The Art of Karatachihi
[Text missing from author's collection]

巾着火之事
The Art of Kinchakubi Drawstring Leather Purse for Fire
[The recipe and construction for the skill described above]

胴之火之事
The Art of the Donohi
[A *donohi* is another form of fire-carrying tool, normally a cylinder or package which contains live burning embers.]

無音薬之事
The Art of the No Sound Power
[Recipes of powders that dampen the sound of tools, etc.]

郭公之事
The Art of the Cuckoo
[A shinobi must learn to imitate animal vocalizations; during an infiltration, the shinobi will call out like an animal or insect; anyone in the target house will be familiar with the noise and ignore any movement outside, thinking it is just the "animal" that is getting closer.]

霧之印之事
The Art of Mudra of Mist
[Blinding powders are often kept in small containers, muskets, canes or cloth. The idea is to gain a position upwind from the enemy and then sprinkle the contents on the wind so that the eyes of the enemy will become blurry and they will be confused. These powders can be thrown at the enemy's face or placed inside of fire rockets and projectiles.]

無言薬之事
The Art of No Speech Power
[Recipes for the above]

眠リ薬之事
The Art of Sleeping Power
[Recipes for the above]

眠リ薬之事又ノ法
An Alternative Sleeping Powder
[Recipes for the above]

手火之事
The Art of the Palm Torch
[Recipes for the above]

松明之事
The Art of Torches
[Recipes for the above]

袖松明之事
The Art of the Sleeve Torch
[A form of torch kept in the sleeve; this is normally another way of carrying embers, or it can be a miniature torch.]

水防薬之事
The Art of Waterproof Medicine
[Shinobi need to have at least a basic knowledge of medicinal plants and travel medicines. Recipes to cure sunstroke, vomiting, headaches and aid in coagulation of blood to close wounds are all required alongside other medical treatments and first aid that is needed while out performing a mission.]

刀拭之事
The Art of Cleaning a Blade
[The concept of quick-cleaning and sharpening a blade, normally this is the skin of an animal with crushed stone applied. The shinobi will sharpen their sword or clean their blade with these methods.]

兵粮丸之事
The Art of Hunger Pills
[Working in "the field" for days if not weeks on end, a shinobi needs to maintain physical and mental stability. Hunger pills are common among soldiers in Japan and consist of different recipes that are formed into pills and tablets. These are light and small but calorie packed. They are to be taken to keep a shinobi from starving.]

遠道労ヲ治ス薬
The Art of Medicine to Cure Exhaustion after Extended Travel
[This requirement for energy and medical aid to prevent exhaustion helps to display the extreme conditions under which the shinobi worked. Shinobi were the long-distance scouts, a black ops team in enemy territory that may have had to infiltrate the enemy camp. They were expected to be in the field for extended periods of time with little or no food, and their health was expected to decline.]

灯燈之事
The Art of the Lantern
[There are various lanterns and lights that a shinobi must use; also there is the art of avoiding lights and illumination.]

御符之事

The Art of Charms

[This is where the arts of the shinobi start to become magical and superstitious. All Japanese war arts have an element of magic; however, it must be remembered that a modern English reader is probably from a Christian based country. "Magic" has become divided from "godly." For samurai and shinobi the "magic arts" can be divine and given from the gods. They would perceive nothing heretical about this. Therefore to help shape the image of the shinobi, consider any charms or magical spells to be equal to a European knight's prayer to God for success in battle. Consider it equal to using holy scripture to protect them, or even a cross emblazoned on armor. The samurai and shinobi would also ask the gods for protection in such a manner.]

削火方

The Art of the Shaved Fire

[Further recipes for starting fires]

紙燭之方

The Art of the Paper Candle

[Further fire recipes for illuminating areas]

続松

Torches

[Even more information on the use of torches]

隠形之文大事

The Art of Ongyo no Bun—words of hiding

[*Ongyo* is the art of hiding. It is a collection of spells and mantra's to help a shinobi hide from the enemy in the dark. The power of the goddess Marashiten is called upon to cloak the shinobi from the eyes of the enemy.]

極意口傳之事

The Art of Oral Traditions of Deep Secrets

[Inside a shinobi school—or family—there are deeper secrets that are passed on to only a few of their students. These secrets differ from school to school but normally—not always— they gravitate towards the magical. With the basic skills now achieved, the shinobi can move towards the higher methods of their school, including esoteric Buddhism.]

Kaiden level

The first three scrolls in Akutagawa-Ryu teach the shinobi their skills and tricks. These they need to know to be a good infiltration agent. They have understood some of the deeper magical elements and can call on the gods for aid. However the final stage is the deepest level of "magic," with ancient rites that have been passed down. They were given to the ancients by supernatural beings.

神伝矢車之法
The Way of the Divine Arrow Windmill
[A magical ritual where arrows are placed in a circle—upon a mirror—and connected by thread, allowing the image of the shinobi to be "buried" below ground where it will stay hidden until the shinobi has finished his mission.]

隠形法
The Way of Ongyo Hiding
[Deeper secrets from the tradition of the goddess Marashiten.]

縮地之法
The Way of Shrinking Great Distances
[A ritual which takes place at an altar and grants success and speed on dangerous missions.]

打電抄
Attacking Like Thunder
[The concept of attacking swiftly and striking the enemy with speed.]

芥子之秘法口授
The Oral Traditions and Secret Methods of Opium
[Poisons and drugs are used in secret missions. Different schools have different versions and uses. From the venom extracted from puffer fish to strychnine and opium, these chemicals are put to use in various ways, poisoning water supplies, food, guard dogs etc. The shinobi becomes a form of chemist and administers his deadly toxin. However, in Akutagawa-Ryu this article is an esoteric ritual.]

The above headings are the shinobi curriculum of the Akutagawa clan. The commentaries are of course mine, but they have been placed there to form a detailed idea of shinobi no jutsu. It becomes evident that the above is, primarily, a list of In-nin skills—*classic shinobi infiltration,* and that Yo-nin—*infiltration through dis-*

guise, has not been addressed. However, other Akutagawa scrolls do have a small sample of disguise skills.*

The preceding is a basic understanding of the shinobi curriculum through the Akutagawa family. To give a further example, the next translation is a collection of extracts from a military manual known as *Giyoshu* 義葉集. This was written by Ohara Masanori 小原 正規 in 1690 and is divided into three volumes:

義葉集

The Giyoshu Manual

The *Giyoshu* manual is a collection of military articles that were written in 1690. The original collection is much larger than the selection presented here. To help form a better idea of the shinobi within the context of the samurai and the military, I have extracted any articles that mention the word shinobi and its sub-labels and also any article that is clearly a shinobi skill. In addition to this, any skill that has appeared in other shinobi literature has been retained, including basic scouting skills. Therefore, some of the following are very much connected to the shinobi, while some only show hints of the shinobi, yet all of them provide a window into samurai warfare and how the shinobi fits into that picture. The original Japanese articles have been left *in situ* above the translation; this has been done to aid any research undertaken by others and to help chronicle this important text for the future.

Volume One

霞の粉とハ胡椒の粉み志やくぎの灰あざみの花鉄の摺くすを抹して竹杖尓仕込或ハ布尓包て打振候ヘハ目暮ム者也眠の粉とハ糞虫を影干尓して火尓焼候ヘハ座中皆眠と云

Kasumi no kona—mist-powder—is made of:

- Ground pepper
- Ash of *Mishashagi*[†]
- Flower of a thistle
- Iron filings

Put the ground mixture into a bamboo cane or wrap it in cloth. If you scatter it towards people, it acts as a blinding powder. Also, sleeping powder is made of *kuso-mushi* ("the golden beetle"[‡]), which is dried in the shade. When burnt, anyone present in a room will fall asleep.

---

* These have been published in *The Secret Traditions of the Shinobi.*
† Unknown material, possibly a skull.
‡ Called the *koganemushi* in modern day Japan, the name *kuso-mushi* was used in the text, translates as "excrement insect" and is a relation to the dung-beetle.

忍の者を可防尓ハ鉄蒺藜（ヒシ）を蒔或ハ竹釘を可指也扨又忍の者来るへき道を可知尓ハ砂、秕（ヌカ）なとを蒔て足跡尓心を可附也

Scatter iron caltrops or stab bamboo nails [into the ground] to prevent shinobi no mono [from infiltrating]. Also, scatter sand or rice-bran along the ground so as to identify footprints; in this manner you will know the way that shinobi no mono have passed.

忍の者鼡となり鼬と成て人家尓入と云ハ鼡鼬の行作を本とする故也日の暮夜の明方を第一尓心掛簀子の下尓先屈候也扨四季の眠時を考へ鼬の路を求鼠の足音虫の声抔して匍（ハヒ）入也

Shinobi no mono are said to infiltrate houses by making themselves like rats and weasels because they act like rats and weasels as a foundation. Also, they prioritize infiltrating at twilight or before dawn. They will crouch under bamboo floors and consider [in which way a person will] sleep depending on the season; after this they crawl their way deeper inside, finding the path of weasels and imitating the sound of the footsteps of rats or the sound of insects.

屏を越候時ハ刀の下緒を足尓搦鍔を踏て可越なり惣して高き所へ登り候時ハ上尓専ら心を付て下を厲（アヤフ）ま須゛下へ飛下り候時ハ心を下に置て飛候者也

Tie the cord of your sword around your foot, [prop the sword against the wall], step on the hilt and cross over a fence. Remember, when climbing up to high positions, pay attention to that which is above and not that which is below and when jumping down to the ground, pay attention to that which is below as you jump.

放し囚人の番等二十人三十人宛昼夜替々勤候ハ忍の者を三四人も召連門外裏路等を守らしむへし

When a group of twenty or thirty people stand watch over prisoners that are not bound by day and by night and by taking shifts, have three or four shinobi no mono guard outside the gate and any back alleys.

忍の者昼ハ休ミ夜ハ張番蟠（カマリ）仕寄継（ツナギ）物見の処尓至り可受指図也

Shinobi no mono rest in the daytime but at night they should go out to the same area as guards on duty, ambushes, to man lookout structures in besieging sides, and as monomi scouts—from here they are given instructions.

張番の者番替の時敵合の物見して返る事一例也又ハ忍の者尓被手引敵地の案内道筋等を見覚へ可備也

It is a custom that guards should scout around no-man's-land just before they return or before a change of guards. [These watchmen] should get familiar with the enemy land and remember the routes and be prepared for [battle]. They do this with the guidance of shinobi no mono.

門前或ハ張番処へ乞食来り候ハヽ早々可追出也惣して大事の番所へ他所より来る者をハ親類たり共遠慮尤也

When beggars come to the gate or guardhouse, drive them off at once. Keep away any person from other territories that approach important guardhouses, even if they are relatives.

惣して忍蟠（カマリ）等尓出候てハ退く時を可慎也夜ハ殊更敵の忍の者跡より慕ひ来る事ある者也

You should be careful about retreating when you go on a shinobi or kamari-ambush mission; especially at night, as the enemy's shinobi no mono will often follow people back.

忍ひ行き敵尓逢候時妄尓不可退若顕て難逃（ノカレ）時ハ足早尓近て品を替て可出向也敵も必同士討を厭者也

If you meet the enemy during infiltration, do not retreat without proper reason. Also, if you are detected and it is hard to escape from the enemy, approach the enemy briskly and deal with them by pretending to be somebody else. Remember, they do not wish to kill their own men.

忍の者ハ第一足場道筋尓心を付月夜闇夜尓品をかへ様を改め月影足跡尓も心を用ひ少の木陰尓も先凌（ヤスロウ）者也

A shinobi no mono should primarily observe the footing and route ahead. Depending on if it is a moonlit night or a dark night, the way of acting or outfits should be changed. Also pay attention to the shadows made by moonlight and to footprints. Try to take cover in even the smallest shadow of trees.

忍の者野山尓起伏する者な連ハ常尓丸寝を可好也

As shinobi no mono sleep and wake in fields or in the mountains, they should always sleep in their clothes.

忍尓出候時道具多きハ悪きと云也食物と虫薬をハ必可持也扨焼食を持犬の吠候時投出し竹管尓糸を通し鉤（カギ）を付高き所へ登る尓も自由をなし申事也

When stealing in you should not carry too many tools. Have food and medicine for stomach-aches above all other things. Carry grilled rice and when dogs bark, feed it to the dog. To climb to a high place using a tool, pass cord through bamboo pipes and attach a hook to the end.

忍ひの者ハ常尓猿を能仕入自由をなし申事も有之也

Some shinobi no mono will prepare and train monkeys so that they can control them with ease.

惣して寒天尓川渡する時ハ先水を一口呑て後渡候者也又堀水抔ハ敵も水の動
静尓心を付る者也

When you cross the river in cold weather, sip a little of the water first and then
cross. Remember, the enemy will watch the water of a moat to observe if it has
movement or if it is still.

忍ひの者五三人も組て出候時ハ名府（ナシルシ）目付（道痕）府（シルシ）を可
定也五色の染紙或ハ米豆等を持て両道ある処川渡の処惣して不案内の處尓て
必用候也

When multiple shinobi no mono venture out as a group, they should make arrangements for the "signs for the name" and "signs to attract attention" and "signs for the
route." They should use five [different] colored sections of paper, or colored rice,
beans etc. The above should be done when a road comes to a fork or at the place
where they cross a river or when they are in a place where they need guidance.

家屋へ忍入候尓ハ先門戸を外より錐（キリ）閉尓して窓穴等を切開き或ハ少しツ
ヽ焼抜扨着類を脱て先へ入連跡より入て其まゝ其口を塞き候事也

When you infiltrate a house, secure the door with a drill from outside first. Next
bore a hole or cut out an opening or burn out a window-like hole little by little.
Take off an item of clothing and put this into the opening first; after that, steal in
yourself and close the hole behind you.

忍ひ得て敵の色目尓噪き候へハ却て顕候也又初めの道を遍るより行抜を吉と須
るなり暁ハ人の眠も安醒者なり能行迹府を取て可返也

When infiltrating to gain information, if you make noise because your enemy's
movements have surprised you, the enemy will find you. Also, it is better to go
ahead [to make your way out] rather than exit along the same route from which
you came. Remember that just before dawn people sleep lightly and therefore are
easily awoken. Be effective and return with evidence.

具足を着し忍尓出候時ハ四尺手拭を以て毛算草摺の不鳴様尓上帯して可出也

When you infiltrate wearing armor, tie a *yonshaku-tenugui*, or four-foot cloth,
around the thigh protectors of your armor; do this like an outer sash, so they will
not make sound.

火縄袋ハなめし革を以て四五寸四方尓きんちゃくの如く尓拵へ跡先を明ケ糸を付
て可持也扨雨降又ハ夜討尓出候時鉄砲の火縄の先を此袋の中へ指入て可持也

Construct a pouch for your fuse; this is made like a drawstring purse. This is a
square of four or five sun and is made of tanned leather. Pierce holes, thread [it
with cord] and carry it. When it rains or you commit a night attack, keep the end
of your fuse in this bag.

Written on the twenty-seventh day of the second month in 1690.

Volume Two

三ツ者とハ臭（カギ）物聞目付を云何も犬忍の者の事也

Mitsumono—the three groups, are *kagi*—people who sniff the air, *monogiki*—people who listen, and *metsuke*—people who see. All three are *inu*—dogs* or shinobi no mono.

敵を遠より見を間見と云近き所尓伏て見を見分と云惣して敵味方の利害吉悪を見を物見と云ふ

To observe the enemy from afar is called *kenmi* 間見 ("looking from a distance"). To observe by lying down near the enemy is called *miwake* 見分 ("to distinguish"). Generally, to observe if a [military] situation is positive or negative between your own side and the enemy's side is called *monomi* 物見 ("scouting").

蟠（カマリ）物見とハ竊盗（シノビ）遠聞の者五三人宛物具堅め出候を云

Kamari-monomi—"hidden scouting"—is a way of scouting done by a group of shinobi or *togiki* ("listening scouts")—they do this with armor on.

草を結とハ敵の来るへき道の草を結ひ或ハ菱（ヒシ）を蒔き伏蟠等を出須を云ふ

Kusa wo musubu can mean; to tie grasses together, to scatter caltrops, or lay *fushi-kamari* ambushes along the path or road from which the enemy may come.

伏蟠（カマリ）野伏村蟠里蟠捨蟠抔云ハ何も人数十廿百二百千二千尓ても村里山林或ハ草深処尓陰連居て敵の不意を撃を云何連も伏兵を云也

[There are many names] for those who ambush the enemy:

- ♦ *Fushi kamari*—ambush troops
- ♦ *Nobushi*—samurai bandits
- ♦ *Mura kamari*—those who ambush villages
- ♦ *Sato kamari*—those who ambush hamlets
- ♦ *Sute kamari*—disposable ambush troops

[The above] ambush the enemy by hiding around villages, in forests and in the mountains or grassy places. These groups can be 10, 20, 100, 200, 1,000 and 2,000. [Collectively] they are all kinds of *ambush*.

---

* "Dog" in medieval Japan was a term used to describe an infiltration agent.

打鉤（カギ）ハ柄のなき熊手尓細引を付て可用也屏乗舩軍等の砌専ら用ヒ候也

An *uchikagi* is a rake without a handle and has a thin rope attached to it when used; this is essential for crossing over a fence, in ship boarding and so on.

四尺手拭ハ米の酢尓浸し乾て後可持若餓候時是を刻ミ可為食物也

Soak a *yonshaku tenugui*—four foot cloth—in rice vinegar, dry it and carry it with you. When you become hungry you can cut off a section and eat it.

澁紙（シフカミ）ハ澁油フノリ此三色紙引て可用也或ハ澁尓ドウサを加へ候

Shibugami—paper strengthened by applying a mixture of persimmon tannin juice; apply oil and seaweed glue to paper. A glaze of alum and glue may be added to the persimmon tannin.

桐油（トウユ）ハ油一升石灰二合能抹して四五篇も塗り能干て後可用也

Tung oil is used [to make oiled paper] by applying a mixture of one *sho* of tung oil and two *go* of powdered lime; apply four to five layers on paper and allow it to dry completely before use.

ガクのドウハ張番伏兵等尓出候時の小屋也破竹を以て籠の如く拵へ澁紙トウユ抔尓て蔽候也

A *gaku no dou* is a small hut used by guards or when in position of ambush. Construct frames as if making a basket with cut bamboo and then coat it with tanned paper, oiled paper, and so on.

The annotation:

内ニ一人居テ自由能様ニ如此拵也

This should be constructed as the drawing so that one person can stay inside and move about freely.

陣中鉄蒺藜（ヒシ）モチリ等必可持也

You should always be prepared with iron caltrops, a *mojiri* (a T-bar drill) and so on when you go to war.

鉄ヒシハ常ニハ細縄ニ通シ置候テモ能ク候
You can have caltrops attached to thin rope during normal times.

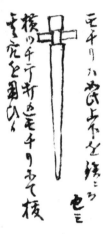

モチリハ如此上下ヲ鉄ニテ包ミ横ツチニテ打込モチリヲ抜其穴ヲ用ユ
Cover the mojiri's upper part and lower part with iron. Drill the mojiri into the
ground by rotating the horizontal T-bar. Take mojiri out and use the hole as you wish.

兵糧乏き時ハ松の甘膚一斤人参一両白米五合右細末尓して後丸して井楼尓て
蒸て十五人尓与へ候へハ三日迄不食しても飢る事更ニ無と也
When food is lacking, make the following:

- ♦ Pine bark—1 kin
- ♦ Ginseng 1—ryo
- ♦ White rice—5 go

When you do not have enough rations, powder the aforementioned ingredients, form it into balls and steam them in a steaming basket. Divide this between fifteen people and they will not starve, even if they eat nothing else for up to three days.

油乏キ時紙燭を拵へ候尓ハ何の木尓ても細くけつり其上を紙尓て巻松脂を解て可塗也或ハ紙小糾を蝋尓て煮しめ可用也

When oil is lacking, make a paper candle. To do this, take thin sticks of any type of wood and roll them in paper and coat it all with melted pine resin. Alternatively, boil a twisted paper string in wax and use that.

雪中尓て手足不寒薬ハ右酒一升生薑六十目皮を去り能刻候て右鍋尓入火を細く焼て半分程尓煉詰小豆程ツヽ手足尓可塗也或ハ酒計を面より手足迄塗候ても防寒者也

A medicine that protects your hands and legs against the cold:

* Sake – 1 sho
* Peeled, chopped ginger – 60 momme

Mix the above in a pot and reduce it over a low heat until it is half in volume. Put an amount the size of an adzuki bean on your hands and legs. Alternatively, use only sake; apply this on your face, hands and legs. These above work for protecting your hands and legs from frostbite.

万毒消ハ青鷺の頭尓ヒルムシロを入黒焼尓志て可用也ヒルムシロとハ海の藻也又第一早く吐出すへき也

The way of making an antidote for all things is to put pondweed into a gray heron's head and char it. Pondweed is a kind of seaweed. Primarily you should spit [poison] out quickly.

血留尓ハ溝三歳（ミソサンザイ）の黒焼を舌の上尓少し可置也

Char a wren and put a little of it on your tongue as a styptic.

同血留尓ハ五八草を流連落たる血の上尓少し可振掛也

Another styptic is to sprinkle *gohasso*—the powder of charred mamushi snake— onto a bleeding wound.

同血留尓松の葉と青木葉の灰を血の上尓可振掛也

Sprinkle the ash of pine and aucuba leaf on the blood of a wound, this is also styptic.

疵（きず）薬ハ膏薬の外妄尓不可用却而痛出る者なり急する時ハ三七葉を捫
（モン）て其汁抔ハ可付也

You should not use other kinds of wound remedies apart from commonly used ointment; this is because they may bring even more pain. In case of emergency, you should crumple the leaves of the chrysanthemum (*gynura segetum*) and rub the juice onto your wound.

白文の書（カキ）様ハ生大豆を能ひしき水を少し入其汁を新筆尓染候て可書也
扨鍋墨を其紙の上尓可振掛始の書たる文字明々尓見へ作那り

The way of invisible writing: mash soybeans and add a little water. Write with this juice and use a new brush. If you apply kettle soot over the paper, the letters originally written will clearly appear on the sheet.

同白文の書様ハ古酒を新筆尓染て可書也扨見候時ハ炭の火尓て焙り候へハ始
の文字明か尓見へ候也

An alternative way of invisible writing is to write with old sake using a new brush. When you want to read this, hold it over the fire and the letters originally written will clearly appear on the paper.

同白文の書様ハ五倍子の不入金の汁を新筆尓染可書也扨見候時ハ水尓浸し候
へハ始の書多る文字明々尓見へ候也

A further way of invisible writing is to write using a new brush with the liquid used for tooth dye without adding the sumac nutgall. When you wish to read it, soak it in water, and the letters that you originally wrote will clearly appear on the paper.

相圖の文書様ハいろは尓ても上の一字を捨てろの字よりいろはと可讀抔約す
る事也

When you write a code, you should make arrangements for the reading of it. For example, every kana character should be read as the one which is one place previous in the "I Ro Ha" Japanese alphabet. For example, the second kana "Ro" should be read as "I."

トウユ尓て長の半頭巾の如く肩迄掛り候様尓拵へ緒を付て可持也

Make a shoulder-length raincoat with oiled paper, styled like a chohan-zukin hood. Attach a cord and carry it.

狼烟を上候尓ハ穴を堀草薬を入狼の糞を加へ火を可掛也煙高く上り遠方の味
方見付候て相図を知る也

When you light a signal fire, dig a hole and add grass and straw to the hole and then add wolf's excrement and ignite it. This smoke will rise up high, and an ally at a distance will see the signal.

同狼烟の方ハ藁三束松葉四分一狼糞三分一鉄砲の薬少し右一ツ尓して火を
付候也

Another signal fire method is to mix three bundles of straw, put together pine
leaves of one fourth of the amount of straw, then add wolf dung to one third of the
amount and a small amount of gunpowder, then ignite it.

同狼煙の方舊畳尓狼糞を加へ其儘火を掛候也扨又狼糞見様ハ糞尓毛交りて
有之者也

A further signal fire method is to add wolf's dung to old tatami mats and ignite
them. To find wolf excrement, know that it has hair in it.

胴の火の方ハ笋の皮を晝夜百日程雨露尓曝し黒焼尓して早稲藁（ハセハラ）を
捫ツトの如く拵へ一方強く結てツント切尓て一方ハ長くして能捫其中へ右の黒
焼を柚の大サ程尓丸して火を付入置上を手拭尓て能包ミ候へハ久敷有之者也

Constructing a *donohi* (body warmer): Expose young bamboo sheaves to the rain
and dew for about one hundred days and nights and then char the mixture. Next,
crumple early-ripening rice straw and make it into a bundle. Fasten one side of the
bundle tight and cut the end off. Leave the other end uncut. Crumple enough [of
the mixture] and char it, [form it into a] ball the size of the yuzu fruit and ignite
it, then place it into the straw bundle. Finally wrap this with *tenugui* cloth and it
will last a long time.

同胴の火の拵へ様ハ奉書の紙を能捫（モミ）引破り丸して燃（モユ）ル火の中へ
投入連惣て火の渡候時別の紙を捫（モミ）置其上を幾重も包ミ火氣の急尓不出
様尓して可懐中也

A further way of constructing a donohi: Crumple hosho paper, which is a thick
paper used for formal documents. Tear it in pieces, forming it into a ball. Throw it
into a fire but then take it out when it ignites. Next completely wrap it with many
layers of crumpled paper; this is so that it does not flare up [and burn out]. Place
this in your kimono.

胴の火の拵へ様ハ苗を能干丸く遍そ尓拵へ其中へ杉原のホクチ尓火を付て
可入也

Constructing a donohi: Dry rice saplings and weave them into a sphere, next create a "belly button" style hollow and ignite tinder made from sugihara paper and
then place the lit tinder within [the sphere].

火口（ホクチ）の拵様ハ舊紙等を両曝尓して塩硝（エンシヤウ）硫黄（イヲフ）尓
て煮合せ可持也用る時ハ少しツヽ切て用候也

Constructing tinder: Expose [and bleach] old paper a few times, boil it in a solu-
tion of saltpeter and sulphur and carry it; tear off a section for use.

同ホクチの拵様ハ奉書の紙を能捫黒焼尓して可用也
A further way of constructing tinder: crumple *hosho* (thick paper), char, and use it.

萬年火の方ハ鞍馬石六匁硫黄三匁二分塩硝三匁二分熊野ホクチ三匁二分 生
脳一匁五分龍脳一匁二分松脂少シ杉原ホクチ少シ右松の甘膚を能煎し其汁尓
て煉固め能干て置扨用ひ候時ハ小刀尓て削り候へハ火出候也
The way of the everlasting fire, mix as follows:

- ◆   Diorite – 6 momme
- ◆   Sulphur – 3 momme 2 bu
- ◆   Saltpeter – 3 momme 2 bu
- ◆   Tinder from Kumano – 3 momme 2 bu
- ◆   Camphor – 1 momme 5 bu
- ◆   Borneol – 1 momme 2 bu
- ◆   Some pine resin
- ◆   Some sugihawa tinder

   Knead and harden the above with liquid made from boiled down pine bark and
dry it. When you use it, ignite it by striking it with a short sword.

矢火矢の薬ハ焔硝八十目硫黄六十四匁灰二十目鉄沙十二匁右からからと研し
一包二七匁宛也
To make powder for fire arrows, grind the following:

- ◆   Saltpeter – 80 momme
- ◆   Sulphur – 64 momme
- ◆   Ash – 20 momme
- ◆   Iron sand – 12 momme

Grind the above together and insert seven momme into each [wooden arrowhead].

此処二口薬二火ヲ付候
Ignite the fuse here.

根ハ木鋒也
The [box] arrowhead is made of wood.

雨火縄拵様ハ生脳一両を挽て其中へ天目尓水二ツ程入候て甞（なめ）候へ者
味の辛程なる時常の火縄を漬して後能干て可用也

Constructing a waterproof fuse: Grind one ryo of camphor and mix two Tenmoku bowls of water with it and then taste. When it tastes pungent, soak a common fuse in the liquid and dry completely so that it is ready for use.

同火縄拵様ハ常の火縄を[?]の中尓七日程漬して後能干て可用也或ハ五倍子の不入カ子尓て能煮て後干て可用也

A further way to construct a waterproof fuse: Soak a common fuse in white lead* for seven days, dry and use. Alternatively, boil it in liquid that is used in dying teeth with which the sumac nutgall has not been added, dry and use.

同火縄の拵様ハ木綿の舊着を縄尓糾（ナイ）塩硝と松脂を水尓たて能く漬して後能干て可用也

A further way of constructing a waterproof fuse: Form the fuse by braiding old cotton cloth into rope, fully boil saltpeter and pine resin in water. Soak the fuse in this liquid, dry it completely and use.

同火縄の拵様ハ椿尓ても藁尓てもアク尓たれ常の火縄を能染よく干て後可用也

A further way to make a waterproof fuse: Soak a common fuse in lye from the camellia plant or from straw; dry it enough for use.

火縄乏キ時蒲の穂の火挟尓合たるを干て其儘可用也

When you lack a fuse, dry the head of a cattail plant and fit in the lock [of the musket] and use it just as it is.

芨（フキ）のからを能両曝尓して後火縄尓糾可用也

Expose the stems of the giant butterbur plant in the sun. These can be made into fuses by braiding them.

松明の拵様ハ枯竹を以て如常拵へ火先の方尓十文字ニ串を指て可用也

Constructing a torch: Make this of dried bamboo as is normally done, pierce it with skewers in the shape of a cross, insert them at the flame end and then use it [by throwing it, note that it will keep the flame upright].

又松明の拵様ハ檜杉禿松の三色を能破候て笋の皮尓て包ミ処々結候て可用也

A further way of constructing a torch is to have three types of wood thinly split;

---

* The ideograms for this are not recorded; the ideogram is made of both 女 "woman" and 粧 "make up," therefore it appears to be white "make up" which was based on white lead.

cypress, Japanese cedar and double-leaf pine. Wrap them within a bamboo sheath [which is found at the base of bamboo], tie it up at places and then use.

又松明の拵様ハクヌギの青き時能扣て後能干て如常拵へ可用也
A further way of constructing a torch is to beat sawtooth oak when it is still green. Dry it and make a torch in the usual way and use.

松明の方ハ塩硝其儘七十目硫黄三匁二分炭三匁二分松脳二匁一分松の引粉一升 ナモミの實三匁三分艾葉一升松脂三匁三分右何もあらくおろして後艾葉を細尓刻ミ松脂と能合て後惣を一尓して能堅メ大形筒三本尓可持也扨一尓て路三里行積也
Constructing a torch:

The following ingredients are roughly grated:

- ♦ Saltpeter – 70 momme (as it is not refined)
- ♦ Sulphur – 3 momme 2 bu
- ♦ Charcoal – 3 momme 2 bu
- ♦ Camphor – 2 momme 1 bu
- ♦ Sawdust of pine tree – 1 sho
- ♦ Cocklebur seed/fruit – 3 momme 3 bu
- ♦ Mugwort leaves – 1 sho
- ♦ Pine resin – 3 momme 3 bu

Shred the mugwort leaves and then mix them with the pine resin. Next mix it all together and ram into three large bamboo cylinders and carry. You can use one bamboo torch for three ri of distance.

雨松明の方ハ塩硝二十五匁硫黄十二匁灰二匁五分松の節五匁艾三匁松脂二匁生脳三匁引茶三分䑕糞三分也右細抹二して竹の筒尓成程堅く込竹の上皮を薄く削て可用也
The rainproof torch:

- ♦ Saltpeter – 25 momme
- ♦ Sulphur – 12 momme
- ♦ Ash – 2 momme 5 bu
- ♦ Pine wood knots – 5 momme
- ♦ Mugwort – 3 momme
- ♦ Pine resin – 2 momme
- ♦ Camphor – 3 momme
- ♦ Ground tea – 3 bu
- ♦ Mouse droppings – 3 bu

Make the above into powder and firmly ram it into a bamboo cylinder, shave the bamboo to make a thin layer and then use it.

水松明の拵様ハ鹿の角尓[?]（ナモミ）の油を塗て干して五十日程返候て後可用也
The way of making a waterproof torch is to coat oil of cocklebur onto a deer antler, dry it for fifty days and then use it.

忍松明の方ハ塩硝二十目硫黄十四匁灰十四匁右を一番と須松脳十二匁右を二番とす松脂一匁八分引茶一匁五分鼡糞一匁七分右を三番とす松の節粉三匁牛糞三匁右を四番とす如此面〻尓合せ扨一ツ尓合して竹の筒へ堅く込竹の上皮を削り扨竹を二ツ尓破其破口を紙尓て二返張り亦惣を一返張て後可用也是ハ火を付候て打消又振立候へハ燃上り候塀尓成とも地尓成共突付候へハ煙り計二成候古へ祐成夜討時時宗是を持候と申傳也
The way of constructing the shinobi torch:

Step one:
- Saltpeter – 20 momme
- Sulphur – 14 momme
- Ash – 14 momme*

Step two:
- Camphor – 12 momme

Step three:
- Pine resin – 1 momme 8 bu
- Ground tea – 1 momme 5 bu
- Mouse droppings – 1 momme 7 bu

Step four:
- Sawdust from pine tree knots – 3 momme
- Cattle dung – 3 momme

Mix each set first and then combine them all together. Ram the mixture into a bamboo cylinder and shave the outer layer of the bamboo until it is thin. Next, cut the bamboo in two; apply two layers of paper over the freshly cut ends and then wrap the whole thing again. Then it is ready to use.

If you put out the fire after igniting this torch, just swing it, and the flames will sprout up again. Stub it against a fence or on the ground and it will just smoke. In ancient times, when [Soga] Sukenari committed a night attack, Tokimune carried this torch.

---

* A second transcription states 10 momme.

Written on the second day of the third month of 1690.

Volume Three

小物見ハ一騎二騎或ハ三騎馬連て可出也是ハ地形の善悪路次の遠近敵の虚實
人数の多寡備の無惣進む敵可退く敵可戦を討敵可討ぬ敵可陣取敵可陣取ぬ敵
可勢の益敵可益ぬ敵可固る敵可別るゝ敵可襲敵可降敵可弱き敵可強き敵可川
を渡る敵可渡さぬ敵可敗るゝ敵可敗られぬ敵可抔能ゝ見分ケ候事也尤川の浅
深堀の廣狭伏兵の有と無とハ様能可心得也

Ko-monomi—small scouting groups—should ride horses and venture out together
in mounted groups of one, two or three. They should know the following:

- ♦ If the topography is positive or negative
- ♦ The distance of the route
- ♦ If the enemy is substantial or insubstantial
- ♦ If the enemy's force is large or small
- ♦ If the enemy is prepared or unprepared
- ♦ If the enemy will advance or retreat
- ♦ If the enemy will attack or not
- ♦ If the enemy is going to encamp or not
- ♦ If the enemy momentum is on the increase or not
- ♦ If the enemy are formed together or formed separately
- ♦ If the enemy will assault or surrender
- ♦ If the enemy is weak or strong
- ♦ If the enemy should be allowed to cross over a river or not
- ♦ If the enemy can be defeated or not

Also, they should have a good judgement on how to know the depth in a river,
how wide and narrow a moat is, and if there are ambushes or not.

惣して物見使番等立返り御返事申陣尓行時ハ相圖の小旗を用候也馬を強く乗
候へハ必乗倒春事ある也

When monomi scouts and the lord's messengers return to their camp with information, they use a small flag as a signal. This is done because if they ride too hard
they may fall [from their horses] from time to time.

相驗ハたとへハ布を一尺程尓切て風と云字を書て鎧の袖尓可付抔兼てより多
く可拵置也

An example of an identifying mark is:
Cut cloth one shaku in length and write an ideogram upon it, for example, 風 *kaze*
for wind; put these on the sleeve of your armor, etc. You should make a lot of such
signs in advance.

相詞定る事敵可と問ハヽ討と答へよ花可と問ハヽ月と答へよ山かと問ハヽ谷と答へよ墨かと問ハヽ硯と答へよ抔と兼て云安き言葉を多く拵へ夜ゝ尓可改易也

You should make passwords as follows:

- When someone says "*Teki*" (enemy), you should answer "*Ute*" (attack)
- When someone says "*Hana*" (flower), you should answer "*Tsuki*" (moon)
- When someone says "*Yama*" (mountain), you should answer "*Tani*" (valley)
- When someone says "*Sumi*" (black ink), you should answer "*Suzuri*" (ink stone)

Prepare many such word combinations that are easy to say, do this in advance, and change them every night.

惣して夜討尓出候時松明抔不可持鉄砲ハ火縄を袋尓可入也

When you venture on a night raid, do not carry a lit torch and put your lit musket fuse into a pouch.

惣して夜討尓出候事月の夜ハ白く闇の夜ハ黒く可出立也

Concerning night attacks, you should wear white when it is a moonlit night. You should wear black when it is dark night.

夜討尓可出尓ハ前の夜より忍の者を入置相圖の剋馬を放ち或火を放ち敵の躁動する尓乗て可討也

When you venture on a night attack, send shinobi no mono the night before the night raid. They should let horses go or use fire as a signal of attack, then attack the enemy by taking advantage of their panic.

相圖の手繩ハ敵の城戸口ゟ忍者を段々尓付ケ繩を引て次第ゝゝ尓可令知也是敵夜討抔尓出候を可知ため也

The skill of signalling by rope involves positioning shinobi no mono at intervals from a [enemy] castle entrance and for commands to be sent back by pulling on the rope that that they have in hand. This is in order to inform people of when the enemy venture out on a night raid.

伊賀甲賀の忍者ハ敵の城内へ忍ひ入て具尓見候て返る事罕々？也城中よりも出多る忍者尓對面して堅き誓言尓て互尓語合候と那り

Iga and Koka shinobi no mono do not always precisely observe and infiltrate castles. Instead they sometimes meet other shinobi no mono that have come from the castle. They often get information from each other by the use of strong oaths.

火事狼煙等の方角を可見知尔ハ常尓其方角を能見定矢倉勢楼尓上り刻（キザ）
を付置候或ハ竹を四方尓立て縄を張り結目を付ケ方角遠近を可知也

To identify exactly which direction a fire or signal fire is positioned, you should mark out the correct directions by making notches upstairs in a turret or in a watch tower. Alternatively you should mark them out by standing four bamboo posts in a square and stretch rope around them with knots to show the direction or the distance [of the fires].

飛脚（ヒキヤク）燧(違う写本では飛脚かがり)狼煙（ノロシ）或ハ玉火流星等を所
〻高山抔尓備へ置相圖の儀ある時其次〻〻の火を見て遠国まて一時尓知候也

Prepare *hikyakukagari* ("express fire messenger"), *noroshi* ("signal fires"), *tamabi* ("ball fires") or *ryusei* ("rocket flares"), etc., and place them here and there on high mountains in advance. When the need to send a signal arises, the signal will be relayed from position to position so that people in the distant place will know of it immediately.

一陰府陰約ハ皆相府相詞作り文字或ハ通音或ハ白文等を以て書札を認メ衣の
内尓納或ハ脇指の鞘尓収メ或ハ切破笠の緒尓拵へ或ハ鞋の裏尓蔵或ハ魚鳥
の腹尓蔵し或ハ竹の筒尓込ミ或ハ心尓銘し或ハ五體を破て其内尓蔵抔して餘
方の味方尓通る事也其外髪の中肌の帯等を吟味する事也

Secret marks or secret arrangements are ways to communicate with allies in a different place by the use of identifying marks or passwords that have been pre-arranged. Do this by writing in letters using secret code or invisible ink; by hiding the writing in your clothes; in the scabbard of your wakizashi; by cutting it into pieces and making strings of them and using them as cords for a straw hat; on the sole of a straw sandal; in a belly of a bird or fish; in a bamboo cylinder; by memorizing it; or cutting open somewhere on your body and inserting it into the wound, and so on.

Apart from these, check the inside of hair and loincloths to discover them.

色府ハ五色の紙を以て餘所の味方へ意趣を通る事也白ハ請加勢ヲ青ハ請兵糧
ヲ黒ハ殺敵将ヲ黄ハ敵（テキ）強（ツヨク）紫（ムラサキ）ハ請玉薬ノ類也

Color marks are used to inform your side of who is stationed in another place and to transmit intentions. For this, use five different colored papers. For example:

1. White: asking for reinforcements
2. Blue: asking for food
3. Black: to kill the enemy's general
4. Yellow: to say the enemy is strong
5. Purple: to ask for gun powder

惣して敵国へ入らハ必物見を幾重尓も出須事也敵間近き処へ物見を出し候時
ハ足軽の一組も二組も跡より可出也

When you enter the enemy's land, send monomi out repeatedly. When you are near the enemy's position and send monomi in, have one or even two troops of ashigaru follow them.

伏蟠（カマリ）可有と思ふ処をハ先へ乗抜敵の道筋尓心を付物鉄砲抔少掛見
候者也

To know if an enemy ambush is laying in wait in an area where you expect them to be, [go around and] pass on after that area and move deeper [into enemy territory] then examine the route that the enemy may have taken [to identify if there are any signs of their passing]. Also shoot muskets to discover [if they are there].

伏蟠（カマリ）可有処を探り候尓ハ先風下へ廻り物音を可聞定也捨火縄見せ旗
作り人形抔有之者也第一地響尓心を付候者也

To check a place you expect ambushes to be laid, move downwind first and listen for any noise. You may find abandoned fuses and fake flags and also fake figures. You should mainly pay attention to if there are any vibrations in the ground.

物見の習とハ第一人数積第二備の立様第三足場の善悪第四町間第五旗の有所
右無御尋候ても可申上也

The teachings of the scout:

- Estimate how many people there are
- Observe what [the enemy] formation is like
- Check if the footing is good or bad
- Distance
- The position of battle flags

If the general does not ask about the above you should still report it to him.

物見の心掛ハ口上の立派をも不好武者振をも不作只敵の知愚人数の多少地の
利備の前後の次第押敵可引敵可陣取敵可不取敵可戦を好む敵可不好敵可戦を
待敵可不待敵可川を渡す敵可不渡敵可敗るる敵可堅き敵可人数を分る敵可集
る敵可加る敵可落る敵可抔と其位を能見分ケ無疑様尓思考の通り聢々可申上也

Monomi should not "speak fair with insincere words" nor should he distinguish himself on the field of battle.

Monomi should just identify the following:

- If the enemy has wisdom or not
- The number of people they have

- ◆ If the land is tactically beneficial or not
- ◆ Their preparation to the front and the rear
- ◆ Observe if the enemy will attack or retreat
- ◆ Observe if the enemy will encamp or not
- ◆ Observe if the enemy wishes to fight or not
- ◆ Observe if the enemy can wait for beneficial timing in battle or not
- ◆ Observe if the enemy will allow our forces to cross the river or not
- ◆ Observe if the enemy are grouping their forces together or separating them
- ◆ Observe if the enemy approach is unified or divided
- ◆ Observe if the enemy increases or decreases

Monomi should inform on these matters and others, but they should discard their own thoughts and not try to pass on *only* positive information.

民家の焼る煙ハ黒く厚く見へ狼烟ハ細く高く見へ其明ハ大方薄く廣く見ゆる者也

Smoke from private houses that are burning looks black and thick, while signal fire smoke looks thin and reaches high. The light from the fire signal will look vague in color but will still be wide.

夜の物見ハ必忍者を召連て出候者也

When scouting at night, always go with shinobi no mono.

夜の物見尓出候て水の浅深を可知尓ハ細縄の先尓小石を付け所ゝ引破紙を付弓弭（ユハヅ）尓結付て可知也惣して水を渡り候尓ハ七尺深きも二丈三丈深きも同し事也

When scouting at night and you wish to know how shallow or deep water is, attach a small stone to the end of a thin rope. Next, splay the rope a little here and there and place paper through it and tie the rope to the horn of a bow [then dip the stone in the water until it hits the bottom]. Use the same method when you cross water even to the depths of seven shaku, two jo, or even up to three jo.

兵の野尓伏候時ハ飛鳥列を亂り月の夜ハ其方必曇と云也

When soldiers are lying in a field, flying birds will break formation. On a moonlit night, the direction [of the ambush] will be cloudy.

野伏の計略尓鳥獣の真似を成し或小鳥抔を持行事有之也

One trick of *nobushi*—bandit samurai—is that they sometimes mimic the sound of birds and beasts or take small birds or other such creatures with them.

矢倉の辺尓ハ甕の口を能包ミ水の不入様尓埋て可置也若シ敵方より地下を鑿
或ハ夜討抔来り候時右の甕の口尓耳を付候ヘハ其方角能聞ヘ候也

Stretch [material] over the mouth of an earthenware jar, bury it [up to the rim] in the ground, but do not let water into it. When the enemy are tunneling underground or approaching with a night attack, listen with your ear against the [covered] opening of an earthenware pot. You can clearly hear the direction that the enemy are coming from.

物見の矢倉尓ハ相圖の貝鐘太鼓等必可有之也

In a lookout turret there should always be conch shells, bells and drum, etc., for signaling.

堀の内尓ハ水鳥の羽を切て放し可置也敵の間者来候時羽音躁て味方心付候也

Take a waterfowl that has had its wings clipped and put it on a moat. When the enemy's spy approaches, the waterfowl will beat its wings and create a fuss. In this way you will know when the enemy is approaching.

Written on the fifth day of the sixth month in 1690.

The Ways of the Hattori Clan and Doson-Ryu

The name Hattori is well known in the world of the shinobi. It is one made famous by the shinobi scroll named *Shinobi Hiden*, supposedly written by Hattori Hanzo (but most likely by his father).* Furthermore, the shinobi scrolls of the military war manual, *Gunpo Jiyoshu*—a staple in the study of shinobi no jutsu—were heavily influenced by a warrior of Iga called Hatori Jibuemon. However, more Hattori manuals do exist and the following translation is of a manual written by Hattori Doson. The scroll is currently in the collection of the Ikedake Bunko in Okayama University Library. The document is in "letter form" and is housed in tandem with another document titled *Gunpo* ("military code"). The shinobi scroll itself is highly interesting and uses various ideograms to represent the different types of shinobi. It even goes as far as to give the ages and social classes of the various types of spy. While a complex matter, it is echoed in other manuals that clandestine, commando-like infiltration is considered the task of younger shinobi-ashigaru (shinobi foot soldiers). The tasks of conspiracy and classic spying are the realm of the older man. The *Bansenshukai* shinobi manual also makes a distinction between the two, but concentrates on a slightly different angle—that those of the samurai class are better suited for classic spying due to their education. However, this is not considered

---

* To read the English translation of the scroll *Shinobi Hiden* and the shinobi scrolls of the *Gunpo Jiyoshu* manual, see Cummins & Minami, *The Secret Traditions of the Shinobi*.

an absolute rule and many shinobi had to undertake both covert commando missions and those of classic spying.

The following is a translation of the two above-mentioned scrolls, while both are stored as a single document. The first scroll is not shinobi arts but basic military code, but has been inserted here to keep it in its correct historical place. It has great importance due to its connection with the Siege of Osaka. The second manual is the Hattori shinobi scroll from a school called Doson-Ryu. The first scroll, *Gunpo*, has been given a simplistic translation to iron out any of the confusing aspects, for the main focus is the second text. The first manual is concerned with the Siege of Osaka in 1614.

The First Scroll:
軍法
Gunpo
Military ways

Once that all is fixed and arranged between the vanguard, the close retainers to the commander and the right and left flanks—keep your position firm and secure, even if you find your position undesirable.

When taking up position in an open space and there are buildings in that area, do not move to take a stand within the buildings.

The vanguard and the first and second troops should be designated at the end [before the battle].

When determining the order of the troops [front or rear], even if there is a dispute to decide which troop should be the vanguard, the second troop and other formations must be fixed steady and proper order must be given throughout the army.

The entourage troops to the lord or those in the right and left flank should not advance to achieve distinction without the direct order of the lord.

Supplementary:
If group captains give commands, follow what they have ordered after discussing the points in full.

Do not mix in the positions of troops from other provinces [who are stationed within the same army]—if you have to go to such a place then only leave after informing your group captain.

Supplementary:

If someone is opposed to soldiers from another troop, deal with the one from your own troop, without investigating who is right or wrong.

Concerning fights that erupt within your own men—make sure to punish both parties involved.

If a horse is released, or a bird or animal comes out around the position, do not raise your voice or become confused.

Do not allow a horse to bolt when in a battlefield camp.

If the roadways are bad, do not call out and interrupt a *Kudashiuma* (horse messenger) [which has been sent from the lord to the battlefront].

Hachiman Daibosatsu will punish those who violate the above points.

Written on the tenth day of the tenth month of Keicho 19 (1614).
By Harutaka 玄隆*

The Second Scroll:
服部道尊一流/忍之法
Hattori Doson Ichi-Ryu no Shinobi No Ho
Hattori Doson's direct line and school of shinobi ways

- ♦ Know the two concepts of *Insei* 陰盛 (yin and prosperous), and *Yokyo* 陽虚 (yo and insubstantial)—this is an oral tradition.
- ♦ *Shinobi no mono* 竊盗ノモノ should be between the ages of 23 and 35 and [this type of shinobi] are called shinobi-ashigaru—"shinobi foot-soldiers." Great generals supervise and utilize them accordingly—this is an oral tradition.
- ♦ There are also shinobi of disguise 變形ノシノビ and shinobi of speech 言語ノシノビ and these people are from 47–48 to around 60 years old. These shinobi シノビ infiltrate the enemy province and record the topography to see how steep or not or how impregnable a difficult place is. Also, they obtain the manners and customs of the enemy and of the enemy lord's ways. They also observe the entertainment used in enemy provinces and

---

* Ikeda Toshitaka (1584–1616), also known as Harutaka. The first son of Ikeda Terumasa, who had a fief of 500,000 koku and was the lord of Himeji castle. In 1614, Toshitaka took part in the winter Siege of Osaka Castle on the Tokugawa side—the importance of this document should not be underestimated, giving us a great view of the winter Siege of Osaka.

they approach "men of lesiure"* to obtain information on whether the province, town or village in question is strong or weak. [For this type of shinobi] you should choose people who are quick-witted and intelligent to perform this task—this is an oral tradition.

- Knowing the different points to keep in mind concerning animals and birds during both the nighttime and the daytime—this is an oral tradition.
- The art of knowing the distance on a road by night—this is an oral tradition.
- Important points about the *haraita* "abdomen plate"—this is an oral tradition.†
- The art of the two types of fire—this is an oral tradition.
- The art of "asking the earth" 地二問フ事—this is an oral tradition.
- Knowing the different points to keep in mind concerning insects during both the nighttime and the daytime—this is an oral tradition.
- The art of knowing if the topography of an area is beneficial or hazardous to your allies—this is an oral tradition.
- The two different mindsets you should have for shinobi infiltration, depending on if it is an enemy castle or a military camp—this is an oral tradition.
- You should be aware that your object cannot be fulfilled without knowing the routes [around the provinces]—this is an oral tradition.
- The art of ignition—this is an oral tradition.
- Fire according to the four seasons—this is an oral tradition.
- The two types of kagimono—this is an oral tradition.
- There are various ways to prepare throwing torches and powder torches and there are a myriad of versions in the world—this is an oral tradition.
- The art of the *Taratara-bi*—"dripping fire"—this is an oral tradition.
- Points you should keep in mind to make contacts within the enemy force—this is an oral tradition.
- Mindsets shinobi should have, for night and daytime—this is an oral tradition.
- You should mix in with the enemy to know if they are strong or weak, as well as to record their passwords and identifying marks—this is an oral tradition.

Other than the above set of skills, shinobi シノビ also perform the tasks of guards; and kamari ambush troops. In addition to this they also patrol the area around an army on the march, around a castle, and around a military camp. Furthermore, they defend against other shinobi 忍ビ and thieves when a lord is taking lodgings

---

* A man of means who has no need of employment.
† Unknown skill or tool.

during a journey. The details of these skills are written in another manual. Therefore they will not be explained here.

Written on the twenty-eighth day of the third month.

Postscript

The above twenty points are the ways of shinobi, I am now writing to present them to you.

There are details to teach for each point, but I, the writer, am too old to write them all down. I feel hesitant to ask someone to do it in my stead. Therefore, I have written things in the above manner. Furthermore, although it does not seem to be so common, [the lord] heard of me and thought it would be helpful for the younger people and had me serve in the service of our clan [lord]. I wonder if this was helpful.

I have three ways of the shinobi path fully transmitted to me, two of which include many gadgets from ko-ryu—old schools. These are to be constructed. There are a lot of tools [in these latter schools] and there are many things that are not explained in detail. A person (or people) from Doson-Ryu [unintelligible text] accompanied the lord when the lord returned [from battle] to our province and reported [to the lord] in detail.

The man named Doson lived as late as into the reign of Lord Nobunaga. The above person (or people) said there was no other shinobi as good as Doson, anywhere within Iga. After the battle of Sekigahara, Lord Gongen (Tokugawa Ieyasu) formally instructed Yamaoka Doami to retain the descendants of Doson. Doami received the order but Doami informed the lord that there were no descendants of Doson remaining—this I heard from a reliable source.

At the time of the rebellion of Shimabara, the person (those people) offered service to Sir Ogasawara Iki-no-kami as good shinobi シノビノ上手 and he considered it was a good offer and discreetly suggested [their service] to Sir Izu and Sir Sanai about sending the said samurai to infiltrate the castle [as shinobi] and burn the huts down, but [in the end] this was not to be allowed. One of Sir Iki-no-kami's retainers, whose name is Asa... [from here the remaining three lines of the text are unintelligible].

Points of interest found within the above text:
Some of the ideograms used in the text are of great importance in the history of the shinobi. They designate different forms of the term shinobi. They show that the ideograms 竊盗 represent stealing into areas, commando, or thief-style infiltration. The spying forms, in this case, come under the now famous ideogram 忍; others have also been included in the body of the text.

Concerning "dripping fire"—"Tara-tara" is a Japanese onomatopoeia, a word that represents a sound. In this case it is the sound of fluid dripping at speed before it begins to pour, like that of a fast dripping tap not fully on nor off. The addition of *hi* 火 (or *bi*) makes this a "fast dripping fire," most likely a fire that drips down a structure.

The Shoka no Hyojo—Shinobi Extracts

The same samurai who wrote the *Gunpo Jiyoshu* manual of c. 1612–19, Ogasawara Saku'un, authors this manual. The Shoka no Hyojo is the follow-up to the previous work and part of a trilogy of manuals. This writing post-dates the Gunpo Jiyoshu but is still of an exceedingly impressive date, being somewhere in the first two decades of the 1600s. When dealing with shinobi manuals, the rule of thumb is that the closer to the date 1603, the more reliable the information. While other manuals of later times are considered mainly correct, the following information is, without a doubt, transmitted by a samurai fighting during the Sengoku Period, and one who has witnessed Warring States Period shinobi.

外聞きに可遣人之事
Togiki ni Tsukawasu Beki Hito no Koto
The people who should be sent for the job of togiki
An old samurai said:
"*Togiki* is so named because those who undertake this task 'listen to external issues.' Therefore, the job of togiki includes listening to discover the enemy status and situation by moving around the guardhouses. He listens finding gaps in their night patrols, or by stealing in close to the enemy. Also it can be safely said that those who go to an enemy province to conduct military tactics are also called togiki. They investigate and observe the enemy province, their behavior and manners. Although shinobi no mono know this task very well, there are important things that need to be understood when conducting military tactics. These things are difficult to achieve unless [the togiki scout] is a brave samurai who comprehends tactics. In addition to the above, the task of togiki is to judge and return with information on the geography of the enemy province. He is to judge if rumors [concerning] the enemy are suspicious [and false or not] and report if anything is suspicious within their boundaries. This appointment [of togiki] cannot be done in full by someone who is without wisdom or good memory; they also need to have good wit and excellent speech."

関所の番別而念可入事
Sekisho no Ban Besshite Nen wo Irurubeki Koto
Those who guard check points should be extremely cautious

An old samurai said:

"Those who guard checkpoints should not be weak of mind in any way. If someone suspicious comes through, they should be stopped and thoroughly checked. Those who do the job of shinobi and togiki are people of wit and thus are excellent at deceiving people. From ancient times it has been known that those who are from Iga and Koka have mastered this path and that they have various methods of deception. This [warning concerning shinobi and togiki] is important for all those who take up the position of guard, but more so at checkpoints, because many people go to-and-fro and because of this they need to take more care in their duties."

外聞きをたより謀略之事
Tokigi wo Tayori Boryaku no Koto
Using togiki to create deeper tactics

In one province there was a togiki who was captured. One of the capturing retainers said to the togiki: "We are going to spare your life, this puts you in our debt, therefore when we send our own shinobi to investigate your province we will have them communicate in secret with you and you are to give them aid. Also, you yourself should periodically return to us and report. Lastly, do not inform those in your home province of this when you return."

When the togiki returned to his home province he informed his lord-commander of this, to which the lord-commander was greatly pleased. In response this togiki was sent back periodically to the where he *falsely* reported on his own side and of his lord's behavior and [tried to] deceive [the enemy] with such a connection. [But the enemy who had captured him knew that he was lying and] in this way the [true] plans were known to the enemy [and they could see the truth] with the clarity of a reflection in a mirror. [The enemy] did not show or display that they knew these factors but instead they made [the togiki] give false speeches and undertook various tactics and this person deceived and "blinded" [his own side], leading them to ruin.

I must say that this approach is a technique to destroy the enemy plans by pretending to accept that which cannot be accepted, and that if also something has been moved to ruin then you should use such a failure [in a positive way as to integrate it] into your plans. This is essential in skills of war.

夜討白出立ちを仕たる事
Youchi Shiroidetachi wo Tsukamatsuritaru Koto
Dress in white during night attacks

One lord-commander who had with him 300 men fought against another lord-commander who had 1,000 men. There was a small river that lay between the two. The commander of the smaller force advanced to the river but as the enemy was larger in number, he did not proceed to enter battle. The larger army saw the smaller army as insignificant and therefore they also did not take the opportunity to enter combat either. The commander of the smaller army sent shinobi to investigate the status of the enemy—and to find where the shallows of the river were. The shinobi investigated these points, returned, and made their report.

The shinobi said: "Generally I have found that this enemy, from the highest rank to the lowest, are content to rely on numerical advantage. This is because while there were watch fires, there were no men standing by them. It looks as if they are not well-guarded. Also, they are rumoring among themselves that even if we attack, our numbers are so small that it would not have an effect on such a larger number. As there is a small river positioned between our sides they have concluded that we will not attack. The rumors also say that our enemy general has the intention to fight as he has come to the river, but that he has yet to cross it. They continued and said that we are not so proficient and therefore they do not have to initiate combat. They say that if their lord forces our army back with his massive army, then we cannot hold out for long."

At this the lord-commander of the smaller army said that this was indeed fortuitous. He had all ranks of his men wear white jackets, telling them that they would carry out a night raid that very night. No one should strike anyone wearing a white jacket, even if it is an enemy. After this they made a night attack on the enemy camp and won a victory, just as they planned.

敵の窃盗をかりたる事

Teki no Shinobi wo Karitaru Koto

To utilize enemy shinobi

In one battle of the past both lord-commanders were experienced men. They both moved with caution and the battle could not be concluded. One old retainer from one of the sides made his men prepare for night attacks for six or seven nights in a row. Those men did this in various ways but did not actually commit to the attacks. After this period, the leader of the attacks *pretended* to be ill and said:

"I am now extremely ill. If the enemy gets wind of this they will approach with a night attack. Therefore this force of 150 people before me should be split into two groups, taking turns to perform night duties with armor prepared."

On that night he used 70 people to commit a night raid against the enemy (who numbered 200 people). He killed more than one hundred of them, including low-ranking soldiers, while only three people of the attacking side died. At this someone said:

"This is a technique of using the enemy shinobi and has been used since the days of [Kusunoki] Masashige. Beforehand he had his men prepared to night attack for six or seven nights. This was used as a threat to the enemy. These false "attacks" caused the enemy to become defensive, keeping their guard firm. This, in turn, tired the enemy out. At which point the commander pretended to be ill so that the enemy would relax—they were exhausted from suspense. Thinking that a night raid would not come allowed them to take off their armor. At this point the troops came and won their victory. These skills are used when you assume that shinobi have infiltrated your own men, and you wish to deceive them. If shinobi are blind-sighted and know nothing of this skill, then the enemy will be defeated without fail."

Generals and retainers should understand this deeply. They should not rely on the judgment of monomi and shinobi alone, but should not dismiss them either. It can be said that the secret traditions of war are here.

眠薬の事
Neburi Gusuri no Koto
Sleeping powder
Supplementary—protection from sleeping powder

- Bat – 5 momme, charred
- The leaves of a Kiri tree – 8 momme, charred
- Centipede – 5 momme, dried in the shade
- White sandalwood – 5 momme in its natural state
- Cotton plant seeds* – 2 momme in its natural state
- Cloves – 5 momme in their natural state
- Agar wood – 8 momme, in its natural state
- Kigyufun (yellow cattle dung)† – 8 momme fully dried
- Suiginro – this is not mercury but is medicine made from "stone" called ginseki (silver stone) – 3 momme

Powder the above and use it when undertaking shinobi activity. Burn it around a guardhouse and if this smell enters the nostrils of even the most well-prepared warriors they will fall asleep and become unconscious—there are oral traditions for this.

When you burn the above powder, apply the following around your own eyes and nose:

- Sulphur – 5 momme in its natural state
- Borneal – in its natural state
- Bat droppings – 2 momme in its natural state
- Asiatic Ginseng – 3 momme in its natural state
- Cloves – 2 momme in their natural state

---

* 木綿核.
† Possibly Oriental bezoar or its literal translation.

- Kunroku (an amber-like substance) – 3 momme in its natural state
- Benzoin resin – 5 momme, melt this in sake and then transfer it to water to solidify it and then powder it down

Powder the above ingredients, mix it with sesame seed oil and apply this oil around the eyes and nose; even if you smell the sleeping powder you will not sleep. There are oral traditions for this.

水防薬の事
Suibogusuri no Koto
Water sealing substance
This was recorded in the manual *Yoshitsune-ko Kakisute-monogatari* and is a tradition from Yoshimori.

- Oil of toad: On the night of the fifteenth day of the eighth month face the moon when it is not hidden by clouds and place toad(s) in a "red bowl;" erect chains around the four corners of the vessel and light candles in front of the chains. When the lights have gone out, the toad(s) will have secreted oil—there are more oral traditions.
- Camphor – 5 momme, place this in a pot and roast it seven times
- Frankincense – 3 momme, in its natural state
- Pine resin – 5 momme, hard, as it is in its natural state
- Mouse droppings – 8 momme, powder these mouse droppings just as they are
- Cedar resin – 2 momme, in its natural state

The toad oil should equal one third of the above ingredients—mix them together into an ointment and apply it when you swim. Place it around the eyes, mouth and nose—more in oral traditions.

If you apply this above to the rim of a barrel and put the barrel over your head you can move along a riverbed and water will not seep into the barrel—there are oral traditions.

火をとる薬の事
Hi wo Toru Kusuri no Koto
Ignition powder
Those people who are skilled in the way of the shinobi have transmitted this recipe for ignition powder.

- Moxa – 10 momme, soak in water and crumple well until it is soft
- Sulphur – 8 momme in its natural state

- Saltpeter – 5 momme in its natural state
- Kettle soot – 5 momme
- Camphor – 8 momme in its natural state
- Agar wood – 7 momme
- Jisseki* – 10 momme in its natural state

Crumple the moxa until it is like cotton, powder the other ingredients and then mix them together. This ignites amazingly well, especially when you ignite it using the sunshine of a clear sky. Using a flawless crystal ball should ignite this. If shinobi do not carry embers upon them then they should use this ignition powder—this is a secret skill of the shinobi. The above can also be used as tinder or the wick of *tamagohi*—"egg fire."

まき松明の事

Makitaimatsu no Koto

The rolled torch

Supplement to this the powder to be used.

The scatter torch: this is taken from the same tradition as the above ignition powder and is excellent at burning down camp quarters when on a night raid.

The rope that secures the torch should be thin and soft so that it will burn quickly.

Place the above small torches together as one, the more the better. As they burn the rope will snap open and they will scatter and separate. Make sure to apply the powder below to each section in order that the fire will spread quickly.

Recipe for the powder:

- Sulphur – 10 momme in its natural state
- Saltpeter – 8 momme in its natural state
- Camphor – 5 momme in its natural state

Dissolve the above in sesame oil and apply the oil to the torch. In addition to this, you can form a candle-like shape and solidify it, using it [as ignition] for the wick. There is more on this in oral traditions. Furthermore, this recipe will catch fire quickly and when it rains it will not go out when wet.

---

* 実石 Unknown substance, presumably a sort of mineral (stone).

袖松明の事

Sodetaimatsu no Koto

The sleeve torch

This is used on night raids and shinobi missions:

- Sulphur – 8 momme
- Camphor – 5 momme
- Blue vitriol – 3 momme
- Jisseki* – 8 momme
- White lead – 3 momme

Mix the above in sesame oil and apply it to a very old cloth. Then split cherry tree wood into thin sections and roll the cloth around it—this will make a torch of four or five sun in length. Carry this in your sleeve and know that it will catch fire very quickly when you need to use it. It will burn for one ri per one sun in length—more information in oral traditions.

たうの火の事

Donohi no Koto

The body warmer and ember container

The recipe for the *donohi* is a secret tradition of the shinobi:

- Blue vitriol – 5 momme
- Mouse droppings – 3 momme
- White lead – 5 momme
- Charred sugihara paper – 3 momme
- Jisseki† – 5 momme
- Polygonum longisetum – 5 momme, use the root and the leaves together

A Donohi from Natori-Ryu, which is also a copper cylinder

Knead the above with glue [made from seaweed], ignite it and carry this in a copper cylinder—more in oral traditions. This can also be called *kaichu no hi*—"fire in the breast of the kimono."

The latter six traditions have been gathered from various writings and traditions passed down from skilled people. Future students should be hands-on and experiment with them.‡

---

* 実石 Unknown substance, presumably a sort of mineral (stone).

† 実石 Unknown substance, presumably a sort of mineral (stone).

‡ As these quotes are taken from different sections of the original manual, the last six before the sentence

事によするてだての事

Koto ni Yosuru Tedate no Koto

The tactics of using pretext

Someone asked me:

"On a battlefield, some things should be made clear while other things should be performed discreetly. Moreover, it seems that most things should be hidden from the enemy. There is no possibility that your own side and the side of the enemy will not have shinobi. Information on what you do will be speedily leaked to the enemy. If you are to attack the enemy by taking advantage of where the enemy is insubstantial but do not inform your own men, then there will be many people who are not fully prepared. On the other hand, if you give them prior warnings then your plans will be given over to the enemy. All will be in ruins. Thus old man, tell me of this?"

I said to him:

"Tactics are constructed to attack where the enemy is insubstantial. Therefore if things are carried out in secret then there is a true advantage. In this, you must take precautions against those enemy shinobi inside your own forces. That being said, if you do not inform your men but attack the enemy without them having time to properly prepare, disaster will follow as well. For this there is a skill called *koto ni yosuru*."

The questioner asked:

"What is *koto ni yosuru*?"

I answered him:

"An example of this is to pretend to move to the left but in fact you move right, or you advance while pretending to make a retreat. These are examples of *koto ni yosuru*. Also, by taking advantage of [the enemy's negligence due to] snow—as we spoke of earlier*—where a general pretended to retreat and made his rearguard look secure, with the intention to get back to the enemy province [which was a ruse].

"Also, if you plan to attack the enemy before they sit for their meal, have your own men finish their meal [early and get ready] using the cold night to come as an excuse to eat early."

Through these examples, consider what should be done.

敵中をさきたる事

Tekinaka wo Sakitaru Koto

To split the enemy with discord

A commander-in-chief once had difficulty capturing an enemy castle. He was contemplating which military tactics he could use to divide his enemy. A clever man said to him:

---

in question were grouped together.

* The episode is not recorded here.

"It has been said from ancient times by excellent generals that a larger enemy should be divided. However, it looks easy to achieve but in fact it is most difficult to do. As I have discovered a good plan, and if you execute my plan, then know that nine times out of ten doubts will be created within the enemy. The castle will fall."

This was said with confidence. The commander replied:

"How is this to be done?"

The man answered him by saying:

"If you give your patronage to my descendants, my sons and grandsons, then I will be determined to sacrifice my life for you; leaving my fame for these descendants."

The commander shed tears of gratitude and said:

"I think most of such a man like you. I appreciate how much divine blessing is given for such a warrior. Such plans cannot be successful without brave and loyal people to engage in them. In order to ease the suffering of our soldiers and to benefit your decedents, also for your own [honor], conduct these tactics, devoting your life and mind to them. I will never forget the will you have."

This was said and an oath was made. The man accepted this mission with pleasure and infiltrated the enemy castle. When the enemy detected and found him, surrounding him in larger numbers, he intentionally took out a suspicious looking letter from his kimono. He immediately burnt it with fire he had upon him. He then drew his sword and tried to fight them but ended up upon the floor. The enemy pinned him to the ground and captured him alive. They bound him in the *takategote* style and took him to the higher retainers. The retainers said:

"The writing that you took out from your kimono and burnt was probably a secret letter; therefore just confess its contents. If you show signs of lying then we will torture you."

The captured man, carrying out such tactics, laughed at him and said:

"Oh, our enemy retainers know nothing about the way of the samurai! To me in a situation like this, nothing will be considered as pain no matter how much you torture me. If I was not determined to sacrifice my life, how could I have infiltrated an enemy castle? Also, even if I have mastered the skills of the *tengu*—goblin, how could I infiltrate* such a strictly guarded castle like this without aid in my tactics? I would never confess and you will find out the truth of this situation in four or five days anyway."†

This was said out loud, he then killed himself by biting off his own tongue. Listening to this the retainers and their men become worried. Doubts between each other arose until they fully feared one another. The castle fell soon after that.

---

* 窃盗得る.

† I.e., an internal conspiracy will become evident and the enemy will see his castle fall around him—of course the agent is lying, there is no such conspiracy.

内通を請たる行の事

Naitsu wo Uketaru Tedate no koto

The tactics to be taken when having received secret communication

A retainer of a castle received a secret communique from the besieging side. Being tactical in mind, he replied to the enemy thus:

"I agree to that matter to which you sent in secret, therefore prepare secret night attacks where my men are guarding, the night after tomorrow. At this point we shall kill the lord-commander in the confusion this creates. I will do this to prove loyalty to your general; therefore, please keep your word as was said in your letter."

While he sent this reply to an enemy retainer, he had actually shown this secret letter to his own lord-commander and said:

"There is no discussion about whether I would ever betray you, but you may get suspicious of this type of ruse. Therefore I will display how all of this has come about here."

He wrote an oath of loyalty to the lord and signed it in blood, saying:

"I have no intention to take up with the enemy but I have sent a reply that says I have accepted their wishes. This was done to plant a seed of a strategy. If you still doubt me in any way then please place those that you truly trust in my own people and prepare with tactics. Without fail the enemy will rely on me and approach in secret, coming close to the fences the night after tomorrow."

The lord listened to this and said:

"If you have an intention to take the side of the enemy then you would have not shown me this letter. If a generational retainer such as you should change their allegiance then it shows that a general's luck is at an end. If you were false-hearted, then I would fall no matter how much I try to defend myself against it. Also, secret communication from the enemy is not only to gain your allegiance but it is also sent to split a lord from his retainers, and to develop suspicion between them. You will not desert me, of this I have no doubts, therefore you must engage in such necessary measures to gain victory."

Saying this he showed no sign of coldness in his voice. At this, the retainer built a suspended false fence at the gate where his men were guarding. There he waited for the enemy to come on their night attack. At the arranged time, as expected, 100 men from the enemy approached in secret, relying on the secret communications that they had engaged in. When the suspended rope was cut, stones and wood were thrown at them, along with a volley of arrows and musket fire. As it was dark it made it hard for them to withdraw, so the enemy tried to move into the castle, but a double fence had been prepared. They were all shot through the gun ports with projectile weapons. None of the allied force had to move outside of the castle. All of the attackers were killed in the event. A later rumor said that the lord of the besieging side was not really of a tactical mind; he was easily deceived. Also the retainer was righteous, his family was in the third generation of service.

How did [the enemy general even] think that with such secret communications [a generational retainer] would take the side of an enemy? Kiichi's tradition* says:
"An ill thought-out stratagem will ruin your allies."

Tactics should be prepared [appropriately] dependent on the time and the enemy. In conducting this you should use [the enemy's] sense of justice, benefits, sex, money and countless other means; and should not believe that you have succeeded without evidence of such. Also do not assume that you have fully captured the enemy [in your tactics] if the enemy shows a sign of indecisiveness. Thus there is doubt about the saying that "a plan [carried out] without any regrets will win."

危働を凶むべき事
Ayauki Hataraki wo Imubeki Koto
Avoiding risky conflicts
Concerning those who serve as shinobi:
When events change to a time of turbulence there will be no time for those who are shinobi to rest. They are busy moving back and forth to the enemy province. This is especially so just before a lord leaves for war. They have to move around to know the geography of the enemy province and the boundaries of the area, to listen to the rumors taking place; to observe and listen, gathering the information on the enemy tactics. During battles they even infiltrate through arrow and gun ports in enemy castles and move around in all directions [on the battlefield]. Sometimes they remain within the enemy and at other times they go back to their allies. They go forth and return without being noticed, even by their own allies. They deceive the enemy in various ways, and when their own forces move on a night attack, they go ahead of the troops guiding them along the way. At times they will steal the enemy's weapons, deceive the enemy, pass through their checkpoints and do this without sparing their own lives. They will have no concern for any disgrace that they may receive. Even though a Bushi warrior should put the highest priority on loyalty over their disgrace, there are many tasks that carry humiliation in the job of shinobi. It is often the case that people who are not exclusively hired for this job, really do not like to accept such tasks. Sometimes miners, carpenters, blacksmiths and so on are attached to shinobi. The miners are used for digging holes. They make good judgements on where water is to be found. The blacksmiths and the carpenters are used for building watchtowers (or besieging constructions). They also enable the climbing of heights and the flattening of lower places.
Building watchtowers, constructing besieging engines, knowing where the enemy is not strictly defended (to facilitate an upcoming attack), are all measures

---

* In legend Kiichi Hogen was believed to have owned the Six Secret Teachings from China, and was transmitted to Minamoto no Yoshitsune—Kiichi's traditions are also mentioned in the Shoninki—*True Path of the Ninja*.

that should be conducted based on the judgments of the shinobi—remember to be resourceful. These points also apply when building a temporary fort that faces an enemy castle.

進退心得之事
Shindai Kokoroe no Koto
Things to keep in mind when advancing and retreating:

A person committing Seppuku is called a Seppukunin, while the Second (assistant), the person who cuts off his head is called a Kaishaku-nin, and the examining official is called a Kenshi.

- During a night attack shinobi infiltrate from steep areas.
- When defending a castle and the besieging enemy withdraw, you should not end your defense or let your guard down while the enemy are still within a distance of twenty ri. Send shinobi to follow them until there are no doubts left.

君臣たる人ハ侫者に近つくべからざる事
Kunshin Taru Hito wa Neisha ni Chikazuku Bekarazaru Koto
The lord and his retainers should not surround themselves with evil-minded people
In war, shinobi should be sent, and/or monomi are sent out to scout to discover the enemy's intention. They observe the topography of the land before any orders are given to a force. Likewise, in times of peace *yokome* ("investigators") should be used to investigate the talk and behavior of those of other provinces before any judgement in governing is decided.

Indeed, victory in war is secured by the ability of these shinobi and monomi. It rests on their ability to identify [the truth of a situation]. Also if they harbor no evil intentions then the lord's tactics will unfold positively and they will fulfil a complete victory. If they are lacking in the power of observation, and their minds are not righteous, then these tactics will fail. Ruin will immediately follow.

窃盗の者嗜みの事
Shinobi no mono Tashinami no Koto
Shinobi no mono should maintain discretion
As a Bushi warrior, you should harshly restrict yourself from falling into evil-mindedness. This applies especially to those who have mastered shinobi ways and conduct various tactics. All of which are justified no matter what tactics are deployed, as long as they are done for loyalty. If you achieve loyalty with such skills, luck will follow and you will gain honor. Alternatively, if you plot with evil intent and have a mind to your own desires, then you will ruin yourself and become a notorious enemy. Therefore, study the correct way of *bu*—"the path of the samurai."

Generally it is more than fair for a samurai to be prepared with any kind of art. If the art of the shinobi is mastered, it is no way a bad thing. Knowledge of shinobi ways can be used as a defense against shinobi or at times it has to be used in tactics to fulfil loyalty. Military skills should not be turned to *majutsu*—"skills of evil magic." Even those who are known to have mastered the shinobi arts, if they used these arts for their own desires, severe punishments will find them. If a common person uses *shinobi no jutsu*—"the skills of the shinobi"—for evil intent, then their sins will be tenfold over those who exclusively perform shinobi skills as a profession. Therefore, maintain your discretion.

修身を以て成忠孝事

Mi wo Osamuru wo Motte Chuko to Narubeki Koto

Truly honing yourself perfects loyalty and fidelity

… Therefore, in any art, even if it does not look so wondrous, it should have some virtue if it truly has value. For example, [*it is said*] those who do shinobi tasks can even transform themselves to mice or birds, which should be no way believable. However, in the saying "they do such wonders," there should be something beneficial to be found. Thus, birds can fly with excellence and mice can pass narrow paths with ease. Therefore, there should be excellent benefits found in human skills. Those who guard should keep their eyes wide open and their minds active; never let their guards down so that shinobi will not be able to do any harm, no matter what exquisite skills they use. Even if enemy shinobi come to see your camp or castle while scouting, and if they see or listen how well-prepared your allies are, it will turn out advantageous for you in the end. This is because if your allies band together as one, and if you are well disciplined, holding fast to the given role of lord and retainers, the enemy shinobi will find this outstanding. In turn, they will report it back to their own side. Doing this makes the enemy fear and become drawn to your side with respect, or even to communicate with you secretly, from such there will only be desirable effects. Nothing that would make them despise or hate you. Thus it seems that the enemy shinobi can bring you an advantage. Be fully aware of this and make sure to continue in the fulfilment of your own duties.

The above translation is a formidable window into early shinobi writings and leads us directly on to another, presumably early, writing.

The general samurai community were well aware of the name Fukushima Masa-nori, but few were aware of his connection to the shinobi.

Fukushima Masanori

The "Lost" Shinobi Scroll of Fukushima-Ryu

The next scroll to be translated has an elusive history. During my research I found myself in Tokyo at the Japanese National Diet Library (NDL) many times. Inside the NDL collection listings is the name of a Fukushima-Ryu shinobi scroll. After ordering a viewing of the manuscript, Yoshie Minami and myself sat in the wait-ing area with excitement. The clerk, a Japanese gentleman in standard shirt and tie, reported back to us. He informed us that the scroll has been missing for over fifty years and that there is no copy available. So, down but not out, I continued the search. A search that led me back to the same place it normally does, the Iga Ueno Museum (home to the largest collection of shinobi scrolls in the world). That line was a dead end. Then, time passed and a few years later, a gentleman by the name of Rein de Rooij contacted me. Rein told me that he had heard of my research and that he had been at the above museum in the early 1990s, visiting the late Mr. Okuse, the Mayor of Iga. He very kindly offered to allow me to see scrolls that he had copied during his visit, and as I looked through the list, a spark of excitement lit within me again. In the list was a copy of the missing Fukushima-Ryu shinobi scroll. Copied in classic 1990s photostat, I had the scroll re-transcribed by Mieko, my trusted helper and friend. Excitedly, translation was under way.

The scroll is broken into two sections. The first section is the original scroll and the second an annotated addendum, the latter being dated to 1797.

They are listed as:

Part One
福嶌流忍術之書
Fukushima-Ryu Shinobi-jutsu no Sho

Part One—the alternative title used in the text
福嶋流忍之巻
Fukuashima-Ryu Shinobi no Maki

Part Two—the annotated scroll
福島流忍之注書第一
Fukushima-Ryu Shinobi no Chusho Daiichi

The above sections have been amalgamated in this translation to make one solid and complete scroll. Originally the first scroll simply had a skill name and at points a very limited explanation—or memory hook. The second scroll with its annotations has been placed below each relevant section. These annotations are all below each title and can be identified by the repeat of the skill title. These have been placed in italics to show the start of the annotations.

The scroll claims to be the collected shinobi skills of a well-known Sengoku Period warlord called Fukushima Masanori, skills which were recorded by a samurai called Nojiri Narimasa. If Fukushima Masanori did indeed collect these shinobi skills—and there is little reason to think he did not—then it makes the skills old, indeed, when thinking in terms of shinobi records.

Fukushima Masanori (1560–1624) was born in the Owari province and was a renowned warrior of the Sengoku Period. He served under Lord Hideyoshi and then Lord Tokugawa Ieyasu. Fukushima Masanori rose to fame during the Battle of Shizugatake in 1583 as one of the *Seven Spears of Shizugatake*. It was this battle that earned him a celebrated status. After campaigning with Lord Hideyoshi he was granted Iyo province and took part in the invasion of Korea. He performed sieges on the holy mountain Koya-san and also later became the lord of Kiyosu region in Owari. During his career he gained the Nojiri family as retainers—of whom Nojiri

Narimasa was the author of the following shinobi manual. Fukushima Masanori then went on to serve Lord Tokugawa Ieyasu and was both at the legendary Battle of Sekigahara and the Siege of Osaka. He was a famed warlord and general, and for many years the name Fukushima has always been associated with these above deeds. However in "ninja circles," the name Fukushima, Nojiri, and the school Inko-Ryu all cry out the image "shinobi." Fukushima Masanori died in 1624.

The scroll itself should be seen like any other shinobi scroll, not as a full school but as a shinobi supplement to another school's art. The Fukushima and Nojiri samurai were just that—samurai trained in the arts of war. Their education also included the addition of deep, secretive shinobi no jutsu—"the skills of the shinobi." The scroll itself is one of the more difficult for a modern reader to "digest" as it is arranged in an apparently random format. It is quite an eclectic skill set. It can jump from skills for climbing over a fence to the mutilation of dogs (in performing spells of invisibility). It even includes substances that will make a shinobi believe he is a demon in the night—bloody terrifying stuff. As stated above, this scroll should be tempered by the knowledge that the skills were considered deep and ancient. These arts of infiltration were used by the very experienced samurai descendants of the Fukushima clan, and their retainers.

A note on the images:

The illustrations for this scroll are at times extremely ambiguous and difficult to decipher, while some are straightforward. The versions used here are copied from the manual in the Iga Ueno Museum and have been redrawn by Koizumi Meiko, and while difficult to interpret they have been left in their original form to preserve them.

福嶋流忍術之書
Fukushima-Ryu Shinobi-jutsu no Sho
A Record of Fukushima-Ryu Shinobi Skills

The annotations say:

This writing is based on a selection made by Lord Fukushima Saemon-dayu [Masanori].

Shinobi means *kanja* ("spy"), and the use of spies is performed in order to obtain information concerning the enemy, so that you can judge if or where an enemy is substantial or insubstantial—this allows you to gain victory in any battle that you fight. Therefore it is regarded as a task of importance. Sun Tzu wrote:

"Without subtle ingenuity of mind, one cannot make certain of the truth of [a spy's] reports. Be subtle! Be subtle! And use your spies for every kind of business."

福嶋流忍之巻第一
Fukuashima-Ryu Shinobi no Maki Dai Ichi
The Shinobi Scroll of Fukushima-Ryu: Part One

夢相通
Musotoshi
Transmitting dreams

- On the fourteenth or fifteenth day of the seventh month, collect pine wood charcoal which has been burnt [for illumination] around a grave – 2 momme
- Take moss from a grave – 5 bu
- Collect dewdrops that have formed on the leaves of the Taro plant which is growing to the east of your own house
- Charred meno – newt: there are oral traditions for if [the target] is male or female
- Your own earwax

Mix the above into black ink.

Musotoshi is a writing that makes a target dream as you wish them to dream. Use charcoal of pinewood that has been used to light a grave—any grave will do. The moss from the grave can also be from any grave. To take dewdrops from taro leaves, trace the ideogram 伊 before you take them. *Meno* means *imori*, which is a newt, and the oral tradition for this is as follows; depending on the gender of your target, switch the gender of the newt you use. For example, use a female newt for a male target. To know if a newt is male or female, know that male newts have a blue belly while a female newt has a red belly. Concerning the above tradition of the newt, you should capture male and female newts when they are mating and separate them, next put them in a bamboo tube but have them separated by an internal wall joint. Close the openings and leave them for three days; after these three days you will find that they have bitten through, making a hole [in the bamboo joint]. Take them out and you will notice that they will be together, joined as one [in copulation]. Divide them again and then char them separately. Whether the target is male or female will determine which one you need to use. To make the ink, powder the above four ingredients listed and then solidify them by mixing in the dewdrops from the Taro leaves. When you rub [the ink stone] to make ink, any pottery can be used, but you must use

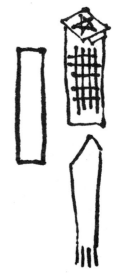

pure water. The brush should be made from the weeping willow tree [and with this brush] write down the details [of what you wish the target to dream about]. Write the ideogram 伊 on to the weeping willow tree brush before you use it. The way to make the document is the same as a *musubijo*—"tied letter." Draw the sign of Seimei pentagram* on the folded knot and then the Doman grid† on the rear.‡ Put the target's name on the top [of the folded paper] and then put your own name below it. If there is a sea or a river around the gate [of the target], write the ideogram for ship 舟 on the underside. This document should be placed in any graveyard.

下馬落
Gebaotoshi
Dismounting a man from a horse

[The spell]

逢坂ヤ八坂サカ中鯖一サシ行基ニクレテ駒ヤハラヤム

Osaka ya Yasaka Sakanaka Saba Hitosashi Gyoki§ *ni Kurete
Kuma Yawarayamu*

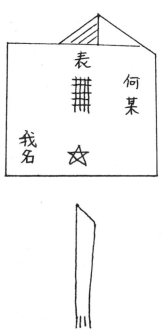

---

* A pentagram. Presumably, the name "Seimei" comes from a famous Japanese yin-yang diviner in the tenth century, Abe no Seimei. This sign is well known and also known as "Seman."
† A grid of five horizontal lines and four vertical lines. The name "doman" comes from a famous yin-yan diviner, Ashiya Doman, who lived in Heian Period.
‡ This could be taken as "bottom."
§ A famous monk (668-749) who aided the construction of the Great Buddha in Nara.

Gebaotoshi is to cause a horse that an enemy is riding to have trouble.

Form a toothpick out of the lintel of a Torii gate [from a Shinto shrine], then write the ideogram 伊 for Ise 伊勢 three times. Before writing the poem from the above text, form a paper package as you would form a medicine package. Write the target's name on the front with the kuji grid, then on the rear draw a pentacle and write your own name. Dig a hole in the hoof prints of the [target enemy] horse and bury the above [talisman] and the toothpick within it. When this is done the horse will keel over and will find itself in trouble.

To remedy this trouble, chant the following poem and then dig up and recover the buried items:

逢坂ヤ八坂坂中鯖一差行基ニクレテ駒ハイサナン
*Osaka ya Yasaka Sakanaka Saba Hitosashi Gyoki ni
kurete Koma wa Isanan*
In the middle of Osaka or Yasaka hill, give Gyoki a bundle
of mackerel and the horse will become spirited

At this the horse will immediately recover.

村雨明松
Murasame Taimatsu
The rain shower torch

- ♦ "Flower" 花 – 10 momme
- ♦ Sho (camphor) – 7 momme
- ♦ Pine [resin] – 10 momme 5 bu

Murasame Taimatsu—this is a rainproof torch. "Flower" here means the Japanese anise tree. Soak this wood in water for one hundred days before you powder it. "Pine" means pine saturated in resin, but I would say that this is simply resin?* "Sho" is camphor. Finely powder the above three and put the mixture into a paper bag and then wrap it in six or seven layers of paper—this is done so that the fire will not be extinguished.

---

* The author of the annotated script is questioning the recipe.

打明松
Uchitaimatsu
The attack torch

- ◆ Camphor – 10 momme
- ◆ Saltpeter – 9 momme
- ◆ Sulphur – 3 momme
- ◆ "Flower" 花– 10 Momme

Uchi Taimatsu – Camphor 10 momme, saltpeter 9 momme, sulphur 3 momme, "flower" [as described in the previous tool] 10 momme soaked in water for 100 days; also, include pine, resin 9 momme 1 bu. Prepare this in the same manner as the above Murasame taimatsu torch. If you insert [horseshoe shaped] needles in a cross form and throw it, it will come to land correctly and burn well.

タ〃三橋
Tatamibashi
Folding ladder*

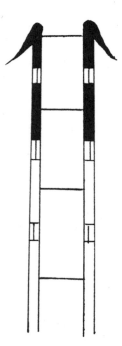

The *Tatamibashi* is used when crossing over a moat and the like. It should be construed so that it can be folded, making it less cumbersome. Place hinges so that it can be extended and have metal latches with *tsuku* [forked shaped fasteners in place]. Attach a thin rope to the end which has a three pronged grapple tied to it and use it to ascend.

---

* The ideogram for bridge is used here but often "bridge" and "ladder" are interchangeable.

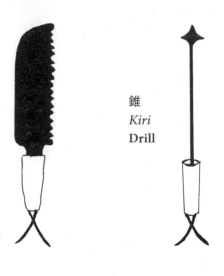

鋸
Nokogiri
Saw

錐
Kiri
Drill

Nokogiri are multi-purpose and there are many points within oral tradition.

第二之巻
Dai ni no maki
Part Two

露之印
Tsuyu no In
Mudra of Dewdrops*
This is used with muskets.

Tsuyu no in is a musket without a bullet and has the purpose of catching an enemy alive. First insert gunpowder and then add a good amount of ash on top of that. Shoot with careful timing so that the enemy will be blinded and disoriented.[†]

明破[‡]
Meiha
Gate breaking
This has three bullets.

Monyaburi—[this works] the same as a fuse burns with saltpeter. Make the bullets and insert the fuse through these three bullets while positioning gunpowder between the balls. Firmly wrap the bamboo cylinder and secure the outside with bamboo rings, like in the construction of a bucket. Place the above balls inside. When in a position close to the enemy, ignite the fuse from behind the cylinder so that they are expelled with a blast, one by one. This is also called *rendama deppo*— "successive musket bullets."

---

* It is possible that this is a transcription error and should be "Mudra of Mist" 霧之印.
† Literally, "a loss of the ten directions," i.e., without awareness of all that is around.
‡ Meiha literally means "bright breaking." In the annotations below, it is called Monyaburi 門破 "gate breaking".

城工入事
Shiroe Iru Koto
Infiltrating castles

- ◆ Crossing steep areas
- ◆ Concerning shinobi-gaeshi—"spiked defenses"
- ◆ Moving into the horse stables

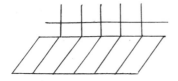

These images were placed in the original scroll as memory hooks; one image is of a sword and the other is a basic image of *shinobi-gaeshi* ("defensive spikes").

Shiroe iru koto means to infiltrate an enemy castle. Enter through the rubbish shute, or, alternatively, cross over the *shinobi-gaeshi* ("defensive spikes"). If you are going to cross over a wall, take advantage of these places. When inside the castle move into the stable—in this way you can know if the horses have been prepared, which will allow you to immediately confirm if a night raid is about to commence. When in the stable stay behind mounds of grass or straw—it is a transmitted teaching to stay in those places mentioned above.

Shinobi-gaeshi wo koshiyo is about shinobi-gaeshi that are on the top of an outer wall. Throw the sageo cord of your sword over the shinobi-gaeshi spikes, then hold on to the cord and cross over. Make sure to use the hilt of your sword as a foothold.

源氏入黒*

Genji no Irezumi

The tattoo of the Genji Clan

Use the oil of Namomi—cocklebur

Genji no Irezumi is to take "oil of cocklebur" and apply it on to a cane or other such things so that when you strike with it, it will break through anything.[†]

矢打留様

Yauchi Tomeyo

To stop arrows striking

This is made of bamboo.

Using a large wheel made of bamboo is *Yauchi tomeyo*, this is like the wheel of a *kinawa no hikiguruma*—pulling cart. Put a hole at the hub of the "wheel" and insert a cane, then rotate the wheel so that using it will stop arrows.

咽乾ヌ薬

Nodo Kawakanu Kusuri

Thirst pills

- ◆ Unripe green plum which has been processed to become "frost plum"[‡] – 1 [measurement]
- ◆ Toboshi—Unhulled mocha rice – 12 [measurements]

Powder equal amounts of the above and make pellets the size of soya beans [to keep thirst at bay]; take one pellet with some water.

Nodo no Kawakanu Kusuri—the ingredient "Toboshi" is *taito mochi*[§] rice in its husk and you should take this every morning. It is advisable to take this before you go into combat.

中ノ大ヲ迯術

Naka no dai wo Nogaruru Jutsu

A skill to escape a crisis on your journey

Bow three times in the direction you intend to travel. It is written [that you should use the following spell]:

---

* In the annotations, it says 入墨, which means tattoo.

† Possibly for digging out clay walls or as a battering ram.

‡ "Frost plum" is a direct translation of the Chinese. This is a traditional medicine for sore throats, which is made of unripe plum, salt, Gleditsia sinensis, dried Chinese bellflower, Arisaema, pinellia (tuber) and liquorice.

§ Unknown, possibly a kind of mochi rice.

武士ノ腰ニ差タル鍔刀事ノツマツキアラセ給ナ

*Bushi no Koshi ni Sashitaru Tsuba Katana Koto no
Tsumazuki Arase Tamona*

May there be no failure or disaster [through or with
my] hilt [and] katana that I wear as a bushi warrior

Naka no dai wo nogaruru koto—cut the kuji grid, cut to the left and the right.

人ノ宅エ入事

Hito no Yaka e Iru Koto

Infiltrating a person's house

Remove both the eyes of a dog, be it still alive or dead. Then string them on the hair from a horse's tail and apply a layer of mercury.* Next soak it in lacquer and dry in the shade for 100 days. Carry this in a crimson bag [when you infiltrate]. There are oral traditions to follow.

Hito no yaka e iru koto—This is the way in which a shinobi† protects himself from being detected by people. Move in with the crimson bag attached to your forehead. This will allow you to see an enemy clearly while the enemy cannot see you.

綱朽之事

Tsuna Kuchiru no Koto

Ruining rope

- ◆ Mica (Unmo)
- ◆ Mercury
- ◆ Oil of hanzaki—ray fish

During ritual suicide many things are reversed in order. The pouring of the sake, the way knots are tied, etc., are all things that are done in reverse to the way they are normally done.

Apply this mixture to rope and the rope will immediately decay.

Tsunakuchi no koto—This is a substance that rots through rope and rope-like things. The ingredient "unmo" is kirara-mica. Also the ingredient "oil of hasaka/hansaki" means "oil of the ray fish."

夜物ノ躰ヲ知事

Yoru Mono no Tei wo Shiru Koto

Observing what something truly is during the night

---

* Literally, "liquid silver."
† 忍人 Shinobi hito.

The following has been recorded:

ヒトフタミヨイツムユナヽヤコヽノタリモヽチヨロツ*
Hito futa mi mi yo itsu muyu nana ya kokono tari momo chi yorozu
1, 2, 3, 4, 5, 6, 7, 8, 9, 10, 1000, 10000

Chant the above three times and then put both hands together in prayer—there is something that needs to be done at this point [which is explained below]. Next, move your hands into "diamond"† position and observe what is there by looking [through your hands].

Yoru mono no tei wo shiru koto is to know what something truly is at night. To put your hands together means *gassho* ("putting your hands together in prayer"). Then open out your palms to make a diamond shape—if you look through this gap then any excitement you have will calm down, allowing you to become more settled. When a person is settled then a proper understanding will follow, leading to a deeper judgment. Chant the poem in the text three times.

太刀落ス之事
Tachi Otosu no koto
Disempowering a tachi sword

The most important factor to remember when dealing with history is that history books concentrate on the terrible and the glorious, which leads to extreme and unbalanced views of history.

- ◆ Collect 33 "Dairyo" spiders, put them in a cylinder, starve them until they die.‡
- ◆ The blood of a newt
- ◆ Fruit of the Shikunshi—Chinese honeysuckle

Mix the above together [and apply it to your hands]—in this way your hands will not be cut. This is also called *Shiraha Dori*—"to receive a blade with the hands."

Tachi otoshi no koto—"shikunshi" is an ingredient used in medicine and can also be called *toronashi*.

鬼ト見スル術
Oni to Misuru Jutsu
The art of becoming the demon

---

* Most likely an ancient Shinto prayer representing the process of the creation of the Universe. Literally meaning 1, 2, ... 10,000.

† To make a "diamond" shape with your hands together and held out to the front.

‡ "Dairyo-gumo" is an alternative name of the *Kogane-gumo* spider (*gumo* meaning "spider"), Argiope amoena.

- ◆ Capture fireflies and toads on the seventh day of the seventh month.
- ◆ On the fifth day of the fifth month, extract "oil of the rat"* and harvest the liver of bats.

Make pills with this mixture and consume them, in this way you will make yourself look like a demon for the period of a night.

Oni to misuru jutsu is a way to help you and your mind avoid cowardice.

Samurai armies include "peasant" soldiers, the ashigaru. Some samurai lead them into battle.

太刀燃ル術
Tachi Moyuru Jutsu
The skill of the "glowing" longsword†
Mix oil of cocklebur with water and apply it to [the sword].

Tachi moyuru jutsu is about applying a substance to your tachi sword. This makes the facing enemy *think* that your sword is "glowing"—the purpose of this is to take away their spirit. This is made from cocklebur.

門出之大事
Kadode no Daiji
The principle of departing through a gate

丑未戌辰分テ行ク何カシ神ノ子ナレハ方ハ嫌ハシ
Ushi hitsuji inu tatsu wakete iku nanigashi kami no ko
nareba hou ha kirawaji
Choosing the direction of Ox, Ram, Dog, or Dragon, whichever god
protects whichever direction—no direction should be shunned

Chant the above three times.

Next, draw the ideogram for "victory" 勝 in your left palm three times with your [right] finger and then close it into a fist. When you have journeyed two or three ken from the gate then open your palm again, saying:

---

* Throughout this manual it refers to "oil of *x*" such as "oil of toad" which is a common item; however, "oil of rat" and "oil of human" are used in this writing. These are considered to be extracts from the creature mixed with oils or fats or the oil and fat of the specific animal listed, or are the names for remedies from Chinese medicine that may not be connected to the animal in question. Therefore they have simply been translated here as they appear in the original scroll.

† Literally, "burning"; however the ideogram was also historically used to mean "glowing" and with the addition of water this is most likely a way to have the sword appear "ghostly" in reflected light.

サカキバニヱウトリシデヽ打佛ヒ道ニケカレヤ雲キリモナシ*

Sakakiba ni Yutori shide de uchiharai michini kegareya kumo kiri mo nashi

If you attach cotton shide† onto the branch of *Cleyara japonica* and use it for purification, there will be no impurity, no clouds and no mist in your way

Chant the above three times.

Kadode no daiji is to not look back behind you until you have ventured two or three ken, at which point open your clenched fist and lick your palm.

秘極之薬之事
Higoku no Kusuri no Koto
The deepest and most secret medicine

- ◆ Soak a large amount of the root of the Japanese rush (*Acorus gramineus*) in sake
- ◆ Gather a medium amount of the peel of a Satsuma (*Citrus unshiu*)
- ◆ Soak a medium amount of *Sapium japonicum* in water
- ◆ A medium amount of fire-roasted Asiatic ginseng

To put samurai society into perspective for today, most readers of this book would be peasants or merchants and not in the samurai class.

Powder the above and make pills.

If you drink alcohol then make pills by using sake; if you are a non-drinker then use tea or water; and in war [make pills] by using the stickiness of rice broth.

The above medicine should be used in battle or any other important situation. In addition to this it works for all diseases, especially as a restorative or as a stimulant.

Higoku no kusuri—sekishobu from the text means *daisegishobu—*greater *sekishobu*.

---

* There is an old poem on which this version is based. To complete this English translation, the alternative version has been used.

† A chain of cut white cotton or paper suspended from the straw rope marking off a sacred area of a Shinto shrine.

第三之巻
Dai san no maki
Part Three

息ノキレヌ薬—人 *
Iki no Kirenu Kusuri—Hito
Medicine for shortness of breath—person
Iki no kirenu kusuri is to apply "oil of human" or "oil of toad" to your lips; alternatively you can hold toad skin in your mouth.

夜物音ヲ聞事—風
Yoru Monooto wo Kiku Koto—Kaze
Listening to sounds at night—wind
Yoru monooto wo kiku koto is to listen by crouching downwind. It is difficult to hear from a windward position.

忍入時之事—八
Shinobi Iru Toki no Koto—Yatsu
Times to infiltrate—eight
Shinobi iru toki no koto is done in the eighth hour of the night[†] as people will sleep deeply at this time. During the day the eighth hour[‡] is when meals are served and is a period of quiet—therefore infiltrate at the eighth hour.

Also for the above—infiltration can be done during the hour of the animal sign of the year that the [enemy] lord-commander was born. The hour of the sign of the year that the lord-commander was born has an element of the insubstantial and therefore, if the enemy lord-commander was born in the *year* of the Rat then infiltrate at the *hour* of the Rat.

敵之心騒セ申事—夢
Teki no Koto no Sawagase Mosu Koto—Yume
Disturbing the mind of the enemy—dreams
Teki no koto no sawagase mosu koto is to use the skill of musotoshi ("transmitting dreams") and to have the enemy lord-commander dream of difficulty. Alternatively this can be to write [on the spell-paper] that a certain retainer of the enemy is in secret communication with the allied side; this will appear to the enemy lord-commander in a dream.

---

[*] This section contains words that act as memory hooks at the end of each title; in this translation the Kuden (oral tradition) has been recorded and the reason for the use of these memory hooks can be seen in each of the annotations.

[†] 2 am

[‡] 2 pm

忍ニアハヌ薬―生 [姜]

Shinobi ni Awanu Kusuri—Shoga

Medicine to protect yourself from other shinobi—Ginger

This can be used for all things.

Shinobi ni awanu kusuri—grate ginger, spread it thinly into a one sun square on paper and put it with thin glue tightly onto your *hori*—belly button.* This is a medicine to prevent sleep and it can be used to work against coldness and heat— have no doubts about this, for it is a great and wondrous medicine.

行燈ノ火カクス事

Andon no Hi wo Kakusu Koto

Hiding the light of a lantern

Andon no hi kakusu koto—use tweezers or other such things and grip it so that the light does not show.

城内又ハ人ニ知ラレヌ書状書様　付タリ見様ノ事

Jonai Matawa Hito ni Shirarenu Shojo Kaki Yo

Details on how to write secret letters that are to be sent into an enemy castle and cannot be read by others

Supplementary to this: how to read them.

Jonai e okuru matawa hito ni shirarenu shojo kakiyo no koto—this skill is used when someone is detached from their allies [and correspondence with them is needed]. This [letter] should be written with ground soybeans or with the liquid used to strain teeth, or even with the juice of the Yuzu fruit. To read [such a letter] hold it over a fire or soak it in water. The liquid used to stain teeth cannot be seen unless it is soaked in water. I must state that to read the letters written with this tooth staining liquid you should coat the underside of the paper in ink; this is because the characters will not absorb the ink, making them clear to see.

[Untitled]

Use the ideogram for Cockerel 酉 seven times

The ideogram 酉 should be written on the left and right of your pillow at night.

The annotations state the point of using "cockerel seven times." No matter what time [you wish to awaken] trace the ideogram 酉 seven times on each side of your pillow while praying and asking to be "startled" at the exact time you wish—then you may sleep. The ideogram *hiyomi no tori* 酉 means cockerel, this is because the cockerel will inform you of the time. This is a magical ritual.

---

* Presumably *hozo*, the belly button, a recurring practice in shinobi literature.

Use a toothpick made from the *Sakaki cleyera japonica* plant and use *torimichi ni kaku* to write on the road [where people] walk.

The annotations state: 通道二書* *torimichi ni kaku* means "to write on the passing road." To do this, have a manushi snake "bite a new ink stone" and write with that ink, by doing this anything that you write will come to pass. Do this by capturing a live manushi and securing it, open the mouth and have it "bite" a new ink stone. Then put [the ink stone] into a pot jar and close it with a lid and bury it under a road where people walk for seven days. Finally take it out and write anything you wish with this ink—your wish will come true.†

水練之事

Suiren no Koto

Aquatic training‡

The measurement is 1 shaku 4 sun

Suiren no koto is a way to stay underwater as long as you like without taking a breath. Make [a device] that is 1 shaku [4 sun] that is made of leather coated with tung oil. Make a mouthpiece of deer horn like a gunpowder flask used for muskets, so that you can hold it in your mouth. The tip of the mouthpiece should be made of copper. Make [a mouth seal] of toad skin to protect against water on the both sides and put a ball of lead in the bag.

Labels from left to right:
1. Toad skin
2. The ball inside
3. Deer horn here

---

* This one is written as 通達 meaning "notification." However, every other equivalent one is 通道, so it is presumed as a transcription error of 通道 torimichi.

† This can be seen as either milking snake venom onto a stone, or opening the snake's mouth around an inkstone and having it bite down upon the stone.

‡ The manual has no instruction on training and only discusses tools. The tool probably allows for a very limited number of extra breaths, which will allow a skilled diver to stay underwater longer.

鹿ノ一足
Shika no Hitoashi
The leg of the deer

- Arsenic – 10 momme—collect this from a silver mine
- Young Japanese five-lined skink (*Eumeces latiscutatus*) – 2 momme dried in the shade
- Sheep Bot flies* – 2 momme charred
- Root of the Japanese butterbur – 3 momme powdered and raw
- Komyoshu cinnabar[†] – five momme

The above should be kept in thin paper.

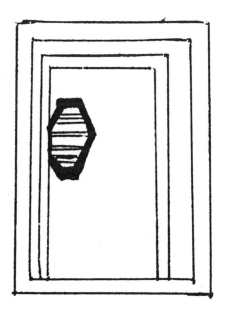

Shika no hitoashi—powder the five ingredients above. Make a paper bag like a tea bag and put the mixture in it. Carry the bag holding it in a folded tissue paper. If you sprinkle it onto the enemy, the enemy will suffer hardship, becoming disoriented, or they may even die. Take precaution not to get it on yourself. The drawing above shows what the tissue paper should be like.

---

* Oestrus ovis.
† Imported cinnabar from China.

堀渡舟之事

Hori Watashi Bune no Koto

Moat crossing boat

Hori watashi bune no koto—make four boxes that slot into one another and cover them with a thin wooden plate like that of the *hasamibako*—clothes carrying box. These can be [connected together] to make the shape of a boat.

Latches and plates should connect them with each other. The oar should be jointed like a fishing rod.

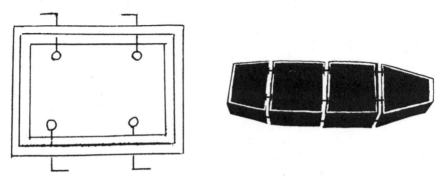

A basic mock-up of the boat latched together

浮沓之事

Ukigutsu no Koto

Floating aids

This should be made in the same manner in which a lantern is made with rings and should be made of whale fin*—there are oral traditions.

Ukigutsu—this should be made of leather and coated with tung oil. It should be attached onto the waist and to the wakizashi.

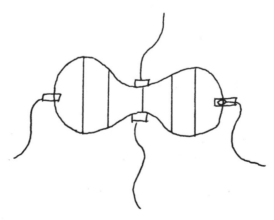

---

* Presumably baleen or other whale products.

第四之巻
Dai yon no maki
Part Four

忍之火持之事
Shinobi no Himochi no Koto
The shinobi method of carrying embers

- ◆ Charred sheaves of young bamboo shoots – 1 momme 5 bu
- ◆ Camphor – 4 bu

Mix the above and solidify it with thin glue. Next, cut bamboo into a five sun section and make a hole in the end. When the mixture is truly dry, push it into the cylinder and ignite it at the open end—if you carry it in this fashion then it will last three days and three nights.*

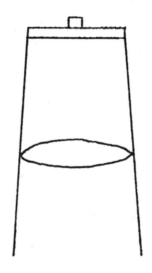

Shinobi no himochi no daiji—Scrape the surface of the bamboo and apply [paper] with glue, with persimmon tannin mixed in.† The bamboo cylinder should have joints both on the top and the bottom. Pierce a hole in the joint on the bottom and ram a mixture of the two ingredients in tightly. Put a small hole on the top joint as an air vent. This is also called *Kaichu no hi*—"fire within the kimono."

---

* The wrong ideogram is used but is presumably a transcription error and means "night."
† For waterproofing.

忍之薬

Shinobi no Kusuri

The Shinobi substance*

- ♦ "Crow snake"
- ♦ Hoya—[to be found on the roots of *Artemisia capillaris*].
- ♦ "White snake"

Mix equal amounts of the above and soak in "oil of [unidentifiable ideogram]"[†] for seven days and dry it in the open air. Powder the mixture and place it into a bag made of paper; light it to a windward direction.

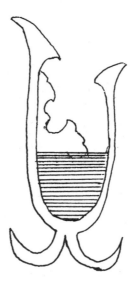

Shinobi no kusuri is sleeping powder. "Hoya"[‡] can be found on the roots of the *Artemisia capillaris*. Put [the mixture] in a paper bag and have a woven bamboo [cover] for it, then wind it with thread and cover it with paper.

- ♦ *Karasu hebi*—"crow snake" means black snake.
- ♦ *Hakuja*—"white snake" means a snake that is white.[§]

---

* A form of sleeping gas.

† Non-existent ideogram, possibly whale or shark.

‡ Presumably *Orobanche coerulescens Steph*. This plant grows on the roots of *Artemisia capillaris* as a parasite.

§ Albino snake; there is also a form of Chinese medicine called "white snake" but the grammar here makes it a "snake that is white in color."

If you burn this substance from the windward side, everyone will fall asleep and their defense will be insubstantial; in this way it is easier to steal in. There is a way to keep you from going to sleep while doing this—put the ginger mentioned in part three onto your belly button so you will not sleep, as is shown in the drawing.

手負ノ血留
Teoi no Chidome
Stopping a wound from bleeding
Fold paper so that it has eight layers* in total and apply it with pressure to the injury. There are oral traditions for the holding of breath while doing this.

[The oral traditions are:]

To stop the bleeding of the injured, trace the ideograms [unknown ideogram] and 冬 for Yamabuki on the forehead of the injured person while holding your own breath. Then hold the bleeding part with the above-mentioned paper and add pressure.

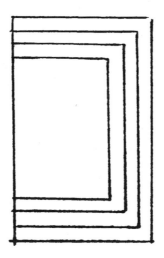

忍火手内ニ持事
Shinobi Hi Te no Uchi ni Motsu Koto
Holding shinobi fire in the palm†
Take eight or nine spines of the feathers from a Japanese crested ibis bird and cut them to the length of the width of your fist and tie them together with string in a bundle. Pour mercury to the amount of eight tenths in each of the [stripped feather] cylinders.

---

* That is, fold it three times.

† This is also known as "Yoshitune's Everlasting Torch," sometimes translated as "Yoshitune's Immortal Torch."

Shinobi hi te no uchi ni motsu koto is also called *Enmyoko* ("round bright light"), or *Shinobi no tebako* ("the shinobi's portable box").

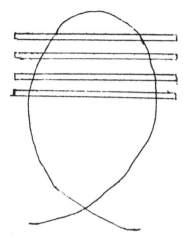

Imagine this as a collection of feather spines, filled with mercury that have been tied together in a buddle with the string in this image.

The box should be 2 sun 9 bu square in size and 2 sun 5 bu in height. Spread mercury* in a thin layer on the inside of the box. Then paste five layers of good quality gold leaf over it. Cut the spines of the feathers of a Japanese crested ibis (*Nipponia nippon*) to the length of the box and in such a number as can be laid within. Next, add mercury into the spines to a measurement of eight parts in ten. Put them together by entwining them with thread and place the bundle in the box. This gives off light when you wish to observe something.

壁外之火取事
Kabesoto no Hi Toru Koto
To take fire beyond the wall

Connect twelve pieces of Yoshino paper together and apply oil from the castor-oil plant. Let it dry in the shade for about thirty days. When you see a small light coming through a gap, paste this paper over the hole.

 Kabe no Soto no Hi no Torukoto—the drawing shows how the paper should be put together.†

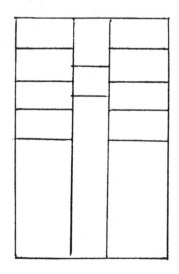

---

* The ideogram used in the text is not extant. Presumably a transcription error of 汞, meaning mercury.
† This tool is ambiguous and is lacking further explanation.

福嶋流心意工夫之巻
Fukushima-Ryu Shin'i Kufu no Maki
Fukushima-Ryu—A scroll for the improvement of your mind and will

Shinobi-mono do not [only use] *myo* ("wondrous magic"), however; before they use [myo] they should first utilize *the five constant factors** alongside wisdom, benevolence, and then bravery to execute their tactics. If they try to obtain results with [only] wondrous skills, then they will be trapped in their own fabrication, losing *honshin*—"original mind." Thus in shinobi no jutsu [it is correct] to obtain results with righteousness.

Shinobi-mono observe the enemy. Then with the element of surprise—and by working independently—they strike at that which is insubstantial in the dark of night. They contemplate with fidelity and reach the truth. "Correct bravery"[†] should not be restrained while "brute courage"[‡] should be admonished. [This means that] a little cowardice [and caution] should be applied and used as a "medicine for ease."

When the skills [recorded here] have been mastered, in addition with the [the above] short set of principles, your *ki* will be enhanced. Benefits will be acquired. To defeat an army, contemplate and use the "established path,"[§] and know that to obstruct the enemy's plans is an excellent military skill—there are countless cases of this.

Obtaining victory through attacking is not a way of excellence. However, if it is not possible [to obstruct the enemy's plan], you need to attack. [Even with] "brute courage" you can win a hundred out of a hundred battles if you perform using the "principle of emptiness"[¶]—in this way the original mind will not be lost and benefits will still be obtained.

The above scroll is the foundation of the shinobi and contains the essential elements needed in disciplining your mind. The previous four scrolls contain those elements that are *myo*, and also include reasonable skills.

Nojiri Jiroemon Narimasa
Okita Sukeshiro Naomichi
Nojiri Saburoemon Masatsugu
Okimi Jirobei
Miyake Juzo

———————————

* The five constant factors are the concepts from the *Art of War*: (1) Moral Law; (2) Heaven; (3) Earth; (4) The Commander; (5) Method and Discipline.
† 上勇.
‡ 血気之勇.
§ The Japanese word in the text for this is *Kayoimichi*, which literally means "the road that people walk."
¶ 空之理.

The annotations state:

1. Benevolence 仁
2. Righteousness 義
3. Courtesy 礼
4. Wisdom 智
5. Fidelity 信

Govern with these virtues.

[All the annotations within this scroll were written] on an auspicious day of the fourth month in the summer of 1797—the year of the Snake.

By Terasawa Naosaku Yukihiro—the ninth descendant of Hyogo no Kami and transmitted to Ishikawa Yamato Minamoto no Ason Kotoku and kept in secret.

Further transcribed on an auspicious morning of the tenth month in the winter of 1824—the year of the Monkey.

Kept in the collection of Fujita Seiko—the fourteenth generation of Koka-Ryu.*

The deep secrets of Sekiguchi-Ryu

Sekiguchi-Ryu was discussed on page 65 along with its headmaster, Yamada Toshi-yasu. Mr. Yamada is the inheritor of Sekiguchi-Ryu Battojutsu—the sword-drawing branch of the school. Sekiguchi-Ryu was founded by the Sekiguchi family and was a comprehensive martial school. However, it was later divided into separate sections, some taking over the grappling skills, while others took over the swordsmanship, etc., allowing for multiple branches to form. Mr. Yamada—and one of his predeces-sors—have endeavored to rediscover the "lost" parts of their school and in doing so the have had the opportunity to transcribe different Sekiguchi-Ryu manuals. One of Mr. Yamada's predecessors, Mr. Aoki Norio, transcribed some manuals from a branch school transmitted in Awa province (present-day Tokushima prefecture). Those manuals include *gokui* ("deep secrets"), which were transmitted directly from Wakayama Katsumasa—who was a direct inheritor from Sekiguchi Ujimune, the founder of the school. These manuals have some very shinobi-like skills yet the word shinobi is not used in the manuals (apart from the shinobi torch). Skills such as walking at night, sleeping powders, poisons and blinding powders are all extremely shinobi-orientated. Therefore, some of the following selections of skills are the most shinobi-related, while others are on the boundry of the shinobi arts (and have been translated here for the first time). Luckily Mr. Yamada—with his assistant Takara Takanashi—still teach and welcome students from all over the

---

* This was added by Fujita Seiko—his claims to a ninjutsu lineage have, to date, not been substantiated.

world. For more information search social media sites for Sekiguchi-Ryu Battojutsu or see their website www.sekiguchiryu.com

Mr. Yamada of Sekiguchi-Ryu Battojutsu and their scrolls.

The deepest secrets of Sekiguchi-Ryu presented by Yamada Toshiyasu:

軍中忍松明之伝
Gunchu Shinobi Taimatsu no Tsutae
The tradition of the military shinobi torch

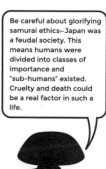

Be careful about glorifying samurai ethics–Japan was a feudal society. This means humans were divided into classes of importance and "sub-humans" existed. Cruelty and death could be a real factor in such a life.

Part 1:
Saltpeter – 20 momme
Sulfur – 14 momme
Ash – 10 momme

Part 2:
Camphor – 12 momme

Part 3:
Pine resin – 1 momme 8 bu
Ground tea – 5 bu
Mouse droppings – 1 momme 7 bu

Part 4:
Cattle dung – 2 momme
Mix each of the above recipes and then mix together; now firmly ram it into a bamboo cylinder. Scrape the surface [of the bamboo thinly] with a knife. If it is extinguished, it will flare up again if it is swung. If you want to put it out, stub it against

a wall or the ground and the fire will immediately go out. This torch is a tradition used by Soga brothers* from ages past.

鶏卵ニテ敵一時殺之法
Keiran nite Teki Ichiji Korosu no Ho
The art of temporarily killing an enemy with an "egg"

Remove the contents of an egg, clean [the inside] with shochu liquor and fill with the poison [below]. Twist paper [into a string] with gunpowder wrapped within it [and put it into the hole of the egg] then ignite around the hole.

The recipe of the powder is as below:

Mix equal amounts of:

- Saltpeter
- Lime
- Pine resin
- Sulfur

Mix the above and powder it finely. Put it into the said egg and throw it at the enemy after igniting the fuse; this will shoot out poison and all your enemies will be "killed" [fall unconscious] for a while. To protect yourself from this, keep 3 bu of crystal sugar in your mouth, applying the oil of the Japanese anise tree onto the nine openings of the body.

眼昧之法
Ganmai no Ho
The art of blinding the eyes

Char the livers of boars and moles and powder it down.† Mix these two ingredients and powder them finely. Wrap with silk cloth or paper and carry it in your kimono at all the times. [When needs arise] blow it over the enemy or throw it. Make sure to do it very quickly.

毒酒茶水知法
Doku Sake Cha Mizu Siru Ho
The art of detecting poison in your sake, tea or water

Look at the reflection of yourself in the sake, tea or water. If it has poison in it, you cannot see your reflection. Know [if it is poisonous] with this method.

---

* The same brothers and torch are mentioned in the *Giyoshu* manual presented earlier.

† Charred and powdered mole is called *Doryuso*, was well-known and was used for multiple reasons.

修利法之口伝
Shuri Ho no Kuden
The oral tradition of on the way Shuri
This is about a paper cylinder.

- ◆ Alum – 2 momme 5 bu
- ◆ White lead – 1 momme 3 bu
- ◆ Marble ["smooth stone"] – 2 momme 1 bu

Powder the above finely and mix it with starch of the "devil's tongue" plant. [Apply this and] wrap the paper [into a cylinder] so that there is a hole in the center. This is also called *harideppo*—the paper musket.

The bullet should be made of rice bran. Shoot it at the face of the enemy [to render them helpless].

聴中三日火縄之事
Chochu Mikka Hinawa
The chochu three day fuse

- ◆ Sweet hydrangea (Amacha) – 20 momme
- ◆ Camphor – 8 momme
- ◆ Moxa 120 momme
- ◆ Alum 10 momme

Powder the above and add it to a roll of sugihara paper, then glue it to secure it. Use rice glue with alum mixed in to make this fuse.

水鉄砲ヲ以テ敵ヲ生捕事
Mizudeppo wo Motte Teki wo Ikedoru Koto
The art of capturing the enemy with the water musket

- ◆ Saltpeter
- ◆ Ground tea

Use an appropriate amount of each.

Put an appropriate amount of water in a cylinder and shoot at the enemy.

If the caliber of a musket is a 3-momme bullet, use 3 momme of the two ingredients. For all amounts, apply this ratio. Shoot it at the enemy's eyes and while the enemy is unconscious, capture them alive.

走時息之切ヌ法

Hashiru Toki Iki no Kirenu Ho

The way of not losing your breath when running

There is a secret skill orally transmitted.

Say the word "kuma" (bear) three times when running. Keeping ginseng in your mouth should also work.

竹松明之事

Taketaimatsu no Koto

Bamboo torch

There is an oral tradition for this.

Scrape the surface skin of bamboo that is 6 or 7 sun in diameter.

Mix camphor with oil and apply it onto the surface of the bamboo. Next put paper around it and use it as a torch. If it is lit, it will not go out, no matter how windy it is.

夜歩行之法

Yoru Hoko no Ho

The method of walking at night

This is an oral tradition.

[Untitled skill]

我是鬼

Trace the above three ideograms on your gate. Then write them again with your right little finger onto your left palm and pray with your hands above your head and then sleep. This works wondrously well, you will not be bewitched by transformed raccoon dogs.

水松明之法

Mizutaimatsu no Ho

The way of the waterproof torch

There is an oral tradition for this.

Skin an eel and put camphor into the [tube of the] skin and secure it with strings. Place sulfur at the ignition end—it will not go out when wet.

人ヲ眠ラス法

Hito wo Nemurasu Ho

The art of making people sleep

There is an oral tradition for this.

Sprinkle whale baleen by crumpling it onto the person's breast—that person will fall into a deeper sleep. This works divinely.

雨中火縄之事

Uchu Hinawa no Koto

Rainproof fuse

Apply lime onto a bamboo fuse with persimmon tannin. Cut paper to an appropriate length and roll it with two or three layers. Use this fuse for the above "old" water musket.

雨中松明の事法

Uchu Taimatsu no Koto Ho

The art of rainproof torch

Take notice that "men of the cloth" do not appear in the Japanese social system—they are outside of the secular world and class systems. In reality, however, they could be very active in the political world.

- ◆ Saltpeter – 2 momme
- ◆ Sulfur – 12 momme
- ◆ Ash – 2 momme 5 bu
- ◆ Pine tree knot – 5 momme
- ◆ Moxa – 3 momme
- ◆ Pine resin – 2 momme
- ◆ Camphor – 3 momme
- ◆ Sawdust – 3 momme
- ◆ Mouse droppings – 3 momme

霞之鞭

Kasumi no Muchi

The rod of mist

The rod of mist is a cane or rod with poison embedded in its tip.

- ◆ Flowers of a thistle
- ◆ Powdered whitewash (calcium carbonate)
- ◆ Iron filings
- ◆ Unslaked lime

Mix the above and powder finely, then insert the mixture into a rod. Swing and flick the rod towards the enemy while considering the "wind and the wave."* Use this in war or in combat.

團扇霧霞之法

Uchiwa Kiri Kasumi no Ho

Fan of mist

Tie a maw worm (intestinal parasite) to a branch and above that place a red and

---

* I.e., take the weather and environment into account.

white insect/worm—the one which lives in drainage systems and which hide in water and flutter about when human footsteps pass. Catch this worm and place it above the maw worm, tie them by winding with string. Next wait until mushrooms grow around it. The first mushroom should be thrown away; take the second one and dry it in the shade, then powder it down. Next powder Japanese tiger beetles and mix it together. Blow this powder with a fan over your enemy and they will immediately die. The worm is not a leech or the larvae of a mosquito. If a human hand is placed near it, it will submerge.

満地之鞭
Manji no Muchi
Rod of Manji

- ♦ Put arsenious anhydride in half [of the inside of the cane]
- ♦ Put arsenopyrite in the other side [of the inside of the cane]

Place the two ingredients into the tip of a rod or cane and swing and flick this at the enemy.

Further Shinobi Quotes

The following short selection of quotes from historical manuals will further help to illustrate the shinobi and the tasks that they perform. Each one comes from different backgrounds and purpose but all shed light on the shinobi.

> *A lord should not try to fulfil his appointed tasks without knowing the job of the shinobi. Lord Takeda Shingen used to make his plans with ease and had complete victory in every battle he ever entered throughout his life. His retainers Baba mino no Kami, Yamagata Saburobei and Yamamoto Kansuke had a secret meeting about [the teachings of the shinobi]. Lord Shingen told them to pass on their suppa (shinobi) family traditions to others.*
>
> *Iga-ryu Koka-ryu Shinobi Hidensho*

Concerning Having Shinobi Infiltrate—on their Advantages and Disadvantages

Do not fail to have [shinobi] infiltrate before [a night attack] and after they have infiltrated, know that you cannot communicate with them without fire—that is while they are inside and you are outside. Strictly avoid telling the troops of the upcoming night attack about these shinobi; this is because if they know this fact, they will count on this and if they rely on them too much, they will be less inclined towards the task at hand.

While you are waiting for the fire from inside but if no fire ignites, it is most likely because the *shinobi no mono* has been killed or for other reasons, therefore you should still attack directly when the appropriate time comes.

When you get to the bamboo fences and you try to attack the inside of the camp and as you know there are allies on the inside, then know that this gives you momentum and that you should attack as the fire rises on the inside, making the external and internal assault correspond to each other. However, take note: it is not advisable to over rely on shinobi.

> Extracts by Hattori Naoyoshi &
> Hattori Naofusa of Owari, c. seventeenth century

On Shinobi Horsemanship

It goes without saying that shinobi should detect gaps in the enemy camp. To add to this, sometimes you should send one or two horses with their tongues tied and drive them into the enemy camp to cause confusion within. Also, you should send shinobi to release any horses, no matter what number of horses there are. This is called "close taking."

> Extracts by Hattori Naoyoshi &
> Hattori Naofusa of Owari, c. seventeenth century

城の内による鉄砲をうたするな鳥のたつまに忍びこそいれ

Do not fire guns from your castle at night. While the birds are flying off, a shinobi will infiltrate.

> Samurai war poem c. seventeenth century

The Oniwaban

The Guards of the Inner Castle Gardens

On the periphery of the identity of the shinobi is the word "Oniwaban," half in the shadow of the shinobi and half in normal Japanese life. The origins of the Oniwaban began when the bloodline of the Tokugawa shogun failed and an heir was needed to replace the main family branch. Luckily the Tokugawa family had planned for this possibility. The Tokugawa clan had set up three major houses to support them. In the case where an heir was not given by the main line they could take a male from one of these other branches. The seventh shogun presented just such a case and, to find the eighth shogun, the clan had to look to one of the three great houses of the Tokugawa family. The eighth shogun was found in the Kishu branch and was put into position as shogun in 1716. When he moved from Kishu he took his own men and among these were the "gunpowder handlers." When the new shogun set up in Edo castle he gave these gunpowder handlers the status of *Iga-mono* (a form of ninja). This entitlement gave them permission to move around the inner sections of Edo castle where others could not. This new group were renamed as Oniwaban—"guards of the inner castle gardens." They wore black jackets, traditional samurai trousers and a sword. Their main task was to secure the gates at night, to patrol the area around the main castle and gardens, and to oversee the gardeners and craftsman that were needed to upkeep the inner areas.

The groups were eventually divided into the main-Oniwaban and the west-Oniwaban. The Oniwaban originally consisted of families from Kishu, some of which collapsed and were replaced by second sons who established their own lines. On top of overseeing the manual work that was undertaken when the lord was absent from the gardens and inner palace, a selection of the best of the Oniwaban was given further tasks. Firstly, they would investigate and vet anyone who was to work in the inner castle, martial arts instructors and teachers, etc., making sure that all were of the correct caliber, reputation and background. In addition to this, the lord or an intermediary gave secret missions to some, but not all, members of the Oniwaban. If rumors abounded about a Japanese warlord somewhere, signs of deception or treachery surfacing, then the Oniwaban would be sent. They would go disguised to discover the truth of the matter. Upon their return they would submit a report that was crosschecked before it reached the lord himself. Furthermore, if an official delegation was sent by the shogun to oversee certain matters in another province, two members of the Oniwaban would take on disguises. They would follow behind the delegation to investigate and observe matters. This system included having agents—who were not Oniwaban—living in Kyoto and Osaka, as well as having a contract with an express messenger firm. These express messengers often moved between Kyoto, Osaka, and Edo delivering post and messages. Therefore, if the Oniwaban needed to move out in a pair they would hire an express messenger to guide them to and around one of the cities, where they could take up lodgings with their secured agents in either Kyoto or Osaka. With this system in place they could investigate and report on the major daimyos and report either directly to the lord or to the intermediary.

Often the Oniwaban are confused with actual gardeners, but this is fictitious. The Oniwaban were half-samurai who oversaw all work, including the gardeners themselves. They were in fact one of the *ban* divisions, *ban* meaning "guard." The reason that they were given the rank of Iga-mono is because of an imaginary line drawn in society around the lord. Everyone fell into one of the following brackets:

1. Omemie-ijo—those who are allowed an audience with the lord.
2. Omemie-ika—those who are not allowed an audience with the lord.

Being of the rank of Iga-mono meant that the Oniwaban could be in the presence of the lord. In fact some of the Oniwaban's ancestors worked as grooms for the shogun's horse—i.e., in close proximity, and all were from established, well-trusted families whose sons inherited the role. This factor is the reason that they are given this status of Iga-mono. It ensures that men of Kishu protected the shogun and his family. This was so that the guards of the garden did not have to leave every time the lord entered. In this way, if the lord so wished, he could give them orders directly, from mouth to ear. The Oniwaban continued to work in that role until the fall of the samurai in 1868.

The Oniwaban being of the status of Iga-mono must not be confused with the actual Iga-mono at the castle. A distinction must be remembered. This should be between the one hundred Iga-mono who worked at the "one hundred man guard house" (at the entrance to Edo castle)—which was nowhere near the inner palace—and the Oniwaban (also Iga-mono) who worked at the center of the castle. The one hundred Iga-mono were the descendants of those samurai who had helped Tokugawa Ieyasu cross Iga when his life was in danger. The Oniwaban were families from Kishu chosen from the "gunpowder handlers" within Kishu—who were classed as Iga-mono serving Kishu Province.

It is interesting to know that the word shinobi—to date—never appears next to Oniwaban. While their ancestry may have been connected to the shinobi in some way, and even though they do undertake secret missions, records never directly connect them to shinobi. They are a form of inspecting officer, or secret service, that have a distant connection to the ways of the shinobi. Oniwaban may have started from the Koka-mono of Kishu castle in modern-day Wakayama.

The Picture of the Shinobi

The above selection of shinobi translations, quotes and statements will have now made apparent the arts of the shinobi, and how they fit into samurai life. The image of the samurai or foot soldier trained in special military ways, and very much a part of Japanese military culture, is self-evident. The shinobi were those warriors who had that extra skill, their actions were dreaded by some, hated by others—but were known to all as a fearsome art form.

As an army moved out, some shinobi would have already been positioned within the enemy for months or years in advance. Other shinobi would be marching out with the allied forces, scouting ahead. When camps had been formed and fortresses built, the shinobi would sleep in the day but venture out in the dead of night, playing "cat and mouse" with enemy shinobi and guards. Moving through the moonlit or moonless night, stalking in the grass, listening and "feeling" for others, they would intercept and construct plans, deceive and fool the opposition and venture deep into hostile territory. They would raid camps, burn stores and perform "black arts." The shinobi devised vicious strategies. They constructed deep plans. They conspired and formed spy networks. They ran between the enemy and their own army, then sat down to an evening meal within the company of their own— but awoke eating breakfast with the enemy, having infiltrated during the night. The shinobi were the warriors between, they were the men who looked for and moved through gaps—just as the sun moves through the gap of an open gateway.

Part IV

THE RESURRECTION

The Return of the Samurai

aving now torn apart the myths of the samurai and shinobi into basic building blocks, we have illuminated the core elements of both the identity and
function of the medieval warrior. Having reconnected and rebuilt a truer
image of both the Japanese knight and the commando-spy the question remains,
what to do next? The central goal of my work is to allow the truth of Japanese medieval warfare to break through into the twenty-first century. This is to put to rest
all the mistruths and fantasy, so as to give it the educated and serious respect that
it deserves, as a comprehensive art of war. This goal is achieved through the various translations of both samurai and shinobi scrolls, specifically through historical
analysis of those translations. The main aim is for all people who have any interest in warfare, history or martial arts, to move past the clichéd idea of the samurai (which was propagated in the 1980s and 1990s), to truly understand just how
dangerous and sophisticated—and even cruel—samurai life was. The best way to
achieve this goal is to translate, publish, and reestablish a historical samurai war
school. It is a method that will fully display the internal workings of the social and
military structure of the warriors themselves. In short—*let them tell their own story*.
Therefore, to truly set this movement in motion and to develop the understanding
of a full samurai school of war, I have sought out permission from a samurai family
to reconstruct such a school. I, with this permission, have resurrected the samurai
and shinobi school known as Natori-Ryu.

Natori-Ryu
Natori-Ryu was already established in the Sengoku Period when one branch of
the family served the Takeda clan in the second half of the sixteenth century. The
country then was at war. After the fall of the Takeda family, the Natori warriors,
along with many others who served the Takeda clan, moved to serve the future
shogun, Tokugawa Ieyasu. From here the Natori clan separated into further sub-
branches and served in places such as the capital, Edo, and in Kishu—present-day
Wakayama. In or around the 1640s, Natori Sanjuro Masazumi was most likely born
and later started to serve the clan, becoming an instructor of *gungaku*—military
study. He revolutionized the school system and was a prolific writer, capturing the

then declining military skills of the last generation. (The last generation being those who had seen active service in the wars, or who had studied directly under them.) His aim was to amass and accumulate the teachings, the valuable skills of the samurai, and to allow his school to flourish. He became known as a *Chuko no So*—"a grandmaster of rejuvenation"—and was known by the name *Issui sensei*. Issui sensei would write on a wide and comprehensive range of subjects, all of which were dedicated to the arts of war. He went on to write one of the most important shinobi scrolls in history, the now famous Shoninki, which has been published in English under the title *True Path of the Ninja*. The school was eventually abolished during the Meiji Restoration and closed its doors under the tide of a new form of warfare. However, in libraries and collections across Japan his writings and teachings have lain on shelves in darkened rooms. For the first time in over 150 years they have been brought back together with renewed life.

To fully immerse into the samurai mind, and the details of samurai warfare, a student of military arts must have an understanding of a samurai school in full. This understanding is *not* just a liking for swordplay or hand-to-hand combat—a usual outlet for samurai enthusiasts. Therefore I set about the task of resurrecting Natori-Ryu and have succeeded in collecting the works of Natori Sanjuro Masazumi. Because of these things, we now have the full opportunity of that understanding before us.

Antony Cummins at the grave of Natori Masazumi

In 2012, my translation partner Minami Yoshie and I discovered the lost grave of the shinobi-samurai Natori Sanjuro Masazumi. We gained a connection with the grave keeper, the monk Yamamoto Jyuho. He was at that time unaware of Natori Masazumi but is now extremely involved in the preservation and promotion of the history of the Natori clan.

From here a bond with the last remaining members of the Natori clan was established. On the May 5, 2013

The monk Yamamoto Jyuho—keeper of Natori Masazumi's grave.

the family and monk signed both an agreement and blessing to allow me to publish Natori-Ryu, reestablishing it as a working military school. This reestablishment allows the English-speaking world to study a complete samurai school of war for the first time. This new opportunity has created an exciting movement in the world of martial arts and Japanese historical research. Members across the globe have actively participated in the reestablishment. I would like to invite you, the reader, to become a part of this movement and to become fully involved with the correct interpretation of these once lost skills. This worldwide community is open to everyone, and is founded on the principles of communal study and mutual benefit to all students. The skills of Natori-Ryu include all the military learning needed in samurai tactics and military campaigns, including a full shinobi curriculum. To contribute in adding life to this authentic samurai school, see the author's website along with other social media for more information—these sites will provide guidance on becoming involved.

The Natori-Ryu logo, with family crest and name in Japanese.

名取流（新楠流とも号する）は石取家家祖
名取與市之丞正俊を流祖とし　中興の祖
名取三十郎正澄によって総合的軍術の流派と
して確立され紀州藩に幕末まで伝えられた
ものです
名取流は武士の道を正しく伝え、軍学を深く
追求し、さらには人としてより意義のある
人生を送る道を示唆しています
名取流元祖名取家および最後の後継者
蓑笠家の直系の子孫である私たちは名取流の
教えが現在と未来にわたり世界中の人々の
心に届き響くことを祈念し名取流軍学を
伝書に基づいて甦らせ伝承しようとしている
アントニ、クミンズ氏の仕事を心から声援します

名取家

朝川政子
日根裕子
石垣勉
石垣茂

平成二十五年五月五日

立合人　山本寿治

Top, The blessing for the reopening of Natori-Ryu by the last members of the Natori family.

Above, Antony Cummins and a museum curator, Nagayo Toshihiko, with some of the Natori-Ryu manuals.

Left, Minami Yoshie, cofounder of the Historical Ninjutsu Research Team, and Nagayo Toshihiko examining some of the same manuals.

A New Understanding of the Samurai and the Shinobi

As the Western knight underwent such a radical change in our understanding, so this book should now have cleared away the debris from the distortion of samurai history. With the "field of battle" cleared there should be an open plain in our minds, so that we can start rebuilding a solid picture of the samurai and of the shinobi. This time building from the ground up.

A New Picture

First, insert the land, the ancient and history-filled country of Japan. Include its surrounding islands, the ancient forests and natural riverbanks (which are almost all gone today). The movement of the four seasons give a dramatic display with snow-covered mountains. Spring brings the wind-swept cherry blossom, and then intense summer burns up the ground with insects screaming at full velocity, to only die off with the arrival of the cold. The cool winds of autumn carry golden leaves into the snow of winter. Next is the placement of buildings within the landscape, some new, some under construction, but many old and in various states of decay. Some are under maintenance, while a few that are beyond the count of years, almost falling back into nature as the spread of deep green moss swallows them. Next, towns, cities, or rural hamlets nestled on plains, in valleys, or in the mountains. Vast graveyards contain stone obelisks covered in a cloud of incense and smoke. Lights burn by night, and crows keep chorus by day. All of the above are subject to the weather, the famed Japanese earthquakes, the hails of rain, deep mountain mists, a humid vision-distorting heat, and even the dreaded tsunami—which all take their toll on the landscape. Finally add to this picture the people of Japan, a people who came from mainland Asia in waves, bringing with them a culture that has had thousands of years invested in it, which is then reshaped by new movements and other people bringing Buddhism and other mainland influences.

The sun vomits through the sky in a crescendo of centuries as our picture arrives at the Sengoku Period in the 1500s. In the rest of the world the Americas had just been discovered by Europeans, Queen Elizabeth I has ascended the throne of England, and while the complexities of European history play out, a very bloodthirsty time has erupted in the once tranquil land of Japan with revolution and establishments being overthrown. To this image and time, enter the samurai! A warrior class who have been in control of the land for over five hundred years, their rule is absolute and established with rods of iron. "Recently" (in the Sengoku Period), lower samurai and those who wish to take up arms and become powerful have turned the order on its head and the once aristocratic families are being thrown from their seats of power and a new order is upon the field. These deep mountains and snow-rimmed lakes are filled with beetle-like figures in dark carapace armor, bright flags bending in the wind and furled about them as they move through our "oil painting," moving through the seasons and the years, falling in battle while new graveyards are erected—a time of man and the assent of his power. At the top of this movement, great names rule the divided nation: Takeda, Uesugi, Hojo, Oda, Asakura, Mori, Tokugawa, all of who look back to the great names of the past for inspiration: Kusunoki, Genji, Fujiwara, Heishi and Tachibana.

Our image clarifies as we focus on a mountain castle, on one unnamed night when the moon is but a slight crack in the sky. The castle is fixed into the natural rock of the mountain and its black walls support tiny figures on patrol, each carrying a blazing torch in the light snowfall. At the base of the mountain an enemy camp is in a nighttime hush, the well-constructed bamboo barricades lead up to the temporary gateways where guards stand by, trenches and pits have been laid out, traps and defenses are in position. Moving through the gateway past the old and experienced guards, we move at ground level through the mud, the tents in rows, the braziers giving off sparks as the mercenaries huddle around fires, sat at the edges of the camp with dogs whose eyes reflect this fire as they hide in the shadows beyond them. Moving closer into the center, we pass all the different huts for all the different tasks—*one of which is empty*. The picture moves up to the main war curtains, snow drifting past a great family crest as we peer through a small hole in this material division to see that which lies beyond. A prince sits upon a stool and a few of his most trusted men are at his side, ready to defend him at all times. Before him are the occupants from an empty hut, the *shinobi no mono* of his army. His command is given by mouth directly to the ear of these specially-trained samurai with their specially-trained foot soldiers in support—they are the shinobi of Japan. They move out of the camp, moving into the snow and the dark, their faces blacked out with powder, their clothes without heraldry and armed with ladders, rope and explosives. They sling their swords on their backs to make ready for the mountain climb, off they move, to do what they do best—*infiltration*.

The Round Up

The samurai was a highly trained professional soldier who deserves the true telling of his story. With a sense of honor that was dominated by the ethics of his time, this was a captain and officer among men, an independent combatant with his own men-at-arms, and a lord at his back. Housed in knightly abode and a lord of his own land, he was a full-time warrior with all the trappings of his office. He held the spiritual beliefs of his era. Above all this was his love and dedication to sophisticated warfare and military action. An equestrian gentleman or esquire on foot his equipment was sturdy and solid, his sword thick with quality, and his furnishings rich with his family history. However, the latter is not his true weapon: below his helm and the skin on his head, housed inside his skull—*which may one day adorn a spike*—lies years of knowledge held inside his brain; this was the weapon of the samurai, a trained mind. Skilled in Chinese classics, having knowledge of tea and ritual, understanding the art of the brush, and the pleasure of the fine arts are all balanced amidst a structure of military strategy. He loves the planning of war, the movement of the formations, the chase through the forest at night, the high-speed mounted scout run, the charge into battle, and the achievement of praise. Above all he loves to collect decapitated human heads and the power that lies in such success. Gold and silver have an appeal, land he wants more. Above all things in his mind, he wants to walk off the field of battle with a bag of heads in his hands, emerging out of a gunpowder fog. A hero to some, a murderer and rapist to others, a champion to his people, and a demon to the enemy, with homicide as a specialty and killing as a business, he is the samurai—the knight of Japan.

The shinobi was a subsection of samurai culture. Like all warriors of his time he could have been of the samurai class or of the foot-soldier class, or even with one foot in both worlds. While being from the samurai world—even though many shinobi were of samurai status—they were also on the outside. This external position was not because of any class divide but because of the nature of their job—which was *clandestine*. Secrets have a way of alienating people and placing them on the fringe. This was evident with the shinobi. The shinobi may have been an undercover agent in a far off territory, away from comrades, away from family and away from his life. He may have been a hidden warrior within his own or enemy army, again, outside of his own life, away from the people he knew, waiting in silence for his activation. The shinobi may also have been hired in public, placed with a group of other shinobi but this time separated by function and task, given their own quarters in battle; specifically taken away from regular tasks. A group such as this would operate in their own setting, just outside of the normal warrior. To be a shinobi took a special skill and a special personality. Those who did not match the grade were filtered out by the grim reaper in times of war and only the highest caliber shinobi achieved what was considered a hellish existence—like that at the height of the Warring States Period. With the foundation of samurai military ways in their make up, these specialists would study language, codes, explosives, infiltration, ritual magic and many other aspects in addition to the normal teachings. They were not frontline soldiers, but those who dared to go beyond enemy lines, either in open disguise or in stealth. If the business of the "pure" samurai was murder, death and the exchange of heads, then the occupation of the shinobi was in destruction, intelligence and secrets. The working shinobi was not among the princes of Japan, he was not found in the generals or in the higher echelons of the samurai world. He was found stood outside the door to the hall in which these ranks met, he was the man who was not on the path *to* high society but the man who had the key to the backdoor, an aid to princes and generals, and agent of information trafficking—he was the commando-spy of Japan.

The Boring Stuff

Conventionally, introductions, explanations, and aides to helpfulness are found at the start of most books. However, without question they are skipped over as the reader finds the "juicy cuts" of the book and returns after their "appetite" has been appeased. For this reason they have been moved to the back of the book, waiting in the "correct" position.

Measurement

All translations of measurement have been given in their original Japanese form; the following table has been constructed to allow you to make the correct conversions.

Measurement	Ideogram	Metric	Imperial
Lengths			
rin	厘	0.3 mm	0.01 in
bu	分	3.03 mm	0.11 in
sun	寸	3.03 cm	1.19 in
shaku	尺	30.3 cm	11.93 in
ken	間	1.81 m	5.96 ft
cho	町	109.1 m	357.9 ft
ri	里	3.92 km	2.435 miles
Mass or Weight			
bu/fun	分	0.37 g	0.013 oz
momme	匁	3.75 g	0.132 oz
ryo	両	37.5 g	1.32 oz
kin	斤	600 g	21.16 oz

Measurement	Ideogram	Metric	Imperial
Volume or Capacity			
shaku	勺	18.04 ml	0.63fl oz
go	合	180.4 ml	6.34fl oz
sho	升	1.8 liters	3.17 pt
to	斗	18.4 liters	31.74 pt
koku	石	180.4 liters	317.4 pt

Numbers from one to one hundred are mainly given in the written form. Numbers above one hundred or those given in dates or recipes have been given in numerical form.

Library lists and catalog numbers

The translation of the *Giyoshu* manual is taken from multiple transcriptions including the Okayama Prefectural Library. The originals can be seen with the following catalog numbers:

Version one:
上 0002120335 – KW399.2.1
中 0002120327 – KW399.2.2
下 0002120319 – KW399.2.3

Version two:
上 0002120681 – KW399.3.1
中 0002120699 – KW399.3.2
下 0002120707 – KW399.3.3

The *Iike Gunki*
    This manual can be found at the Japanese National Archives.

The *Hattori Doson Ichi-Ryu no Shinobi No Ho* manual
    This manual can be found in the Ikedake collection at Okayama University Library with the catalog number:
    H2-105

The locations of the remaining manuals have been referenced in the text or are found in private collections or have been previously published.

About the Author

Antony Cummins is from Lancashire, England, and is the author of multiple books on Japanese history and the ways of the shinobi. Antony has a Bachelor's degree in Ancient History and Archaeology and also a Master's degree in Theoretical Archaeology. He leads the Historical Ninjutsu Research Team and is dedicated to the reinterpretation of historical samurai ways and the promotion of medieval Japanese culture. For more information, visit his website and other social media sites: www.natori.co.uk.

"Books to Span the East and West"

Tuttle Publishing was founded in 1832 in the small New England town of Rutland, Vermont [USA]. Our core values remain as strong today as they were then—to publish best-in-class books which bring people together one page at a time. In 1948, we established a publishing outpost in Japan—and Tuttle is now a leader in publishing English-language books about the arts, languages and cultures of Asia. The world has become a much smaller place today and Asia's economic and cultural influence has grown. Yet the need for meaningful dialogue and information about this diverse region has never been greater. Over the past seven decades, Tuttle has published thousands of books on subjects ranging from martial arts and paper crafts to language learning and literature—and our talented authors, illustrators, designers and photographers have won many prestigious awards. We welcome you to explore the wealth of information available on Asia at www.tuttlepublishing.com.